# COLONIZATION AND CONQUEST:
## British Florida in the Eighteenth Century

*by*
*Lawrence H. Feldman*

CLEARFIELD

Copyright © 2007 by Lawrence H. Feldman
All Rights Reserved.

Printed for
Clearfield Company by
Genealogical Publishing Co.
Baltimore, Maryland
2007

ISBN-13: 978-0-8063-5322-7
ISBN-10: 0-8063-5322-8

*Made in the United States of America*

## CONTENTS

Counting People in the English Period .................... 1–2

East Florida, Late Arrivals and Quick Departure .................... 2

  1. Saint Augustine, February 1776 .................... 2–4
  2. Refugees, November 1776 .................... 4–7
  3. Saint Augustine, January 1778 .................... 8–12
  4. Importance of Province of East Florida, 1782 .................... 12–19
  5. Refugees from Georgia and Carolina, 1782 .................... 19–20
  6. Saint Augustine, June 1783 .................... 20–25
  7. Refugees from Carolina, July 1783 .................... 25–29
  8. Refugees from Georgia, July 1783 .................... 60–77
  9. Petition, Saint Augustine, September 1783 .................... 77–81
  10. Evacuation of East Florida, 1784 .................... 81–82
  11. Saint Johns, January 1785 .................... 82–84
  12. Saint Augustine, February 1785 .................... 85–86
  13. Saint Augustine, March 1785 .................... 87–89
  14. Emigrants from East Florida, 1785 .................... 89

West Florida, Many Lands and Increasing People .................... 90

  15. West Florida, Merchants Memorials, 1768 .................... 90–91
  16. Province of West Florida, 1769 .................... 91–95
  17. Observations on Stockade Fort of Pensacola, 1769 .................... 96–97
  18. Delegates to Council at Pensacola, November 1777 .................... 97–98
  19. Request Burial Grounds in Pensacola, November 1777 .................... 98
  20. Election of the Council at Pensacola, 1778 .................... 99
  21. West Florida, Petition, August 1779 .................... 100–104
  22. Pensacola, Request Militia, September 1779 .................... 104–105
  23. West Florida, Persons...against...Chester, 1780 .................... 105–106
  24. Pensacola, Inhabitants, February 1780 .................... 106–109
  25. Pensacola, Satisfied with Chester, February 1781 .................... 110–111
  26. Pensacola, Householders at Capitulation, May 1781 .................... 112–114
  27. Natchez, Anti Indian, January 1779 .................... 114–117
  28. Natchez Inhabitants, October 1779 .................... 118–119
  29. Mobile Inhabitants, [1770] .................... 120

30. Mobile Enfranchisement, November 1778 ............................ 121
31. Tombecbec under English (1779) and Spanish (1780) .... 122–125
32. Tensa and Mobile under Spanish, 1780 ................................ 125
33. Inhabitants of Mobile District, Neutrality, 1780 ............... 126–128

Spanish/English War: West Florida Campaign (1779–1781)

Annotated Bibliography .......................................................... 129–130
  1. Manuscripts .................................................................. 130–231
  2. Articles ......................................................................... 232–249
  3. Books ........................................................................... 250–268

References Cited ..................................................................... 269–277

# Counting People in the English Period

In 1991 I published a volume entitled "Anglo-Americans in Spanish Archives: Lists of Anglo-American Settlers in the Spanish Colonies of America." It provided lists of census data for Anglo Americans who settled in the Second Spanish period (1784-1821) in West Florida (mostly Natchez, Mobile, Tombeche, Baton Rouge, Nogales [Vicksburg], New Madrid, Pensacola), in East Florida (some Saint Augustine material), Belize and Delaware (Swedes who shipwrecked in Puerto Rico).

In 1998 I published a book entitled "The Last Days of British Saint Augustine, 1784-1785," which was about a Spanish Census of the English Colony of East Florida. Now I am providing information for the Anglo Americans who settled between 1763 and 1784 (British period) in the Floridas. The data comes from the Public Record Office files of London England, copied for the Library of Congress, in the 1920's. But two aspects distinguish this work from earlier studies.

The first is that I did the survey and compilation of data in five months. Actually I did it in two and a half months. This was not because I am more proficient in this material. On the contrary, having worked with Spanish and not English records, I was much less familiar with English records of this period. In fact, my intention was to do something quite different, namely a study of the English/Spanish war of 1779/84. What I soon discovered is that this topic has been done by others. There are a series of books on the topic, and I would be wasting my time to do another.

Hence I gravitated to doing another study of census documents, this time for the English period. What I discovered is that the English did not do census documents. There were compilations of people for one task or another; but, with the partial exception of people entering East Florida toward the end of this period (who were loyalists fleeing the "rebels"), there were no census documents as such. Therefore this work is dependent upon these partial semi-census documents.

The second subject is that there are fewer settlements in the British period. For East Florida there was Saint Augustine, but West Florida had Pensacola, Mobile, Tombeche, Tensa, and Natchez. Other communities were settled in the 2nd Spanish period (Baton Rouge, "Nogales") or were never under British control (Saint Louis, New Madrid, Saint Genevieve). This does not mean that there were very few British settlers, there were in fact many, but they came in late and often left with the British flag. I begin my survey with East Florida.

## East Florida
## Late Arrivals and Quick Departures

The British arrived in East Florida in 1763. They got it in exchange for Cuba. East Florida was immediately adjacent to their other colonies (e.g. Georgia) and this made it easy to hold East Florida. Although there were earlier migrations, the earliest compilations of people coming into East Florida for which I have records date from 1776 and 1778. We also have a list of the prior British inhabitants of this colony.

### 1. Address of the Inhabitants of the Province of East Florida. 27 February 1776. PRO CO 5. 556

Most Gracious Sovereign,

We, Your Majesty's most dutiful and loyal subjects, the inhabitants of East Florida, impressed with the most grateful sentiments for the protection and assistance which Your Majesty has graciously afforded this infant colony; and deeply deploring and disavowing the present unhappy and unnatural rebellion, which prevails through most of Your Majesty's other colonies on this continent, beg leave to approach the throne, and to assure Your Majesty that we will not only studiously avoid every connexion and correspondence with or support of the persons engaged therein (notwithstanding the very great distress which many of us do now feel from the want of those necessary supplies, which we used to derive from those colonies) but that we shall be always ready, and willing, to the utmost of our weak abilities to manifest our loyalty to Your Majesty's person and a due submission to Your Majesty's government and the legislature of Great Britain.

Wishing for a speedy and happy Reunion of all the parts of Your Majesty's great Empire, the submission and return of the deluded multitude in America to their Allegiance and the Re-establishment of Order and Tranquility through the whole of Your Dominions; we heartily pray the Almighty God to grant that Your Majesty may long enjoy the blessings of health and peace to rule of an united, happy and grateful people. Saint Augustine, the 27$^{th}$ of February 1776.

| | | |
|---|---|---|
| Bachop, Peter | Doran, John | |
| Barns, James | | Laidler, Ralph |
| Barton, Enoch | Fatio, Francis Philip | Lowthrup, George |
| Bernard, Charles | Fatio, F. P. Junior | Lundie, Arch. |
| Bisset, Alexander | Fatio, Lewiis | |
| Bisset, Robert | | Man, Spencer |
| Brown, James | Grant, Alexander | Marshall, Abraham |
| Bunkley, John | Grassell, George | Mason, John |
| Bunkley, John | | McLean, Donald |
| Broomhead, Joseph | Hares, Henry | Michael, Joseph |
| Clark, Thomas | Henderson, James | Mills, William |
| Cooke, Abraham | Higgins, Thomas | Moncrief, James |
| Cookson, John | | Mott, Jonah |
| Cuenoud, Lewis | Johnson, Thomas | Mowbray, Ino. |
| Dayton, William | Johnson, William | |
| | Justin, Thomas | Newcomb, John |
| Daniel, Alexander | | |
| Delap, Charles | Kip, Jacobus | |

| | | |
|---|---|---|
| Penman, James | Sherwood, William | Taylor, William |
| Pouly, James Isaac | Short, William | Tennant, John |
| Powell, G. Mid. | Sill, Richard | Tims, James |
| | Simpson, George | Turnbull, And. |
| Reddy, William | Smart, Thomas | Turnbull, And., Jun. |
| Rivas, Isaac | Smith, James | Waights, James |
| Robinson, Patrick | Sowerby, Henry | Watson, William |
| Rolfes, Frederick | Speir, John | White, Stephen |
| Rolphes, George | Stafford, Robert | Williamson, Thomas |
| Ross, John | Stout, Joseph | Wilson, William |
| Roworth, Samuel | | Woodvill, W. |

A. Turnbull for upwards of two hundred families of Greeks and other Foreigners in the Smyrna settlement. [This is] in Mr. Turnbull's letter of May 10th

2. Humble Address and Petition of several Refugees (Planters, Merchants and others) from the Province of Georgia now residing in East Florida, 1 November 1776
PRO CO 5. 557

May it please Your Majesty

We, Your Majesty's most dutiful and truly loyal subjects, late planters, merchants and others in the province of Georgia now residing in East Florida, most humbly presume to approach Your Majesty with Our most grateful acknowledgments for many blessings we have enjoyed under Your Majesty's most auspicious Reign and mild government and to lay before Your Majesty the circumstances of Our present distressed situation.

From the first commencement of these seditious troubles and unnatural rebellion which now prevails in America we have at the risk of our lives fortunes diligently watched and firmly opposed the pernicious measures of the ringleaders, and animated with a spirit of loyalty, little known in America, we have preserved in our breasts, and recommended to others that veneration for a well poised constitution and a king whose principal concern is the happiness of his people, which the rebels at first affected to have.

While we had the smallest prospect of being useful by every means in our power we endeavored to preserve and restore peace and affection to your Majesty's person and government in the province of Georgia, a colony in a flourishing state from Your Majesty's bounty and the assistance of the good people of England till unable to bear repeated insults and persecutions from Our old friends and neighbors. We found that we must either submit to the arbitrary and unjust exactions of a lawless new modeled government (where the lowest of the people bear sway) or forfeit what we shall ever hold most sacred, our allegiance to Your Majesty.

Deeply impressed with gratitude for the attention Your Majesty has shown to the persecuted Friends of Government in the Colonies in Rebellion, under the authority of your Majesty's Governor of East Florida proclamation dated the second of November one thousand seven hundred and seventy five, we fled to East Florida as an asylum and to share of Your Majesty's royal bounty in getting gratuitous grants of land as there in expressed. The expense, risk and difficulties we me with in removing we considerable, some fled with part of their property, others almost without any, and all leaving considerable debts and effects in that province.

With hearts replete with gratitude towards his Excellency Governor Tonyn, we think it our duty to bear the fullest testimony of his unwearied zeal for Your Majesty's service, and the kind reception we met with by every assistance and protection in his power which he has upon all occasions shown to your Majesty's persecuted loyal refugees, thereby humanely fulfilling as far as in him lay Your Majesty's most gracious intentions towards them.

May we, most gracious sovereign, presume to represent to your Majesty that the State of this province is such that from large tracts of land being granted on the East Coast, and the most valuable lands near Latehaway being claimed by the Indians, Your Majesty's petitioners, and many others well affected to Your Majesty who want only a safe opportunity of removing their effects into this province, cannot reap the benefit of Your Majesty's royal bounty or take up lands in this province with any benefit to themselves and family's until land is in Congress ceded by the Indians to Your Majesty.

We sincerely wish that Your Majesty's deluded subjects in America may soon be convinced of their error and delusion and return to their allegiance, that under Your Majesty's paternal care and fostering protection we may with Our fellow subjects enjoy our usual liberty, peace and affluence.

And not doubting that upon Your Majesty will with your wonted humanity take into Your Royal consideration, the situation of your loyal petitioners, persecuted for their attachment to Your Majesty's Person and mild government, and grant them such relief as in your royal wisdom you shall think meet.

| | |
|---|---|
| Anderson, Thomas | Brown, William |
| Barry, George | Christie, James |
| Begbie, Alexander | Club, George |
| Begbie, James | Club, William |
| Bethun, John | Cock, Charles |
| Brown, Edward | Deas, David |

Edwards, Peter
Finlayson, Henry
Forrester, J.R.
Gibbon, Dan
Harvey, J.
Jemeson, Thomas
Johnston, A.
Johnston, Lewis, junior
Jones, Lewis
Knight, Chat
Knight, Jermyn
Leake, Richard
Macculloch, Chas.
MacDonald, Alexander
Mackinen, Chas. Hm.
MacQueen, Alexander
Martin, James
Martin, John
Mincham, Charles
Moodie, John
Munro, Robert

Oldis, H.

Panton, William
Paterson, Alex
Peacock, John
Phelps, James
Renny, Patrick
Richardson, Thomas
Stewart, John
Thomson, Alexander
Thomson, Thomas

Watson, James

Weech, George
William, Samuel
Wood, John
Wylly, Alexander

Yonge, Henry, junior

Endorsed in Governor Tonyns of 1st November 1776.
Copy sent to Plantation Officer.

3. Saint Augustine, 19th January 1778, East Florida.

PRO CO 5: 546

To His Excellency Patrick Tonyn Esquire, Governor Captain General and Commander in Chief in and over His Majesty's Province of East Florida, Chancellor Vice Admiral and Ordinary of the Same.

The humble address of the Inhabitants of this and the Refugees from the neighboring Provinces now in this Province:

May it please your Excellency: We His Majesty's most dutiful and loyal subjects, the inhabitants of this and the refugees from the neighboring provinces, truly sensible of the many blessings we have enjoyed under the mild, just and auspicious government of our most gracious Sovereign, humbly conceive it to be our indispensable duty, at this alarming Crisis, to renew our assurances of fidelity and attachment to your Excellency.

Convinced Sir, that it has ever been your unwearied study to promote the true Interest and Welfare of this Province and that the service of your Royal Master and the Laws of your Country but acknowledge with the warmest gratitude, the seasonable and vigorous efforts of your Excellency to put this Province in a Respectable state of defense, previous to a daring invasion by the Rebels; to which in spite of the Machinations of our Enemies we owe, under God, the preservation of our laws, our liberties and lives.

We, the Refugees, are peculiarly sensible how much we owe to your Excellency's Goodness. We humbly beg leave to express our unfeigned acknowledgements for the kind relief and support many of us have received at your Excellency's hands.

With pleasure we reflect that your Excellency in fulfilling the intention of the best of Princes only complied with the generous emotions of a benevolent Heart.

Professions of loyalty by Us have long characterized the American Petitions to our most Gracious Sovereign. We flatter ourselves your Excellency will never be deceived; our late and future conduct will bear testimony of our sincerity and loyalty.

Happy shall we esteem ourselves ever to convince Your Royal Master, that we are equal Enemies to sedition and Rebellion. And that from a firm and zealous attachment to the and Constitution of our Country, we are ready and willing to co-operate with Your Excellency in the support of the Honor and Dignity of the Crown at the expense of our Lives and Fortunes:

Adams, Samuel
Alexander, William
Allen, Willis
Anderson, James

Bachofo, Peter
Begbie, James
Bethune, John
Bethune, Malcum
Bonsall, Robert
Bremner, John
Bride, Thomas

Brown, Thomas

Christie, James
Clegg, Samuel Camble
Clubb, George
Cooke, Abraham
Crichton, Thomas
Crighton, Alexander

Demere, Raymond
Doran, John

Edwards, Peter
Finlayson, Henry
Forsyth, John
Fryermer, John Adam

Gillies, Euan
Grey, Alexander
Grindrod, Will

Haley, In.
Herrera, Lu. De
Hewitt, William
Hunt, William

Iynes, Harris

Jenkins, Owen

Kelly, William
Kennedy, Donald

Kennedy, John
Kosmer, In.

Laidler, Ralph
Levett, Francis
Leslie, John

Love, John
Lyford, William

Maccalloch, Charles
Mack, George
Mackie, In.
Mackinen, Charles
Mackinnon, Donald
MacLeod, Rodk
MacQueen, Alexander
Marlin, Edward
Mason, John
McDonald, James
McKay, John
McKenzie, Collin
McKenzie, Hugh
McLaurin, Euan
McPherson, Alexander
Michael, Joseph
Mill, Alexander
Millar, George

Miscoves, Henry
Moses, David
Moss, William
Munro, Robert
Murphey, John

Nixon, Thomas, junior

Oldis, William

Osborne, Geo.

Pantop, William
Park, Robert
Paterson, Alexander
Payne, R.
Peavett, Joseph
Penn, John
Price, In.
Prince, Charles

Robinson, Joseph
Roworth, Samuel

Samson, James
Samson, John
Sanchez, Francis
Scott, Robert
Shong, William
Skinner, Alexander
Smith, James

Smith, Robert
Solona, Emanuel
Stevens, Richard
Stewart, Walter

Stubbs, Wade

Taylor, William
Tennant, John
Thomson, George

Wallace, James

Watson, James
Webley, Edward
Welch, George

Welsh, Patrick
Witter, Jacob
Wood, John
Wright, Jermyn

Yonge, Henry, junior
Yuguet, Charles

N. Besides the above, one hundred and twenty five desired to sign by Proxy as will be observed by the copies transmitted annexed to the proceeding of Council.

Endorsed   East Florida.   In Governor Tonyn's (Number 50) of 19th January 1778.

*What does these lists tell us? Two documents were by petitioners who, upon the revolt of the inhabitants against the King, fled into East Florida. These petitioners were mostly from the adjacent colony of Georgia. The third document has no locality of origin but it is also from people fleeing the Rebels. It is interesting to note that it includes a man, David Moses, who was not Christian but Jewish (for further details on him see Feldman 1998).*

The documents refer to need for new land, since they had abandoned all upon fleeing into East Florida. The third document notes "how much we owe to your Excellency's Goodness. We humbly beg leave to express our unfeigned acknowledgements for the kind relief and support many of us have received" from the governor of the colonial province. All of these refugees were Crown Loyalists who fled to East Florida. But some arrived before the American Revolution. One of them, a British inhabitant of East Florida, offered his own thoughts on the value of East Florida.

4. Considerations on the Importance of the Province of East Florida to the British Empire (on the supposition that it will be deprived of its Southern Colonies) by its situation, its produce in Naval stores, ship lumber, and the asylum it may afford to the wretched and distressed loyalists. 1782. PRO CO 5: 560

### East Florida's Advantage to the Enemy in War Time

In war time with France and Spain, it is obvious to say much of the advantage of that Peninsula; the loss of which would shut for ever the return to Europe of any vessels from Jamaica and the West Indies through the Gulf, the Bahamas, the Havana, Cuba etc, on one side East Florida, on the other at the narrow entrance to the gulf stream, would prevent any ship without convoy to attempt a passage; any light vessel, or whale boats, armed in the guays, would first attempt her, and a few frigates would secure any number.

### First Plan of Settlement very Advantageous and well Reflected

The province of East Florida being settled on the plan suggested by His Majesty's ministers at the conclusion of Last War, would have made it one of the most valuable colonies in North America, I mean having settlements on the Gulf of Mexico, as well on the Atlantic, the Bays and Harbors of Spiritu Sancto, off Carlos and others will afford Ports and retreats safe and secure, for any number of ships almost of any dimensions, the country from Apalachicola to Fort Saint Mark is fertile even to the seashore, and was the principal settlements of the Spaniards before their long and inveterate war, with the Indians, their pious schemes of extirpating every heretic Indian, was checked by the brave Creeks and Choctaws.

The Province ... is not occupied above 25 miles from the Sea along the coast

As the province stands now we are cultivating in East Florida the most ungrateful soil of the whole province; no plantation at this very day is beyond 25 miles from the sea, and it is well known that on the southern coast of America, as far as Chesapeak[e] Bay the whole tract at that distance from the Sea (few swamps excepted) is a mere sandy barren land.

The Seminole Indians, the present Inhabitants, are not legal possessors of land

The Indians who now occupy the fertile lands of East Florida are not the aborigines of the country. They are called by the Creeks, Seminoles or in their language Wild Indians. The scum of the several tribes of the Apaloches or Blue Mountains, a vast tract of back country between Georgia and West Florida, as called [by the] Creeks. The Seminoles are vagabonds and despised by these natives and never permitted to intermix or to join with them in any talk with the Europeans.

The Yamousies who Inhabited East Florida before Seminoles were almost destroyed by Creeks [who] conquered aborigines

The Yamousies who drove away and exterminated the Florida Indians had been almost looted out by the Creeks; a few of them at this present time are settled in the island of Cuba and seldom venture on the continent with the Spanish fishermen who yearly visit the coast, chiefly on the Gulf of Mexico. The Creeks, having been reduced lately to a very low ebb by a long and inveterate war with the

Choctaws and having but a gloomy aspect of the good will toward them of the Georgians and Carolinians, would be easily prevailed to recall the Seminoles back to nation to reinforce them. It is not long ago that the Creeks made some advances toward it. By negotiation well managed by the Superintendent with both nations, a value for the purchase offered, perhaps not above two years presents a fair acquisition of the whole peninsula to the British Empire. Would be ascertained without any suspicion of those base contracts by which most of America been vested into European hands against rum in a drunken meeting so justly reflected upon and reproached to the possessors.

East Florida is limited to the west of Apalachicola River on the borders of which the Spaniards had formerly a capital settlement called Santa Maria d' Apalachicola. The country all around it is fertile upon a rising ground. The beginning of the Grand Apalaches is Fort Saint Mark, abandoned only in 1772, not far from Saint Carlos Bay. From thence the communication by land to Saint Augustine was supported by a few blockhouses and Houado Fort in the country called Saint Mathew Uttota Attachua and Puolata on the East side of Saint Johns river, distant about 30 [leagues] from Saint Augustine. Returning from this last place, travelers and traders have the advantage of a navigable river called Little Savannah that with canoes goes a short time into the Gulf of Mexico near Saint Mark.

The barren lands now occupied in East Florida produce the best naval stores in all America. Saint John's River, navigable near 300 miles, running parallel to the Atlantic and nowhere distant more than 25 miles, will produce any quantity of tar, pitch and turpentine. It would be easy to find substantial contractors for 100/m barrels a year sorted by different species allowing a reasonable time at first, as the exportation in 1781, has not exceeded 30/m barrels.

Experience has taught us how to remedy so that vast destruction of timber by such crops. Therefore provincial laws should be made to prevent setting on fire the pine bearing lands, to regulate the boxing of trees for turpentine, to prohibit the extirpating the young saplings and to fix the number of trees that should always remain on every acre. The straggling hunters and cattle keepers set these pine bearing lands on fire in the winter and early in the spring to make new pastures for the cattle who graze the whole year round; or to prepare the hunting grounds and attract deer. Unless the planters have thoroughly cleared and cleaned their turpentine tracts from all weeds, dry grass and other combustibles, the fire catching coagulated turpentine and rosins on the trees destroy in an instant the trees prepared for green tar when the extraction of turpentine is completed and waste immense tracts of land useless for ages to come.

East Florida is now the only province of North America belonging to the Crown where naval stores can be made. The immense quantity of Live Oaks on the Salts fit for timber of the largest ships of war is another object worth the attention of government.

In the year 1769 or 1770 a frigate was sent to Saint Mary's river with ship carpenters to survey the Live Oaks, and search for the proper pieces for 74-64 gunships and frigates. They were found at the plantation of Jermyn Wright Esquire on Saint Mary in a few hours time. Without running half a mile, Live Oak on the Salt Water Creek, or Islands is far superior to those on fresh water with less sap and a fine grain of wood. A difficulty attends the working of that timber, it must be done while green [since] no tool can be found to hew it when once seasoned by the air and time. Live Oak is made use on at Toulon in France, the south of Province and Italy produces such trees [but] none so lofty or valuable as in Florida or Georgia. The timber is seasoned in basin filled up with water. Each piece is taken out as it can be worked up. It rots and decay's in the water and so only the heart is used [for this purpose]. The Live Oaks of East Florida produce the best timber and a cargo of it was sent in 1774 to Philadelphia. Those not sorted [was] sold to advantage.

When the tree is straight, it may be sawed while green and makes valuable board and something for gun barrages and mortar beds that are to be permanent and exposed to the inclemency of weather. The Yellow Pine of East Florida is remarkably large, straight and of a fine grain [and] remarkably large, straight and fine grain, rather heavy for single stick or large mast. For made masts I humbly apprehend it would be very proper, as it is easy to find large trees free of all kinds

of knots from 40 to 50 feet in length. For deck planks no wood is equal to it. I had some sawed above 40 feet, free of knots and clear of heart shake.

The present emigration of wretched and distressed refugees from the most fertile land in North America, calls aloud for some arrangement in East Florida to assign them better spots of Land, to raise provisions for the inhabitants and to supply in time our West Indies islands.

The land on Nassau River is acknowledged to be equal if not superior to most of the best in Georgia and South Carolina for rice, corn and indigo. Planters of consequence have not yet dared to make settlements on the several branches of that river on account of the frequent eruption of those wild Indians. They are not to be restrained by fear, threatening or any kind of law. They plunder indiscriminately friends and foes and in their executions kill the cattle and livestock of all the wretches they meet with. When intoxicated beat and murder the first man who dares to oppose or to check them.

The north branch of Nassau runs within 4 or 5 miles of Saint Mary [along] the north boundaries of East Florida. The land on that river is better than on Saint John. The navigation is not easy up in the country being very narrow and shaded by the trees. The bar, the entrance and the harbor are the best on the coast,

If Saint Augustine, for the security of the Province, is to remain the seat of government [then] a town at Saint Mary would be the most advantageous for trade being the only Port of the province that can admit frigates and large merchant ships [and so] had been projected by the late Lord Egmont. The lots disposed of among the chief planters. The entry into Saint Mary has on the North Cumberland and Amelia on the South. This last belongs to the family of the late Lord Egmont. In peaceable time its position is very convenient to trade with Georgia, having an inland navigation in schooners and sloops as far as Savannah.

There is 17 feet water on the bar of Saint Mary at low water agreeable to a draft made in 1769 by Lieutenant Fulton of the Navy who surveyed that coast by order of Lord Egmont; the tide rise above 4 feet, the channel straight. The same Lieutenant Fulton, acting agent in East Florida, is actually at Saint Mary taking a new survey. Next to Saint Mary is Nassau, having on the North Amelia and Talbot to the South. The bar is difficult and intricate. There is near 12 feet water on the bar but being very narrow, it breaks all over as any gale of wind blows on the coast. The harbor inside the bar is note safe for large vessels. Small craft may run about 80 miles on both branches of that river.

The inlet between Talbot and Little Talbot Island admits only boats at high water. Between Little Talbot and Fort George island is a little inlet, forded at low water almost joining Saint Johns River. The bar of Saint Johns River is very easy. The channel is wide near the land and the bar not above a cable in length. There is commonly 10 feet at low water. The tide rises 4 feet after a fresh [wind] in the river. At spring tide or after a long N east wind the bar deepens considerably and has often 16 feet water. The navigation on that river is complicated. The tide swells two hours before it flows, and falls two hours before ebb that is called tide and half tide.

High water on the bar is at half flood and very convenient for vessels going in, as they may up, two hours longer with the tide. The same disadvantage attends large vessels going out as they must take the bar at half flood and have a wind to stem the tide. This, by neglect or inattention of the pilot, had occasioned the loss of sundry vessels. Between Saint John River and Saint Augustine there is no inlet whatsoever, the beach runs smooth and straight South by East and North by West, distant from Point to Point 25 miles. The bar at Saint Augustine is very dangerous, shifting almost every hard gale of N East wind, being at a great distance from the Land and entangled by hard ground; breakers, of shelly kind, [cause] the loss of almost every vessel that ground or becalmed on bar.

It is worth the attention of navigators to observe that every time the tide shifts, that instant the winds lull and the vessel is becalmed, the current and tide run toward the breakers. And unless the vessel has a boat with an anchor out, she is wrecked and bulged instantly. South of Augustine, is Matanza Inlet defended by a stone fort built in the middle of the channel, and having an officer and 25 men from the garrison. It is the only inlet accessible for galley or small craft. Coming with forces to attack Saint Augustine the north side is bounded by Saint Anastasia inland, which run quite over against the town, and make its harbor (on the south is a beach) a kind of peninsula going to Mosquito Inlet, about 80 miles from town.

Mosquito inlet has not above 8 feet at high water. There was before the War very considerable settlements on the lagoons that run north and south, such as Dr. Turnbull's, at Smyrna belonging to Lord Temple. Sir William Duncan deceased and others, Peter Taylor, Richard Oswald, Governor Elliot, Lieutenant Governor Moultrie, had very large plantations with a number of Negroes: Smyrna, a large village, is inhabited by Greeks and Minorcans. From thence to India river there is no other inlet, this admit only fishing boats which are chiefly Spaniards from Havana. The coast is very low and full of rocks, at Cape Canaveral a very long ridge of rocks stretched from the point to break at low waters. There is an eddy of the Gulf Stream along the coast well known to Spaniards, which serve them to return to Havana after their fishery.

The Bahamas and New Providence Wreckers frequent that part of East Florida. They rendezvous at little Matacomba, one of the Keys, where they carry the plunders of the poor unfortunates who perish on these rocks. Key Largo is the first seen near Cape Florida, and is remarkable for large clumps of trees, a kind of Scrubby Live Oak. There are several good harbors on the quays but of no service to vessels in boisterous weather, though very safe for those that are in before the gale. These [are a] few observations, made after a residence of ten years in East Florida, humbly offered to Major Morrison by his most obedient humble servant, F. P Fatio, a planter. 14th December 1782, a true copy from original, William Chelfe [sic]

The cutting down of the wilderness, bringing new lands into cultivation, and exports of naval stores, peltry and lumber show its utility to Great Britain. They noted that the lands are fully capable of producing rice, cotton and indigo as well as supporting the local inhabitants. They also could support Loyalists fleeing the American Revolution.

### 5. A Return of Refugees and Their Slaves arrived in East Florida from Georgia and South Carolina.
### PRO CO 5: 560; November and December 1782

| Whites | Georgia | Carolina | Total |
|---|---|---|---|
| Men | 352 | 221 | 473 |
| Women | 195 | 324 | 519 |
| Children | 235 | 338 | 573 |
| TOTAL | 722 | 1383 | 2165 |

| Blacks | Georgia | Carolina | Total |
|---|---|---|---|
| Men | 709 | 741 | 1450 |
| Women | 523 | 495 | 1018 |
| Children | 427 | 445 | 872 |
| TOTAL | 1659 | 1681 | 3340 |

To November 1782

| Whites | Georgia | Carolina | Total |
|---|---|---|---|
| Men | 419 | 788 | 1267 |
| Women | 224 | 347 | 641 |
| Children | 268 | 382 | 650 |
| TOTAL | 911 | 1517 | 2428 |
| Blacks | | | |
| Men | 770 | 819 | 1589 |
| Women | 566 | 532 | 1098 |
| Children | 450 | 472 | 932 |
| TOTAL | 1786 | 1823 | 3609 |

To December 1782

6. Saint Augustine, 6th June 1783, East Florida, Petition, PRO CO 5:560

To His Excellency Patrick Tonyn Esquire Captain, General, Governor and Commander in Chief and over His Majesty's Province of East Florida, Chancellor, Vice Admiral and Ordinary of the same.

The humble address of the Principal Inhabitants of the said Province, may it please Your Excellency

We His Majesty's loyal subjects, having fully and dispassionately considered the calamitous state to which we will be reduced by the cession of this province to the Crown of Spain, and the measures that have been recommended to us by the Right Honorable Lord Hawke, and the other proprietors of Lands resident in London, beg leave to address Your Excellency requesting that you will be pleased to present our most grateful acknowledgements to his Lordship, and them for their early attention to our interest, and to inform him that agreeable to his directions as many of us as the time would permit have made estimates and valuations of our Estates, to request the continuance of that Noble Peers interest, and to assure him that we will most cheerfully contribute our proportion towards defraying the expense that may rise in the prosecution of our claim.

From Your Excellency's long residence amongst us it becomes needless to mention the numberless difficulties we have surmounted and the immense sums that have been expended to bringing this country from an uncultivated wilderness to a respectable state of cultivation. The amazing progress it hath of late made, the exports of naval stores, peltry and lumber fully evince its utility to Great Britain, and to what consequence it might be raised were the more valuable uncultivated parts of the northern and western coasts settled by men undoubtedly well attached to His Majesty's Government, and who would glory in raising a progeny of the same principles. We humbly conceive that neither Nova Scotia nor the Bahamas Islands can answer for commodious habitations to the owners of slaves, and we are well informed that the West Indies is overstocked. Besides, Sir, sensible of your Excellency's zeal for Government and attachment to the Mother Country it is with bleeding hearts we lament that many of His Majesty's Loyal Subjects, soldiers, sailors, and husband-men sinking under accumulated misfortunes, and for want of such a residence as this country if retained would afford will think themselves under the necessity of reverting to American States and growing upon its ruins by industry of these very people who might be so beneficially employed in adding to the strength, and increasing the commerce of Great Britain.

Your Excellency is sensible that prejudices have prevailed against this country, that the lands are well calculated for producing sufficient provisions for the maintenance of its inhabitants, and that they are fully capable of producing rice, cotton and indigo for exportation, that it abounds with Live Oak timber fit for ships of war of any rate, that the bars of Saint Augustine and Saint Johns are not insurmountable obstacles to commerce, and that the Harbor of Saint Mary's, Spirito Santo and Appalachicola are fit for every purpose of commerce as well as for the reception of His Majesties ships, not to mention the advantage of furnishing the West Indies markets with several articles that must otherwise be supplied by the American States, and the entire loss of the numerous tribes of Southern Indians emerging from barbarity, who would in peace consume our manufactures and increase our trade, and in the late war have manifested a fidelity and attachment to the King and a disposition to act agreeable to orders they received, which would do honor to a civilized nation.

Whatever the event be Your Excellency may be assured that we ever shall preserve our loyalty to the King and maintain a grateful remembrance of your Excellency's exertions, and the good offices of our numerous friends in Great Britain, and humbly conceiving that our interest and that of the Mother Country are intimately connected – We are happy in our expectations from the late change in Administration that Right Honorable Minister at the head of the department actuated by that regard to justice and those principles of humanity which ever influenced his conduct, will in his great wisdom adopt measures more beneficial to the interest of the Nation at large, more adequate to our wants, and more suitable to our circumstances than any pecuniary consideration could prove.

Abbott, Edward, R. Art.  
Abbott, F. H., Capt., R. Art.  
Alexander, William  

Allen, Levi  

Amoss, Adam  
Anderson, Thomas  

Ball, Elias (for self)

Ball, Elias (junior)
Barron, Alexander
Bethune, Ferqr.
Bennie, William

Campbell, A., Captain S. C.
Campbell, Donald, Ensign
Campbell, Donald, Lieutenant
Campbell, James
Charleton, Geo.

Charlton, William, junior
Charleton, William
   Lieutenant, R: Arty
Charlton, William, junior

Clark, John
Connell, Redmond

Crookshanks, Patrick

Douglass, Benjamin
Douglass, Jno.
Dow, Thomas

Edwards, Peter

Fatio, Lewis
Fraser, Thomas, Major S.C.
Fotheringham, Alexander

Brown, John
Brown, Thomas
Brown, Thomas

Forbes, John

Grassell, Geo
Gunno, John.

Hale, Thomas
Hamilton, James
Hamilton, Jno. Lt. Colonel
Halloran, Jno.
Holmes, John
Honge, Henry

Humbard, Bernard

Hutchins, Anthony

Johnson, John
Johnson, William
Johnston, Lewis

Johnston, Lewis, junior

Kelsell, R.

Kemp, George
Kerr, John
Kinnen, Lewis, Captain

Lawe, R.
Leggett, Jnt., Captain

Leslie, John
Levett, Francis
Lindsay, Charles Stewart
Lord, Benjamin

Mackenzie, G.
Man, Spencer
Manson, Daniel, Major

Manson, G., Ensign
Marrett, Joseph
Martin, John
Martin, John
McDonald, John
McDonald, Thomas

McGaskill, Alexander
McIntosh, Jn.
McJuer, Colon

McKenzie, George, 60th reg.
McKinnon, Will

McLachlan, Archibald
McLatchy, Charles
McLeod, Murdock, Surgeon
McLeod, Robert
McLeod, William
McLuil, Daniel

McMain, Andrew
McMain, John
McMain, Thomas
McMurray, James


Mitchell, John, junior
Monkeith, Thomas
Moore, Philip
Moreas, Francis
Mortimer, Edmond
Moss, James
Moss, Thomas
Moss, William (for self)
Mowbray, Jno.


Muffett, Robert


Panton, William (for self)
Parr, Thomas (for Dennis Rolle)
Parr, Thomas (for self)
Payne, R.
Pengree, William
Penman, Edward

Perpall, John
Prince, Charles

Robinson, Geo
Robinson, Patk

Ross, John
Roupell, G.
Rowork, Sam

Scott, Robert
Shirreff, Peter
Smith, James

Smith, James
Smith, Josiah, Captain
Smith, Robert
Slater, William
Spence, Robert
Spiers, Alexander J.

Tattnall, Jno. Mullryne
Tattnall, Josiah

Waldron, Lyfford


Wallford, Benjamin
Warrington, Richard
Waters, Thomas
Wells, Wiurtwhat
Winniett, Jno
Withens, Thomas


Wood, John

Wyllay, Alexander C.
Wylly, William, Captain


Yeats, David

*Meanwhile, with the evacuation of South Carolina and Georgia by the British forces, many settlers fled into East Florida.*

7. A Return of Refugees, with their families and Blacks, who came to the Province of East Florida in consequence of the evacuation of the Province of Carolina. July 1783. PRO CO 5: 560

|  | Whites | | | Blacks | | | |
|---|---|---|---|---|---|---|---|
|  | | | | A | | | |
|  | M. | W. | C. | M. | W. | C. | [Men, Women, Children] |
| Abner, Jacob | 1 | 1 | 1 | | | | |
| Abraham, free black | | | | 1 | | | |

|  | M | W | C | M | W | C |
|---|---|---|---|---|---|---|
| Aird, James | 1 | 1 | 1 | 4 | 2 | 3 |
| Allison, James | 1 |  |  |  | 1 | 1 |
| Amos, Adam | 1 |  |  | 2 | 1 | 1 |
| Anderson, James | 1 |  |  |  |  |  |
| Andrews, Samuel | 1 | 1 | 3 | 1 | 1 | 1 |
| Antrobus, Issac | 1 | 3 |  | 1 | 1 | 1 |
| Armour, James | 1 |  |  |  |  |  |
| Artis, Josiah, free black |  |  |  | 1 |  |  |
| Asbell, Isaac | 1 |  |  |  |  |  |
| Ash, Richard Russell | 1 |  |  | 26 | 1 | 1 |
| Aslewood, Isaac | 1 |  |  | 1 |  |  |
| Ashworth, Arthur | 1 | 1 |  |  |  |  |
| Aughtry, Absolume | 1 |  |  |  |  |  |
| Austin, David | 1 |  |  |  |  |  |
| Austin, James | 1 |  |  |  |  |  |
| Austin, Joseph | 1 |  |  |  |  |  |

B

|  | M | W | C | M | W | C |
|---|---|---|---|---|---|---|
| Bailey, James | 1 |  |  |  |  |  |
| Bailey, John | 1 |  |  |  |  |  |
| Bailey, Mathew, junior | 1 |  |  |  |  |  |
| Bailey, Mathew, senior | 1 |  |  | 1 |  |  |
| Baker, Ann |  | 1 |  |  |  |  |
| Baker, Elizabeth |  | 1 |  |  | 1 |  |
| Baker, James | 1 |  |  |  |  |  |
| Baker, William | 1 |  |  |  |  |  |
| Baker, William | 1 |  |  |  |  |  |
| Ball, Elias, junior | 1 |  |  | 30 | 14 | 14 |
| Ball, Elias, senior | 3 | 2 | 4 | 75 | 49 | 59 |
| Ballenger, John | 1 |  |  |  |  |  |

| Name | | | | | | |
|---|---|---|---|---|---|---|
| Barber, Elizabeth | | 1 | 1 | | | |
| Barber, Gasper | 1 | 1 | 1 | | | |
| Barbett, a free black | | | | | 3 | |
| Barlow, William | 1 | 3 | | | | 2 |
| Barrow, Doctor Alex. | 1 | 1 | | | 11 | 6 |
| Bartlam, Mary | | 1 | 2 | | | |
| Bartholomew, Stephen | 1 | | | | | |
| Bates, Ephraim | 1 | | | | | |
| Bates, Joseph | 1 | 1 | 5 | | | |
| Bates, Thomas | 1 | | | | | |
| Bates, William | 1 | | | | | |
| Battles, William | 1 | 1 | | | 1 | 1 |
| Beames, Thomas | 1 | | | | | |
| Beams, William | 1 | | | | | |
| Beasley, Jacob | 1 | | | | | |
| Beasley, James | 2 | | | | | |
| Beasley, William | 3 | | | | | |
| Beaumont, Henry | 1 | | | | | |
| Beckman, Albert | 1 | 1 | 1 | | | |
| Bedford, Jonas | 1 | | | 1 | | |
| Beek, Abraham | 1 | | | | | |
| Begbie, William | 3 | | | 15 | 1 | |
| Bell, Samuel | 1 | | | | | |
| Belton, John | 1 | | | 15 | 4 | 4 |
| Bennie, William | 1 | 1 | | 4 | 5 | |
| Benson, Martin | 1 | | | | | |
| Berry, Michael | 1 | | | | | |
| Berwick, John | 1 | | | | | |
| Biggs, Caleb | 1 | | | | | |
| Billy, a free black | | | | 1 | | |
| Bitter, William | 1 | | | | | |
| Black, James | 1 | | | | | |

| Name | | | | | | | |
|---|---|---|---|---|---|---|---|
| Black, Robert | 1 | 5 | 3 | 1 | 1 | 1 | |
| Black, Thomas | 1 | | | | | | |
| Blackman, Wood | 1 | 1 | | | | | |
| Blair, Robert | 1 | | | 2 | 3 | 3 | |
| Bodley, John, junior | 1 | 1 | | | | | |
| Bodley, John, senior | 1 | 2 | | 4 | | | |
| Boggs, John | 1 | | | | | | |
| Boggs, Robert | 1 | 3 | 5 | | | | |
| Boggs, Simon | 1 | | | | | | |
| Boisseaw, Edward | | | | 10 | 4 | | |
| Bolton, Robert | 1 | | | 1 | | | |
| Bowgan, William | 1 | 1 | | | 1 | | |
| Bowman, William | 1 | 1 | | 2 | 1 | | |
| Boydson, Daniel | 1 | | | | | | |
| Bracker, George | | 2 | 3 | | | | |
| Bradley, Joseph | 1 | | | | | | |
| Bradley, Robert | 1 | | | | | | |
| Brasewill, Robert | 1 | | | 2 | | | |
| Brayn, William | 1 | 1 | | | | | |
| Brewer, William | 1 | | | | | | |
| Brewer, William, junior | | 1 | | | | | |
| Brindley, John | 1 | | | | | | |
| Brinkley, Joseph | 1 | | | | | | |
| Bristol & Greenwick | | | | 2 | | | |
| Brodie, John | 1 | | | | | | |
| Brown, Archibald | 2 | | | 31 | 24 | 27 | |
| Brown, Charles | 1 | 1 | 2 | | | | |
| Brown, Christopher | 1 | 1 | | 2 | 1 | | |
| Brown, Hugh | 1 | 1 | 4 | | | | |
| Brown, Peter | 1 | 2 | | 1 | | | |
| Brown, Stephen | 2 | 1 | | 3 | 5 | | |
| Brown & Mickie | 2 | | | 4 | 1 | | |

| Name | M | W | C | M | W | C |
|---|---|---|---|---|---|---|
| Bryan, Col. Samuel | 1 | | | 1 | | |
| Buchanan, John | 1 | | 1 | | | |
| Buckingham, Elias | 1 | | | 2 | 1 | 1 |
| Buckley, John | 2 | 1 | 2 | | | 1 |
| Bunch, Jacob | 2 | 3 | 4 | | | |
| Bunch, Paul | 1 | 1 | 1 | | | |
| Burcham, Joseph | | | | 2 | | |
| Burchum, Joseph | 1 | 1 | 1 | | 1 | |
| Burkett, George | 3 | 1 | 1 | | | |
| Burney, John | 1 | | | | | |
| Burrows, Ann | | 1 | | | | |
| Burrows, Sarah | 1 | 2 | | | 1 | |
| Burrows, William | 2 | | | 1 | | |
| Burser, Randolph | 1 | | | | | |
| Burts, Michael | 1 | | | | | |
| Byrd, Robert | 1 | | | 1 | 1 | |
| Byrd, John | 3 | 1 | 1 | | | |

## C

| Name | M | W | C | M | W | C |
|---|---|---|---|---|---|---|
| Caeser, Adam | 1 | | | | | |
| Cameron, Jean | | | | | 1 | |
| Campbell, Ann | | 1 | | | 1 | |
| Campbell, Archibald | 1 | | | 1 | 1 | |
| Campbell, John | 1 | 1 | 2 | | | |
| Campbell, Margaret | 2 | 2 | 1 | | 2 | 2 |
| Candiff, Isaac | 1 | 1 | 2 | | | |
| Cane, Benjamin | 1 | | | 1 | | |
| Cantzen, William | 1 | | | | | |
| Cape, Bryan | 1 | | | 14 | 5 | 2 |

| Name | | | | | | |
|---|---|---|---|---|---|---|
| Capers, Gabriel | 1 | | | 25 | 15 | 12 |
| Cargel, Daniel | 1 | | | 1 | | |
| Cargel, Richard | 1 | | | | | |
| Carmichael, James | 1 | | | | | |
| Carr, William | 1 | 1 | | | | |
| Carrier, Thomas | 1 | | | | | |
| Carrol, Thomas | 1 | | | | | |
| Carter, Isham, free black | | | | 1 | 1 | 2 |
| Carter, James | 1 | 1 | 2 | | | |
| Carter, Jeremiah | 1 | | | 2 | 1 | |
| Carter, John | 1 | | | 1 | | |
| Carter, Joseph | 2 | 2 | 3 | | | |
| Carter, Thomas | 4 | 1 | 2 | | | |
| Cashen, James | 1 | | | | | |
| Cassells, James | 1 | | | 13 | 11 | 3 |
| Champlin, James | 3 | 1 | | 1 | | |
| Champney, John | 1 | 1 | | 3 | | |
| Chappel, James | 1 | | | 1 | | |
| Charles, Christopher | 1 | | | | | |
| Cherry, Beley | 1 | 1 | 2 | 3 | 1 | |
| Christie, Harman | 1 | 1 | | | | |
| Clark, Colin | 1 | | | 1 | | |
| Clark, Isaac | 1 | 1 | | | | |
| Clark, Jacob | 1 | 1 | 1 | | | |
| Clark, Robert | 1 | | | | | |
| Clark, Thomas | 1 | | | | | |
| Clarkson, Mary | 1 | 1 | | | | |
| Clatworthy, James | 1 | 1 | | | | |
| Coatney, William | 1 | | | | | |
| Cole, Alice | 1 | 3 | 1 | | | |
| Cole, Baptist | 2 | 1 | 2 | | | |
| Cole, William | 1 | 1 | 3 | | | |

| Name | | | | | | |
|---|---|---|---|---|---|---|
| Coley, Keder | 1 | | | | | |
| Collier, Thomas | 1 | | | 1 | | |
| Collins, Charles | 1 | | | | | |
| Colson, John | 1 | | | 5 | 4 | 4 |
| Commander, Thomas | 1 | 3 | | 3 | 3 | 3 |
| Constable, David | 1 | | | 1 | | |
| Cook, Thomas | 1 | | | | | |
| Cooper, James | 1 | 1 | 2 | | | |
| Courtney, Thomas | 5 | 4 | | 1 | 1 | |
| Cowan, Benjamin | 2 | 1 | | | | |
| Cox, Charles | 1 | 1 | | | 1 | |
| Cox, David | 1 | | | | | |
| Cox, Thomas | 1 | 1 | 1 | 1 | 1 | |
| Crawford, Alexander | 1 | | | | | |
| Crawford, John | 1 | 1 | | 2 | 1 | |
| Creighton, Catherine | | 1 | 1 | | 1 | |
| Creed, Mathew | 1 | | | | | |
| Crocketts, David | 1 | | | | | |
| Croger, Martin | 1 | | | | | |
| Crosier, Thomas | 1 | 1 | | | | |
| Crum, Elijah | 1 | | | | | |
| Crumb, Harman | 1 | | | | | |
| Crumb, Solomon | 1 | | | | | |
| Culp, Jonathan | 1 | | | | | |
| Cuningham, Patrick | 1 | | | 7 | 5 | 6 |
| Cuningham, Robert | 1 | | | 1 | | |
| Cuningham, William | 1 | | | 3 | 1 | 4 |
| Cunningham, Andrew | 1 | 1 | 2 | 3 | | |
| Curry, Joseph | 1 | | | | | |
| Curtis, William | 1 | | | | | |
| Curtis, William | 1 | | | | | |
| Cuthbert, James | 2 | | | 1 | 1 | |

## D

|  | M. | W. | C. | M. | W. | C. |
|---|---|---|---|---|---|---|
| Daniel, James | 1 | | | | | |
| Davidson, Alexander | 1 | | | | 2 | 2 |
| Davies, Elizabeth | | 1 | | | | |
| Davies, George | 1 | 1 | 3 | | | |
| Davies, Mary | | 2 | | | | |
| Davies, Phoebe | | 1 | | | | |
| Davies, Robert | 1 | | | | | |
| Davis, John | 1 | | | | | |
| Dawson, William | 1 | | | | | |
| Day, Benjamin | 1 | 1 | 1 | | | |
| Daynham, David | 1 | 1 | 2 | 2 | | |
| Daynham, James | 1 | | | | | |
| Delashmate, Elias | 1 | | | | | |
| Dennis, Joseph | 1 | | | | | |
| Dennis, William | 1 | | | 1 | | |
| Dennistown, John | 2 | | | 3 | 2 | |
| Denoon, David | | 2 | | | | |
| Derry, John | 2 | 2 | 4 | | | |
| Deveaux, Andrew, junior | | | 1 | | 19 | |
| Deveaux, Andrew, senior | | | 1 | 12 | 19 | 11 |
| Deveaux, Jacob | 1 | | | 5 | 5 | |
| Dewelt, Daniel | 2 | 2 | 2 | | | |
| Dickson, Aaron | 1 | | | | | |
| Dickson, Josiah | 1 | | | | | |
| Dill, Job | 1 | | | | | |
| Dobbins, Isaac | | | | 1 | | |
| Dodgen, William | 1 | | | | | |
| Dorry, George | 1 | | | | | |

| | M | W | C | M | W | C |
|---|---|---|---|---|---|---|
| Dougharty, James | 1 | | | | | |
| Dougharty, John | 3 | 1 | 2 | | | |
| Downer, Moses | 1 | | | | | |
| Downey, Jean | | 2 | | | | |
| Downs, Arthur | 1 | | | 1 | | |
| Doyl, Thomas | 1 | | | | | |
| Drake, Aaron | 1 | 1 | 1 | | | |
| Drew, William | 1 | | | | | |
| Drury, Miles | 1 | 1 | 2 | | | |
| Drysdale, Alexander | 1 | | | 1 | | |
| Duberdue, Solus | 1 | | | | | |
| Duncan, Samuel | 1 | 1 | 2 | | | |
| Duncan, William | 1 | 1 | | | | |
| Duke, John | 1 | | | | | |
| Durban, Elizabeth | | 4 | | | | |
| Dwight, Henry | 1 | | | | | |
| D'Yarbrough, James | 1 | | | 8 | 4 | 2 |

E

| | M | W | C | M | W | C |
|---|---|---|---|---|---|---|
| Eager, Richard | 1 | | | | | |
| Earvin, John | 1 | | | | | |
| Eason, John | 1 | 1 | 4 | | | |
| Eden, George | 1 | 1 | 3 | 1 | | |
| Edie, Rebecca | | | | | 1 | |
| Edwards, Meredith | 1 | 1 | | | | |
| Egan, John | 1 | 1 | | | | |
| Egan, Nathaniel | 1 | | | | | |
| Egan, William | 1 | | | | | |
| Elerby, Isham | 1 | | | | | |

| | M. | W. | C. | M. | W. | C. |
|---|---|---|---|---|---|---|
| Elerby, Mary | 2 | 2 | 6 | 7 | 2 | 3 |
| Elerby, Thomas | 2 | 1 | 2 | 1 | | 1 |
| Elliot, Amos | 1 | 1 | | | | |
| Elizabeth, a mulatto | | 1 | | | | |
| Elmore, John | 1 | | | | | |
| Elmore, William | 1 | | | | | |
| English, John | 1 | | | 2 | 2 | 3 |
| English, Robert | 1 | 3 | 5 | 11 | 7 | 8 |
| Ennis, Rachel | 1 | 1 | 3 | | | |
| Evans, John | 1 | | | | | |
| Evans, Thomas | 2 | 2 | 3 | | | |
| Evans, Thomas | 1 | 2 | | | | |
| Eventer, Goodley | 1 | 1 | 3 | | | |
| Ewing, William | 1 | | | | | |

## F

| | M. | W. | C. | M. | W. | C. |
|---|---|---|---|---|---|---|
| Faircloth, Zachariah | 1 | | | 1 | | |
| Falconer, John | 2 | | | 3 | 5 | 1 |
| Fanning, Abraham | 1 | 1 | | | | |
| Fanning, Col. David | 4 | 2 | | 6 | 2 | 2 |
| Fanning, Jacob | 1 | | | | | |
| Fanning, John | 1 | 1 | 1 | 1 | | |
| Fanning, John, his comp. | 14 | 8 | 6 | | | |
| Farde, George | 1 | | | 6 | 4 | 2 |
| Fatio, Francis Philip | 2 | 2 | | 9 | | |
| Favours, William | 1 | 1 | | | | |
| Feltley, Jacob | 3 | 1 | 1 | | | |
| Felts, Fredrich | 1 | 1 | | | | |
| Ferebee, John | 2 | 1 | | | | |

| | M. | W. | C. | M. | W. | C. |
|---|---|---|---|---|---|---|
| Ferguson, Areal | 1 | | | | | |
| Fiddler, John | 1 | | | | | |
| Fincher, Jesse | 1 | | | 1 | | |
| Finlayson, Henry | 2 | 1 | 3 | | 1 | 1 |
| Fitcher, John | 1 | | | 1 | | |
| Flake, John | 1 | | | | | |
| Flannagan, Michael | 1 | | | 1 | | |
| Flowereu, Francis | 1 | 1 | 4 | | | |
| Floyd, Eve | | 1 | 1 | | | |
| Foisen, Ellias | 1 | | | 2 | 1 | |
| Forcetener, Joseph | 1 | 1 | 1 | | | |
| Foreman, William | 1 | | | | | |
| Forrester, John | 1 | | | | | |
| Fortenberry, James | 1 | | | | | |
| Fortune, Richard | 1 | | | | | |
| Fowler, William | 1 | 1 | | 1 | 1 | |
| Fraser, Hugh | 1 | | | | | |
| Fraser, Isaac | 1 | 1 | 3 | | | |
| Fraser, Thomas | | | | | | |
| Freeman, Abraham | | | | 1 | | |
| Freeman, John | 1 | 1 | | 3 | | |
| Friday, David | 2 | 2 | 5 | 2 | | |
| Frisbee, Abel | 2 | | | 1 | | |

## G

| | M. | W. | C. | M. | W. | C. |
|---|---|---|---|---|---|---|
| Gaits, Robert | 1 | | | | | |
| Ganaway, Marmaduke | 1 | | | | | |
| Gascin, John | 1 | | | | | |
| Gascoyn, Richard | 1 | | | 2 | 1 | |

| Name | | | | | | |
|---|---|---|---|---|---|---|
| Gaul, Robert | 1 | | | | | |
| Gentry, William | 1 | 1 | 1 | | | |
| George, free black | | | | 1 | 2 | |
| Gernon, James | 1 | | | | 1 | |
| Gibbons, Precilla | | 1 | | | 1 | |
| Gigleater, Frederick | 1 | 4 | 3 | | | |
| Gill, Mary | 3 | 2 | | | | |
| Gill, Robert | 1 | 1 | 3 | | | |
| Gillet, William | 1 | | | | | |
| Gilliard, John | 1 | | | 114 | 80 | 64 |
| Ginnings, Peter | 1 | | | | | |
| Glass, John | 1 | 1 | | | | |
| Glass, Soloman | 1 | 1 | | | | |
| Glen, John | 1 | | | 3 | | |
| Glen, William, senior | | | 1 | | 3 | |
| Goff, Charles Barnett | 2 | 1 | | 12 | 4 | |
| Goldsmith, Jesse | 1 | 1 | 2 | | | |
| Goodbread, Philip | 1 | | | | | |
| Goodman, Charles | 1 | | | | | |
| Gordon, James | 1 | | | 5 | 1 | |
| Gray, Agnes | | 1 | | | | |
| Gray, Archibald | 1 | 1 | | 3 | 1 | |
| Gray, Isaac | 1 | | | 1 | 2 | |
| Gray, Jesse | 1 | | | 1 | 1 | |
| Gray, Samuel | 1 | 1 | | | | |
| Green, Uriah | 1 | 1 | 2 | 1 | 1 | 1 |
| Greenland, Daniel | 1 | | | 1 | | |
| Gregory, Samuel | 2 | | | | | |
| Greenwich, Abraham | 1 | 1 | | | | |
| Griffin, John | 1 | | | | | |
| Griffis, Joseph | 1 | 1 | | | | |
| Groves, Joseph | 4 | 1 | 1 | | | |

|  | M. | W. | C. |  | M. | W. | C. |
|---|---|---|---|---|---|---|---|
| Grymes, Robert William | 1 | 1 | | | 1 | | |

## H

| | M. | W. | C. | M. | W. | C. |
|---|---|---|---|---|---|---|
| Hadson, Sherard | 1 | 1 | | | | |
| Hagler, John | 1 | 1 | 1 | | | |
| Hagler, Peter | 1 | 1 | 2 | | | |
| Halbart, John | 1 | | | 6 | 2 | |
| Haley, Nicolas | 1 | | | 1 | | |
| Hall, Philip | 1 | 1 | 1 | | | |
| Hamilton, James | 1 | 1 | | | | |
| Hamilton, John | 1 | | | | | |
| Hardage, Joseph | 1 | | 1 | | 1 | |
| Hardwick, Lewis | 1 | | | | | |
| Harker, John | 1 | | | | | |
| Harmond, Anthony | 1 | | | | | |
| Harmond, David | 1 | 1 | | | | |
| Harris, John | 1 | 1 | | | | |
| Harris, Simon | 1 | | | | | |
| Harris, William | 1 | 1 | | | | |
| Harrison, James | 1 | 1 | 1 | 3 | 2 | |
| Harrison, Capt. Samuel | | | | 5 | | |
| Hart, Ellis | 1 | | | 1 | | |
| Harvey, Thomas | 2 | 2 | 5 | 14 | 9 | 10 |
| Hatch, William | 1 | | | | | |
| Hayes, Robert | 1 | | | | | |
| Haynes, William | 1 | 1 | | | | |
| Heaker, Fredrick | 1 | | | | | |
| Heaker, Fredrick | 1 | | | | | |
| Healms, William | 1 | | | | | |

| Name | | | | | | |
|---|---|---|---|---|---|---|
| Heartley, Fredrick, junior | 1 | 1 | 2 | | | |
| Heartley, Fredrick, senior | 1 | | | | | |
| Heatley, Henry | 1 | | | | | |
| Henderson, Druscilla | 1 | | | | | |
| Henderson, Jean | 2 | | | | | |
| Henderson, Sherard | 1 | | | | | |
| Henderson, Sherwood | 1 | | | | | |
| Hendricks, Micajah | 1 | | | | | |
| Hendricks, William | 2 | 2 | 3 | 2 | | 1 |
| Henry, John | 2 | 1 | | | | |
| Henry, William, junior | 1 | | | | | |
| Henry, William | 1 | | | | | |
| Hersham, Godfrey | 1 | | | | | |
| Hepburn, James | 1 | | | 4 | 2 | |
| Hicks, John | 1 | | | 1 | | |
| Higgins, Reuben | 1 | 1 | | | | |
| Higgins, William | 3 | 1 | 2 | | | |
| Hill, John | 1 | | | | | |
| Hillis, William | 1 | | | | | |
| Hittenbrand, Daniel | 1 | 1 | | | | |
| Hobbs, Augustine | 1 | | | | | |
| Hodgeson, Catherine | | 2 | | | | |
| Hoggan, Daniel | 2 | 1 | | | | |
| Holdsworth, Stephen | | | | 6 | | 3 |
| Holliday, George | 1 | | | | | |
| Holloway, Samuel | 1 | | | 1 | | |
| Hood, John | 1 | | | 1 | | |
| Hopton, Enoch | 1 | | | 1 | | |
| Howard, John | 1 | | | | | |
| Hudson, Joch | 1 | | | 2 | | |
| Hudson, Samuel | 2 | 1 | | | | |
| Hughs, Fredrick | 1 | 1 | 3 | | | |

|                          | M. | W. | C. | M. | W. | C. |
|---|---|---|---|---|---|---|
| Hume, James              |    |    |    | 31 | 19 |    |
| Hume, Peter              |    |    |    | 4  | 4  | 3  |
| Humphreys, James         | 1  |    |    |    |    |    |
| Hungerfreelar, David     | 1  | 1  | 1  |    |    |    |
| Hungerfreelar, Jacob     | 1  |    |    |    |    |    |
| Hungerfreelar, John      | 1  |    |    |    |    |    |
| Hunt, Madderson          | 2  | 1  | 2  |    |    |    |
| Hunter, John             | 1  | 1  | 1  |    |    |    |
| Hurton, Nicolas          | 1  | 1  | 2  |    |    |    |
| Hutchins, Anthony        | 2  |    |    |    |    |    |

## I

|                  | M. | W. | C. | M. | W. | C. |
|---|---|---|---|---|---|---|
| Ingraim, William | 3  | 1  | 1  |    |    |    |
| Ishell, Benjamin | 1  | 1  |    | 1  |    |    |
| Iverson, Samuel  | 2  |    |    |    | 1  |    |

## J

|                              | M. | W. | C. | M. | W. | C. |
|---|---|---|---|---|---|---|
| Jackson, John                | 1  | 1  | 1  |    |    |    |
| Jackson, John                | 1  |    |    |    |    |    |
| Jeffry, William              | 1  |    |    |    |    |    |
| Jennings, Peter              | 1  |    |    |    |    |    |
| Joblin, Ann                  |    | 1  |    |    |    |    |
| Johnson, Bunch               | 1  |    |    |    |    |    |
| Johnson, Elizabeth           |    |    |    | 1  | 1  |    |
| Johnson, Henry               | 1  |    |    |    |    |    |
| Johnson, John, for Dr. Wood  | 1  |    |    |    |    |    |

|  | M. | W. | C. | M. | W. | C. |
|---|---|---|---|---|---|---|
| Johnson, Patrick | 2 |  |  | 1 | 1 | 2 |
| Johnson, Robert, for Colleton |  |  |  | 19 | 12 |  |
| Johnston, Charles |  |  |  | 18 | 16 | 14 |
| Johnston, Elizabeth |  | 1 |  |  | 2 |  |
| Jones, Barbara |  | 1 |  | 2 |  |  |
| Jones, Henry | 1 |  |  |  |  |  |
| Jones, Henry | 2 | 1 |  |  |  |  |
| Jones, James | 4 | 1 | 4 |  |  |  |
| Jones, James | 1 |  |  |  |  |  |
| Jones, John | 1 | 1 | 2 |  |  |  |
| Jones, John | 1 |  |  |  |  |  |
| Jones, Nathaniel | 1 | 2 |  | 3 | 2 |  |
| Jones, Richard | 1 | 3 | 3 |  |  |  |

## K

|  | M. | W. | C. | M. | W. | C. |
|---|---|---|---|---|---|---|
| Kagler, Andrew | 1 | 1 | 1 | 2 |  |  |
| Kagler, Michael | 1 |  |  | 1 |  |  |
| Kebler, Adam | 1 | 1 |  |  |  |  |
| Keef, Daniel | 1 | 1 |  |  |  |  |
| Keller, Gasper | 1 |  |  |  |  |  |
| Keller, John | 1 |  |  |  |  |  |
| Kellian, Andrew | 1 |  |  |  |  |  |
| Kelly, James | 2 | 2 |  | 1 | 1 |  |
| Kelly, John | 1 |  |  |  |  |  |
| Kelly, Robert | 1 | 1 | 1 | 5 | 2 | 2 |
| Kelly, William | 1 |  |  |  |  |  |
| Kembler, Henry | 1 |  |  |  |  |  |
| Kennedy, Robert | 2 |  |  |  |  |  |
| Kerr, George |  |  |  | 6 | 7 |  |

41

|  | M. | W. | C. | M. | W. | C. |
|---|---|---|---|---|---|---|
| Kerr, John, for J. Hepburn |  |  |  | 1 | 3 | 3 |
| Kerr, John | 1 |  |  |  |  |  |
| Kerroy, Elizabeth |  |  |  |  |  |  |
| Kersey, Elizabeth | 1 | 2 | 2 |  |  |  |
| Key, Elizabeth |  | 1 | 2 |  |  |  |
| King, Asberry | 1 |  |  |  |  |  |
| King, George | 1 | 2 | 1 |  |  |  |
| King, Henry | 1 |  |  |  |  |  |
| King, John | 1 |  |  |  |  |  |
| King, Richard | 3 | 2 |  | 3 | 1 |  |
| King, Samuel | 1 | 1 |  |  |  |  |
| King, Sebastian | 1 |  |  | 1 | 1 |  |
| King, Starling | 1 |  |  |  |  |  |
| King, Sugar | 1 |  |  |  |  |  |
| Knox, John | 1 |  |  | 2 | 2 |  |

## L

|  | M. | W. | C. | M. | W. | C. |
|---|---|---|---|---|---|---|
| Laird, James | 1 |  |  |  |  |  |
| Lane, Marrion |  | 1 | 2 | 4 | 2 | 2 |
| Lang, Richard | 2 | 1 | 4 | 3 |  |  |
| Langford, James | 1 |  |  |  |  |  |
| Langham, William | 1 |  |  |  |  |  |
| Lapkin, James | 1 | 2 |  |  |  |  |
| Large, Nathaniel | 1 |  |  |  |  |  |
| Lawes, John | 1 | 1 |  |  |  |  |
| Lawes, Robert | 1 |  |  |  |  |  |
| Leary, Darby | 1 |  |  |  |  |  |
| Le Blonde, Andrew | 2 | 3 | 2 |  |  |  |
| Le Blonde, Henry | 2 | 3 | 1 |  |  |  |

| | | | | | | |
|---|---|---|---|---|---|---|
| Ledford, Fredrick | 1 | | | | | |
| Lee, William | 1 | 2 | 1 | | | |
| Legge, Benjamin S. | 1 | | | 3 | | |
| Legge, Edward | 1 | | | 3 | 3 | 2 |
| Legge, Edward | 1 | | | 2 | | |
| Lekes, George | 1 | | | | | |
| Lemons, James | 2 | 2 | | | | |
| Lewis, John | 1 | 1 | | | | 1 |
| Lewis, Peter | 1 | | | | | |
| Lewis, Peter | 1 | | | | | |
| Lewis staff | 1 | 1 | 1 | | | |
| Liblier, John | 1 | | | | | |
| Lifner, George | 1 | | 2 | | | |
| Lindsay, Sarah & Phillis | | 2 | 1 | | | |
| Lindsay, Thomas | 1 | | | | | |
| Linn, Joseph | 1 | | | | | |
| Lipps, Jacob | 1 | | | | | |
| Little, Niel | 1 | | | | | |
| Lizzett, Patrick | 1 | | | | 1 | 1 |
| Lockwood, Josiah | 1 | | | | 1 | |
| Long, George | 3 | 1 | 2 | | | |
| Lorimere, Alexander | 1 | | | | 8 | 1 |
| Lovegrove, William | 1 | | | | | |
| Lowrey, Lewis | 1 | | | | | |
| Lucas, William | 1 | | | | | |
| Luden, Catharine | | | 1 | | | |
| Lukason, Boston | | | | | 1 | |

## M

| | M. | W. | C. | M. | W. | C. |
|---|---|---|---|---|---|---|
| Madden, Emanuel | 1 | | | | | |
| Madden, George | 1 | | | | | 1 |
| Maltsbey, William | 2 | 2 | | | | |
| Man, Spencer for Edward Fenwick | | | | | 11 | 9 |
| Manson, Duncan | 1 | | | | | |
| Manson, Margarat | | 1 | 1 | 1 | 1 | |
| Mary, a free black | | | | 1 | 2 | 3 |
| Markley, Henry | 1 | | | | | |
| Marshall, John | 1 | | | 1 | 2 | |
| Martin, Martin | 1 | | | | | |
| Martin, Murdoch | 1 | | | 2 | 2 | 1 |
| Martin, William | | | | | | |
| Maser, John | 1 | | | | | |
| Mason, John | 1 | | | | | |
| Masters, Henry | 1 | | | | | |
| Masure, Christopher | 1 | | | | | |
| Mathews, Andrew | 2 | 2 | | | | |
| Mathews, Martin | 1 | | | | | |
| Matlock, Charles | 1 | | | | | |
| Maxwell, William | 1 | | | | 2 | 3 |
| May, Joseph | 2 | 2 | | | | |
| Mayfield, Stephen | 1 | | | | | |
| Mays, Richard | 1 | | | 1 | | |
| Mays, William | 2 | 1 | 4 | | | |
| Melone, Ephraim | 1 | 2 | 2 | | | |
| Messmore, Martha | | 2 | 4 | | | |
| McAulay, Alexander | 1 | | | | | |
| McAulay, Murdoch | 1 | | | | | |

| | | | | | |
|---|---|---|---|---|---|
| McBride, James | 1 | 1 | | | |
| McCall, Paul | 1 | | | | |
| McCan, John | 1 | 1 | | | |
| McCart, William | 1 | | | | |
| McCartney, Nicolas | 1 | | 1 | | |
| McCaskill, Captain for sister | 1 | | | | |
| McCaskill, John | 1 | | | | |
| McCelvey, William | 1 | | | | |
| McConnel, Samuel | 1 | | | 1 | |
| McCullum, James | 1 | | | 1 | |
| McDonald, Angus | | 2 | | 1 | 1 |
| McDonald, Hugh | 1 | | | | |
| McDonald, Isabell | | 2 | | | 1 |
| McDonald, John | 2 | | | 1 | |
| McDonald, John | 1 | | | | |
| McDonald, John | 1 | | | | |
| McDonald, John | 1 | 2 | | 2 | 1 |
| McDonald, Rodrick | 1 | | | | |
| McDonald, Ronald | 1 | | | 3 | 3 |
| McDaniel, James | 1 | | | | |
| McEmery, William | 1 | | | | |
| McEnnery, William | 1 | | | | |
| McFaitter, Daniel | 1 | | | | |
| McFarlan, Parland | 1 | | | | |
| McFarlane, John | 2 | | | | |
| McFarlane for– | | | | | 2 |
| McGee, Elizabeth | | 1 | 2 | | |
| McGill, Samuel | 1 | | | | |
| McHezzack, Daniel | 1 | 1 | | | |
| McInnis, Angus | 1 | | | | |
| McInnis, Donald | 1 | | | 4 | 1 |
| McInnis, Donald | 1 | | | | |

45

| Name | | | | | | |
|---|---|---|---|---|---|---|
| McInnis, Miles | 1 | | | 1 | | |
| McInnis, Miles | 1 | | | | | |
| McInnis, Niel | 1 | | | | | |
| McIntyre, Duncan | 1 | | | | | |
| McIntyre, John | 1 | 1 | | | | |
| McIver, Colin | 2 | 1 | | | | |
| McKay, Archibald | 1 | | | | | |
| McKay, Niel | 1 | | | | | |
| McKenzie, Daniel | 1 | | | | | |
| McKenzie, John | 2 | 1 | 2 | 1 | 2 | |
| McKenzie, Mary | 3 | 1 | | | | |
| McKenzie, Col. Robert | | | | 1 | 2 | 2 |
| McKinnon, Margarat | | 1 | 2 | 4 | 2 | 1 |
| McKinnon, Samuel | 2 | 1 | 2 | 15 | 17 | 14 |
| McLean, Andrew | 1 | | | | | |
| McLean, Mary | | 1 | | | | |
| McLean, Robert | 1 | 1 | 2 | | | |
| McLennan, Alexander | 1 | | | | | |
| McLennan, Henry | 1 | | | | | |
| McLennan, James | 1 | | | | | |
| McLennan, Laughlan | 1 | | | | | |
| McLennan, Rodrick | 1 | | | | | |
| McLeod, Alexander | 1 | | | 1 | 1 | |
| McLeod, Donald | 1 | | | 1 | 1 | |
| McLeod, Mary | | 1 | | | | |
| McLeod, Niel | 1 | | | | 1 | |
| McLeod, Norman | 1 | | | | | |
| McMullen, Ann | | 2 | 2 | | | |
| McMurray, James | 2 | | | 4 | 5 | |
| McNab, Margaret | 1 | 1 | | 2 | 2 | |
| McNair, John | 1 | | | | | |
| McNiel, Daniel | 1 | 1 | | | | |

| | | | | | | |
|---|---|---|---|---|---|---|
| McNiel, Hector for– | | | | 3 | | |
| McQueen, Donald | 1 | | | | | |
| McQueen, John | 1 | | | | | |
| McQueen, Thomas | 1 | | | | | |
| McQuire, Daniel | 1 | 1 | | | 1 | |
| McRae, Alexander for– | | 3 | | 2 | 1 | |
| McRae, Donald | 1 | | | 1 | | |
| McRae, Duncan | 1 | | | | | |
| McRae, Finlay | 1 | | | | | |
| McRae, John | 1 | | | | | |
| McRae, John | 1 | | | | | |
| McRaw, Tarquhar | 1 | | | | | |
| McSennan, Donald | 1 | 1 | | 1 | | |
| McTee, Archibald | 1 | | | | | |
| McVicar, Mary | | 1 | | | | |
| McYomery, Lawrence | 1 | 1 | | 1 | | |
| Mickie, Harry | 1 | | | | | |
| Mickie, John | 3 | | | 4 | 1 | |
| Middleton, Robert | 1 | 1 | | | | |
| Miley, Jacob | 1 | | | | | |
| Miller, Elizabeth | | | | | 1 | |
| Miller, Jacob | 1 | | | | | |
| Miller, Margarat | 2 | 2 | | | | |
| Miller, Samuel | 2 | 1 | 2 | 1 | | |
| Mills, John | 1 | 1 | | 2 | | 1 |
| Mills, Robert | 1 | | | 1 | 1 | |
| Milton, Michael | 1 | | | 1 | | |
| Mitchell, Alexander | 1 | | | | | |
| Mitchell, John | 1 | | | | | |
| Mitchell, John | 8 | 2 | | 5 | 2 | |
| Mitchell, John | 2 | 2 | | | | |
| Moffat, Daniel | 1 | | | | | |

|  | M. | W. | C. |  | M. | W. | C. |
|---|---|---|---|---|---|---|---|
| Molloy, Charles | 1 | | | | 1 | 2 | |
| Montell, Anthony | 1 | | | | | | |
| Moore, Gabriel | 1 | 1 | 1 | | | | |
| Moore, John | 1 | | | | 2 | 1 | |
| Moore, Joseph | 1 | | | | | | |
| Moore, Mary | | | | | | 1 | |
| Moore, Moses | 2 | | | | 1 | 1 | 4 |
| Moore, William | 2 | 1 | 4 | | | | |
| Morgan, Carles | 2 | 2 | 2 | | 5 | 4 | 2 |
| Morris, John | 1 | | | | | | |
| Morris, John | 2 | | | | 1 | 3 | |
| Morrison, Alexander | 1 | 1 | | | | | |
| Morrison, Archibald | 1 | | | | | | |
| Morrison, John | 1 | | | | | | |
| Morrison, John | 1 | | | | | | |
| Mortgridge, John | 3 | | | | 2 | | |
| Mulligan, John | 2 | 2 | | | | 1 | |
| Murphy, Hugh | 2 | | | | 1 | 1 | 1 |
| Murphy, John | 2 | | | | 1 | | |
| Murphy, John | 1 | 2 | | | 2 | 1 | |
| Murphy, Richard | 1 | | | | | | |
| Murphy, Robert | 1 | | | | | | |
| Murphy, William | 1 | 1 | 1 | | 1 | | |
| Murray, Thomas | 1 | | | | | | |
| Muslewhite, Josiah | 1 | | | | | | |

N

|  | M. | W. | C. | M. | W. | C. |
|---|---|---|---|---|---|---|
| Nash, Elizabeth | 1 | 1 | 2 | | | |
| Nash, John | 1 | | | | | |

| | | | | | | |
|---|---|---|---|---|---|---|
| Neilly, John | 1 | | | | | |
| Nelly, Christopher | 1 | 1 | 3 | 3 | 3 | 1 |
| Nelly, Robert | 1 | | | 1 | | |
| Nelson, Ambrose | 1 | 1 | 1 | | | |
| Nelson, Ann | | 1 | 1 | | | |
| Nelson, William | 1 | 1 | 4 | | | |
| Newland, Dennis | 1 | 2 | 4 | | | |
| Niblet, Timothy | 1 | | | | | |
| Nielson, Ann | | 2 | | | 1 | |
| Noble, Peter | | | | 2 | 1 | |
| North, Joshua | 1 | | | | | |
| Norton, John | 1 | | | | | |
| Nowland, John | 1 | | | | | |
| Nun, Joshua | 1 | 1 | 2 | 1 | | |

## O

| | M. | W. | C. | M. | W. | C. |
|---|---|---|---|---|---|---|
| O'Bryan, Samuel | 1 | | | 1 | | |
| O'Niel, Henry | 1 | | | 2 | | |
| O'Niel, James | 1 | 1 | 4 | 2 | 1 | 1 |
| O'Reilly, Charles | 1 | | | 1 | | |
| Odam, Sarah | 1 | 5 | 3 | | | |
| Osten, James | 1 | | | | | |
| Ouple, John | 2 | 1 | | 1 | 1 | |
| Owen, Elizabeth | | 1 | | | | |
| Owen, Jean | | 1 | | | | |
| Ownsel, George | 2 | 1 | 1 | | | |

## P

|  | M. | W. | C. | M. | W. | C. |
|---|---|---|---|---|---|---|
| Panting, Timothy | 3 | 3 | 1 | | | |
| Paris, Richard | 1 | 2 | | 7 | 2 | |
| Parker, Charles | 1 | | | | | |
| Parker, John | 1 | 1 | 2 | | | |
| Parker, Thomas | 1 | | | | | |
| Parker, William | 1 | 1 | 1 | 2 | | |
| Parsons, William | 3 | | 1 | | | |
| Pary, Ishom | 3 | | | | | |
| Patchin, John | 1 | | | | | |
| Patterson, Thomas | 2 | | | | | |
| Pearson, Thomas | 1 | 1 | | 1 | | |
| Peglar, Henry | 1 | 1 | 2 | | | |
| Peglar, Jacob | 1 | 1 | 2 | | | |
| Peglar, Peter | 1 | | | | | |
| Peirce, William | 1 | | | | | |
| Peircy, James | 1 | | | | | |
| Penman, Edward | 2 | | | 4 | | |
| Pentecost, Hartwell | 1 | 2 | | | | |
| Perkins, Christopher | 1 | | | | | |
| Phelps, Frederick | 1 | 1 | | | | |
| Pickering, Francis | 1 | | | | | |
| Plummer, Daniel | 1 | 1 | | 2 | 2 | 2 |
| Pool, Peter | 1 | | | | 1 | |
| Porter, John | 1 | | | 2 | | |
| Povey, Richard | 1 | | | | | |
| Powell, Doctor John | 1 | | | | | |
| Prescot, Aaron | 2 | | | | | |
| Prescot, Jasper | 1 | | | | | |

| | | | | | | |
|---|---|---|---|---|---|---|
| Preston, William | 1 | | | | | |
| Price, William | 1 | 1 | 1 | | | |
| Prichard, Robert | 1 | | | | | |
| Proctor, Edward | 1 | | | | | |
| Proctor, Philip | 1 | 1 | 1 | | | |
| Prow, Peter | 2 | | | 2 | | |
| Prowit, Beasley | 1 | 2 | 3 | | | |
| Pye, Roger | 1 | | | 3 | 1 | |
| Pyne, William | 1 | | | 1 | | |
| Pyner, Joseph | 1 | | | | | |

## Q

| | M. | W. | C. | M. | W. | C. |
|---|---|---|---|---|---|---|
| Quinlin, John | 1 | 1 | | 1 | | |

## R

| | M. | W. | C. | M. | W. | C. |
|---|---|---|---|---|---|---|
| Ramsay, Alexander | 1 | | | | | |
| Ramsay, James | 1 | | | | | |
| Ramsay, Niel | 1 | | | | | |
| Ray, Elizabeth | | 1 | | 2 | 2 | 4 |
| Ray, Thomas | 1 | | | | | |
| Ray, William | 1 | | | | | |
| Rayborn, George | 1 | 2 | 1 | | | |
| Rayborn, Richard | 1 | 2 | | | | |
| Redground, David | 1 | 1 | | | | |
| Rees, William | 1 | | | 7 | 5 | 8 |
| Reeves, James | 1 | | | | | |

| | | | | | | |
|---|---|---|---|---|---|---|
| Reilly, William | 1 | 2 | | | | |
| Remington, William | 1 | 2 | | | 1 | |
| Ren, Thomas | 1 | | | | | |
| Revels, Edmund | 1 | | | | | |
| Reynolds, John | 1 | | | | | |
| Rhode, Godfrey | 1 | | | | | |
| Rhodes, William | 1 | | | 1 | | |
| Rhodes, William | 1 | 3 | | 2 | 1 | |
| Riddle, Andrew | 1 | | | | | |
| Ried, Thomas | 1 | | | | | |
| Riggard, Gasper | 1 | | | | | |
| Right, William | 1 | | | 1 | | |
| Ringer, Henry | 1 | | | | | |
| Roberts, John | 1 | | | | | |
| Roberts, Joseph | 1 | | | 4 | | |
| Robertson, John | 1 | 1 | 2 | 1 | 1 | |
| Robinson, David | 1 | | | | | |
| Robinson, Joseph | | 1 | | 2 | 2 | |
| Robinson, Joseph | 1 | | | | | |
| Robinson, Samuel | 1 | | | | | |
| Rocer, Jonathan | 1 | 1 | 2 | | | |
| Rocker, Jasper | 1 | | | | | |
| Roger, Jasper | 2 | 1 | 3 | | | |
| Romney, Andrew | 1 | | | | | |
| Rose, Hugh | 2 | | | 1 | | |
| Ross, George & Robert | 2 | | | 4 | | |
| Ross, Hugh | 2 | | | | | |
| Rowe, Samuel | 1 | 1 | 1 | 4 | 3 | 4 |
| Rowe, Samuel, junior | 1 | | | | | |
| Rowe, Fredrick | 1 | | | | | |
| Rowles, Silas | 1 | 1 | | | | |
| Rowpell, George | 1 | 2 | | 12 | 13 | |

|  |  |  |  |  |  |  |
|---|---|---|---|---|---|---|
| Runnels, Thomas | 1 | | | | | |
| Rush, Abraham | 1 | | | 1 | | |
| Rush, George | 1 | | | | | |
| Rush, Peter | 1 | | | | | |
| Russell, Samuel | 1 | | | | | |
| Russell, William | 1 | | | 1 | 3 | |
| Rutter, William | 2 | 1 | | 2 | | |

## S

|  | M. | W. | C. | M. | W. | C. |
|---|---|---|---|---|---|---|
| Saddler, John | 1 | | | | | |
| Sailor, David | 3 | | | 13 | 4 | |
| Sallie, Henry | 1 | | | 4 | 1 | 1 |
| Samatt, Leonard | 2 | 1 | | | | |
| Sarah, a free mulatto | | 1 | | | | |
| Scipio, a free man | | | | 1 | | |
| Scott, David | 1 | 1 | 1 | 4 | 5 | 1 |
| Scott, John | 1 | | | 3 | 3 | |
| Scott, Samuel | 3 | 1 | 1 | | | |
| Scurry, John | 1 | | | | | |
| Sfowzal, Alexander | 1 | | | | | |
| Shaver, George | 1 | 1 | 1 | | | |
| Shaver, Philip | 1 | | | | | |
| Shaw, Archibald | 1 | | | | | |
| Shaw, Norman | 1 | | | | | |
| Shelly, Christian | 1 | | | | | |
| Shields, Elizabeth | | 1 | | | | |
| Shirley, Absolume | 1 | 1 | 1 | | | |
| Shoemaker, Daniel | 1 | 4 | 5 | | | |
| Shorter, Richard | 1 | 1 | | 1 | | |

| Name | | | | | | |
|---|---|---|---|---|---|---|
| Shouse, Henry | 1 | | | | | |
| Shuffer, Jacob | 1 | | | | | |
| Siglor, John | 1 | 1 | | | | |
| Silby, Francis | 1 | 1 | 2 | | 1 | |
| Silcocke, John | 1 | | | | | |
| Simmons, Joseph | 1 | 1 | 2 | | | |
| Simmons, Thomas | 1 | 1 | 1 | | | |
| Simms, Edward | 1 | | | | | |
| Simpson, John & Jeremiah | 2 | | | 1 | 1 | 2 |
| Simpson, Thomas | 1 | 1 | | | | |
| Simpson, William | | | | | | |
| Sinclair, Daniel | 1 | 2 | 2 | | | |
| Skinner, Joanna | | 1 | | | | |
| Slater, Thomas | 1 | | | | 1 | |
| Sloan, James | 1 | 1 | | | | |
| Sloan, Patrick | 1 | | | | | |
| Sloan, Robert | 1 | | | | | |
| Small, Thomas | 1 | | | | | |
| Small, William | 1 | 2 | 1 | | | |
| Smalley, Abner | 1 | | | | | |
| Smart, Isaac | 1 | | | | | |
| Smart, William | 1 | | | | | |
| Smiley, James | 1 | | | | | |
| Smiley, Niel | 1 | | | | | |
| Smith, Adam | 1 | | | | | |
| Smith, Arthur | 1 | | | 4 | 1 | |
| Smith, Christian | 1 | | | | | |
| Smith, Drury | 1 | | 1 | | | |
| Smith, Edward | 1 | | | | | |
| Smith, George | 1 | | | | | |
| Smith, Henry | 1 | | | | | |
| Smith, James | 1 | | | | | |

| Name | | | | | | |
|---|---|---|---|---|---|---|
| Smith, James | 1 | | | | | |
| Smith, John | 1 | | | | | |
| Smith, John | 1 | | | | | |
| Smith, John | 1 | | | | | |
| Smith, Levey | 1 | 1 | 3 | 2 | 2 | |
| Smith, Robert | 1 | | | 2 | 2 | |
| Smith, Thomas | 1 | | | | | |
| Smith, William | | | | 1 | | |
| Smythe, John | 1 | | | 18 | 13 | 9 |
| Snell, Henry | 1 | 1 | | | | |
| Snelling, Richard | 1 | 1 | 1 | 1 | 1 | 1 |
| Someral, Henry, junior | 1 | | | | | |
| Someral, Jacob | 2 | 3 | 4 | 2 | 2 | 1 |
| Sommerline, Jacob | 1 | | | | | |
| Somerline, Thomas | 1 | | | | | |
| Sommers, John | 1 | | | | | |
| Southerland, Daniel | 1 | | | 3 | 3 | |
| Spence, Doctor Peter | 1 | 2 | | 2 | 3 | 1 |
| Spencer, Stephen | 1 | 1 | | | | |
| Stage, Fredrick | 1 | 1 | | 2 | 2 | |
| Stamma, Lewis | 1 | | | | | |
| Starling, Francis | 1 | | | | | |
| Steed, Thomas | 1 | | | | | |
| Stephen, William | 1 | | | | | |
| Stepney, a free black | | | | 1 | 1 | |
| Stevens, William | 1 | | | | | |
| Stevenson, George | 1 | | | | | |
| Stevenson, Hugh | 1 | | | | | |
| Stewart, Kenith | 1 | | | | | |
| Stinewinter, George | 1 | 1 | 3 | | | |
| Stockhill, Joshua | 1 | | | | | |
| Storer, Mary | | 1 | | | | |

|  |  |  |  |  |  |  |
|---|---|---|---|---|---|---|
| Storr, John | 2 | 1 |  | 4 | 5 | 1 |
| Stoutimere, George | 1 |  |  |  |  |  |
| Stradford, John | 1 |  |  |  |  |  |
| Strain, William | 1 |  |  |  |  |  |
| Strickland, William | 1 |  |  |  |  |  |
| Stroup, John | 1 |  |  |  |  |  |
| Stuart, Alexander | 1 |  |  | 1 | 3 |  |
| Stuart, Allen | 1 |  |  |  |  |  |
| Stuart, John, estate of |  |  |  | 22 | 22 | 41 |
| Stunder, Jacob | 1 |  |  |  |  |  |
| Sullivan, James | 1 |  |  | 1 |  |  |
| Sutton, Beauman | 1 |  |  |  |  |  |
| Swafford, Thomas | 1 |  |  |  |  |  |
| Swanson, David | 1 |  |  | 2 |  |  |
| Swiney, James | 1 |  |  |  |  |  |

## T

|  | M. | W. | C. | M. | W. | C. |
|---|---|---|---|---|---|---|
| Tackell, William | 1 |  |  |  |  |  |
| Tam, Anthony | 1 |  |  |  |  |  |
| Tatnall, John Mulrain | 1 |  |  | 2 | 1 |  |
| Tattnall, Joshua for Ord, Boom & Colleton |  |  |  | 57 | 44 | 48 |
| Taylor, Elijah | 1 | 2 |  |  |  |  |
| Taylor, Elizabeth | 1 | 1 |  |  |  |  |
| Taylor, James | 1 |  |  |  |  |  |
| Taylor, Robert | 1 |  |  | 1 | 2 | 2 |
| Teague, Israel | 1 |  |  |  |  |  |
| Temple, James | 1 | 2 | 1 |  |  |  |
| Thomas, Ralph | 1 |  |  |  |  |  |

| | M. | W. | C. | M. | W. | C. |
|---|---|---|---|---|---|---|
| Thomas, William | 1 | | | | | |
| Thomason, John | 1 | 1 | 1 | | | |
| Thompson, John | 1 | | | | | |
| Thompson, Peter | 1 | 1 | 3 | | | |
| Thompson, Victor | 1 | | | 8 | 8 | |
| Thomson, James | 1 | | | 4 | 2 | |
| Thowson, Joseph | 1 | | | | | |
| Tinily, Jolin | 1 | | | | | |
| Tinker, Jeremiah | 1 | 2 | | 2 | 2 | |
| Titley, Joseph | 1 | | | 3 | 2 | 1 |
| Torry, James | 1 | | | | | |
| Tree, George | 1 | 1 | | | | |
| Trussell, Charles | 1 | 1 | 2 | 1 | | |
| Trust, George | 1 | | | | | |
| Tufton, Simon | 1 | | | 1 | | |
| Tunne, Thomas | 1 | | | 8 | | |
| Tunno, John | 1 | | | 4 | 5 | |
| Turner, David | 1 | | | | | |
| Turner, Edward | 1 | | | | | |
| Turner, Elijah | | | | | | |
| Tyler, John | 1 | 1 | 4 | | | |
| Tyler, Capt. Peter, his company | 27 | 6 | 7 | | | |
| Tyner, Lewis | 2 | 1 | 3 | | | |

U

| | M. | W. | C. | M. | W. | C. |
|---|---|---|---|---|---|---|
| Ulmer, Jacob | 1 | 3 | 1 | | | |
| Underwood, Benjamin | 1 | | | | | |
| Underwood, Joseph | 1 | | | | | |

## V

|  | M. | W. | C. | M. | W. | C. |
|---|---|---|---|---|---|---|
| Vass, Laughlan | 1 | 1 | 1 | | | |
| Vanhorn, William | 1 | 1 | | 1 | 1 | |
| Vardy, Aaron | 1 | 1 | | 6 | 4 | |
| Verner, Peter | 1 | 1 | 1 | | | |

## W

|  | M. | W. | C. | M. | W. | C. |
|---|---|---|---|---|---|---|
| Wade, James | 1 | | | | | |
| Waggoner, John | 1 | | 3 | | | |
| Wallace, Edward | 3 | 1 | 4 | | 1 | |
| Wallace, James | 1 | 1 | 4 | 6 | 5 | 6 |
| Ward, John | 1 | | | | | |
| Warden, John | 1 | | | | | |
| Warren, Edward | 1 | 1 | | | | |
| Warrington, Nicholas | 3 | | | | 1 | |
| Warshing, Gasper | 1 | | | | | |
| Wasdin, Thomas | 3 | 1 | | | | |
| Washam, Joshua | 1 | 1 | 1 | | | |
| Waters, James | | 1 | 4 | 3 | 5 | 6 |
| Watson, John, his return | 30 | 7 | 1 | 4 | 3 | 1 |
| Watters, William | 1 | 1 | | 3 | 5 | |
| Watts, Gasper | 1 | | | | | |
| Wear, John | 1 | 1 | | | | |
| Weatley, Samuel | 1 | 1 | | | | |
| Weaver, Joseph | 2 | 3 | | | | |
| Webb, William | 1 | | | | | |

| | | | | | | |
|---|---|---|---|---|---|---|
| Wells, William Charles for John | | | 3 | | | |
| Wells, William Charles for self | 3 | | | 1 | 1 | |
| Welsh, David | 1 | 1 | | | | |
| West, James | 1 | | | | | |
| Westman, Jacob | 1 | | | | | |
| Wetherden, John | 1 | | | | | |
| Whitacre, John | 1 | | | | | |
| White, Alexander | 1 | | | | | |
| White, James | 2 | 1 | | 1 | 1 | |
| White, James | 3 | 3 | | | | |
| White, Soloman | 1 | | | | | |
| Whiteman, William | 1 | | | | | |
| Whitesides, Thomas | 1 | | | | | |
| Whittey, Moses | 1 | | | 6 | 4 | 1 |
| Wiesenhunt, Conrad | 1 | | | | | |
| William, Hezekiah | 1 | | | | | |
| Williams, Henry | 3 | 1 | 4 | 7 | 4 | 1 |
| Williams, John | 3 | 2 | 3 | | | |
| Williams, Samuel | 3 | 1 | | 5 | | |
| Williamson, Jonathan | 1 | | | | | |
| Wilson, Robert | 1 | | | 3 | 5 | |
| Wilsone, Alexander | 1 | 1 | 3 | 2 | | |
| Wilsone, Samuel | 1 | | | | | |
| Wilsone, William | | | | | | |
| Wimberley, Abraham | 1 | 1 | | | | |
| Wise, John | 1 | 1 | 3 | | | |
| Wiseman, Grace | | 1 | | | | |
| Wistanley, Thomas | 1 | | | 1 | | |
| Witter, Mathew | 1 | | | | | |
| Wood, Rebecca | | 1 | | | | |
| Woornell, Michael | 3 | 1 | 1 | | | |
| Wray, Joseph | 1 | | | | | |

| | | | | | | |
|---|---|---|---|---|---|---|
| Wrench, Richard | 3 | 1 | | 5 | 3 | |
| Wright, Jane | | 1 | | | | |
| Wyatt, John | 5 | | | 2 | 1 | |
| Wyatt, William | 3 | 1 | | | | |

## Y

| | M. | W. | C. | M. | W. | C. |
|---|---|---|---|---|---|---|
| Yanson, George | 1 | | | | | |
| Yelding, Robert | 1 | | | | | |
| Yeomans, Lery | 1 | 1 | 2 | | | |
| York, George | 2 | 1 | 2 | | | |
| Young, John | 1 | 1 | | 3 | | 1 |
| Young, Samuel | 1 | | | 5 | 2 | 1 |
| Young, William | 1 | 1 | | 3 | 2 | 4 |
| Youngblood, Jesse | 1 | | | | | |

Received from Gentleman Leslie, 15 July 1783

| | Whites | Blacks |
|---|---|---|
| Men | 1117 | 1281 |
| Women | 499 | 800 |
| Children | 402 | 482 |
| Totals | 2018 | 2563 |
| GRAND TOTAL | | 4581 |

8. A Return of Refugees, with their Negroes, who came to the Province of East Florida in consequence of the evacuation of the Province of Georgia. July 1783.
PRO CO 5: 560

|  | Whites | | | Blacks | | |
|---|---|---|---|---|---|---|
|  | \multicolumn{6}{c}{A} | | | | | |
|  | M. | W. | C. | M. | W. | C. |
| Agnew, widow | 1 | 1 |  |  |  |  |
| Anderson, Margaret | 2 | 1 |  |  |  |  |
| Anderson, Thomas | 2 | 1 | 3 | 5 | 3 | 2 |
| Andrew, a free black |  |  |  | 1 | 3 | 4 |
| Armstrong, James | 1 |  |  |  |  |  |
| Ashley, Nathaniel | 3 | 2 | 4 | 5 | 2 | 3 |
| Aston, Edward | 2 |  | 4 |  |  |  |

B

|  | M. | W. | C. | M. | W. | C. |
|---|---|---|---|---|---|---|
| Bailey, George | 1 |  |  | 4 | 4 | 1 |
| Ballard, Samuel | 1 |  |  |  |  |  |
| Barnard, James | 1 |  |  | 1 | 1 |  |
| Barns, George | 2 |  |  | 2 | 1 |  |
| Barrier, Barbara |  | 1 |  |  |  |  |
| Barrier, Susana |  | 1 |  |  |  |  |
| Barrow, Richard | 2 | 1 |  |  |  |  |
| Barrow, Thomas |  |  |  | 15 | 17 | 8 |
| Belliew, Isaac | 1 | 1 | 3 | 13 | 8 | 5 |
| Bennett, Mrs. |  | 1 | 2 |  |  |  |

| Name | | | | | | |
|---|---|---|---|---|---|---|
| Bennett, William | 1 | | | 2 | | |
| Bethune, Angus | 1 | | | | | |
| Bingaman, Christian | 1 | | | | | |
| Blackwell, Nathan | 1 | | | | | |
| Blunt, Eloe | 2 | 1 | 2 | 1 | 1 | |
| Blythe, John | 1 | | 1 | 9 | 6 | 4 |
| Bonhill, Elias | 1 | 2 | | | | |
| Boon, Caleb | 1 | | | | | |
| Booth, John | 1 | 1 | 2 | 2 | | |
| Bradey, Martha | | 1 | 1 | | | |
| Brandon, Samuel | 1 | 1 | 1 | | | |
| Brayett, William | 1 | | | | | |
| Braywell, Robert | 1 | 1 | 1 | 1 | | |
| Bremer, John | 1 | | | | | |
| Briggs, John | 1 | 1 | 1 | | | |
| Brown, Burrard | 1 | | | | | |
| Brown, James | | | | 9 | 9 | |
| Brown, John | 1 | 2 | | | | |
| Brown, Michael | 2 | 1 | 1 | 2 | 1 | 1 |
| Brown, Sarah | | 1 | | | | |
| Brown, Col. Thomas | 1 | | | 21 | 10 | 6 |
| Brownhill, Thomas | 1 | | 1 | 2 | 2 | |
| Browning, Benjamin | 1 | 1 | 1 | 1 | 1 | 1 |
| Browning, John | 1 | | | 1 | | |
| Brownson, Daniel | 1 | | | | | |
| Bryan, Zachariah | 2 | 1 | 3 | 2 | 2 | 1 |
| Bushup, Elijah | 2 | | | 1 | | |
| Bynham, James | 2 | | | | | |
| Byrn, Gerald | 1 | | | 4 | | |

## C

|  | M. | W. | C. | M. | W. | C. | |
|---|---|---|---|---|---|---|---|
| Cadiack, Luis | 1 |  | 1 |  |  |  | |
| Caid, John | 1 | 1 |  | 1 | 1 |  | |
| Cairney, Arthur | 1 |  |  |  |  |  | |
| Caldwell, John | 1 | 2 | 5 |  |  |  | |
| Caldwell, Mathew | 1 |  |  |  |  |  | |
| Cameron, John | 1 |  |  |  |  |  | |
| Campbell, Charles | 1 |  |  |  |  |  | |
| Canada, John | 2 |  |  |  |  |  | |
| Cannon, Willoughby | 1 |  |  |  |  |  | |
| Carpenter, Jacob | 1 |  |  |  |  |  | |
| Carrey, Alexander | 2 | 1 | 1 |  |  |  | |
| Carsewell, Edward | 1 |  |  |  |  |  | |
| Carter, Alexander | 2 |  |  |  |  |  | |
| Case, William | 1 |  |  |  |  |  | |
| Clark, Catherine |  | 1 | 3 |  | 2 |  | |
| Clark, James | 1 | 1 |  |  |  |  | |
| Clark, Thomas | 1 | 1 | 5 | 2 | 2 | 1 | |
| Clark, William | 1 |  |  | 2 |  |  | [Augusta] |
| Clark, William | 3 |  |  | 19 | 7 | 7 | [Picolatta] |
| Clark, William | 1 | 1 | 3 | 2 | 4 | 3 | [Turtle river] |
| Clark, William | 1 |  |  |  |  |  | [in town] |
| Clarke, Alexander | 1 |  |  | 1 |  |  | |
| Clem, Valentine | 3 | 1 | 4 |  |  |  | |
| Club, George | 1 | 1 | 2 | 1 |  |  | |
| Club, Thomas | 1 | 2 | 3 | 14 | 15 | 13 | |
| Club, William | 1 | 1 |  |  |  |  | |
| Codrey, Thomas | 2 | 2 | 2 |  |  |  | |
| Collins, David | 2 | 1 | 3 |  |  |  | |

| Name | M. | W. | C. | M. | W. | C. |
|---|---|---|---|---|---|---|
| Collins, Hezzekiah | 1 | 1 | 2 | 1 | | |
| Collins, William | 3 | 3 | | 2 | 1 | |
| Combust, Simon | 1 | | | | | |
| Cooke, Ralph | 1 | 1 | | | | |
| Corker, William | 4 | | | | | |
| Cornick, Joseph | 1 | | | | | |
| Correy, Robert | 1 | 1 | | | | |
| Coutch, Joseph | 1 | | | | | |
| Cowan, Robert | 1 | 1 | | | 2 | |
| Cox, Patience | | 1 | | | | |
| Cox, Robert | 1 | 1 | | | | |
| Crawford, Edward | 2 | 2 | 1 | 2 | 3 | 1 |
| Cree, Moses | 1 | 2 | | | | |
| Crosbey, John | 2 | 1 | 1 | | | |
| Crutchfield, William | 1 | | | | | |
| Cuningham, Alexander | 1 | 2 | | 6 | 3 | 3 |

## D

| Name | M. | W. | C. | M. | W. | C. |
|---|---|---|---|---|---|---|
| Dampier, Stephen | 1 | 1 | | | | |
| Davies, Ephraim | 1 | 2 | | | | |
| Davies, Richard | 1 | | | | | |
| Davies, William | 1 | 2 | 1 | 2 | 1 | |
| Delegal, Sarah | | 1 | 4 | 10 | 8 | 5 |
| Dinkens, Henry | 1 | | | | | |
| Douglas, James | 6 | | | | | |
| Douglas, Col. John | 1 | 2 | | 5 | 4 | 5 |
| Downer, John | 1 | | | 1 | | |
| Drury, Thomas | 1 | | | | | |

| | | | | | | | |
|---|---|---|---|---|---|---|---|
| Duberry, Thomas | 1 | | | | | | |
| Dun, Cornelius | 1 | 1 | 1 | 6 | 4 | 3 | |
| Dyer, Elijah | 1 | | | | | | |

E

| | M. | W. | C. | M. | W. | C. |
|---|---|---|---|---|---|---|
| English, Elizabeth | 1 | 2 | 2 | 1 | | |
| English, John | 1 | | | | | |

F

| | M. | W. | C. | M. | W. | C. | |
|---|---|---|---|---|---|---|---|
| Farley, Samuel | 1 | 1 | 1 | 1 | 3 | 7 | |
| Ferguson, Henry | 1 | | | 9 | 4 | 6 | |
| Flannagan, John | 1 | 1 | 2 | | | | |
| Flemming, Thomas | 1 | | | 2 | 1 | | |
| Flemming, Thomas | 1 | | | | | | junior |
| Flyersmouth, John A. | 2 | | 1 | 2 | 1 | | |
| Forbes, James | 1 | | | 1 | | | |
| Forte, Drury, junior | 1 | 1 | 1 | 1 | 1 | | |
| Forte, Drury, senior | 2 | 1 | 1 | | | | |
| Foulke, John | 1 | | | | | | |
| Fowlis, John | 1 | | | 3 | | | |
| Fox, Benjamin | | | | | | | |
| Fox, Jean | | | | | | | |
| Fox, John | | | | | | | |
| Fox, Thomas | | | | | | | |
| Fradget, Aden | 1 | | | | | | |

| | M. | W. | C. | M. | W. | C. |
|---|---|---|---|---|---|---|
| Friend, Robert | | | | | | |
| Fryer, Aaron | 1 | 1 | 4 | 1 | 1 | 1 |
| Fulford, Ann | 1 | 1 | 2 | 2 | | |
| Fulsom, Ebenezer | 1 | | | | | |
| Furlow, John | 4 | | | | | |

## G

| | M. | W. | C. | M. | W. | C. | |
|---|---|---|---|---|---|---|---|
| Garnard, John | 1 | | | | | | |
| George, Moses | 1 | | | | | | |
| Gibbons, Emilio | | 1 | | | | | |
| Golphin, John | 3 | | | 16 | 17 | 12 | |
| Graham, John | 5 | 3 | | 190 | 128 | 147 | self & others |
| Graham, Walter | 1 | 1 | 2 | | | | |
| Gregory, Richard | 1 | 1 | | | | | |
| Green, Thomas | 1 | | | 1 | | | |
| Green, William | 2 | | | 2 | | | |
| Gresham, George | 1 | | | | | | |
| Grymes, Mary | 1 | | | | | | |
| Guy, James | 1 | | | | | | |

## H

| | M. | W. | C. | M. | W. | C. |
|---|---|---|---|---|---|---|
| Hall, John | 2 | 1 | 1 | 2 | | |
| Hancock, Francis | 1 | 1 | | | | |
| Hannagan, John | 1 | 1 | 2 | | | |

| | | | | | | | |
|---|---|---|---|---|---|---|---|
| Hannah, a Negro | | | | | 1 | 1 | |
| Harrigle, Daniel | 1 | 1 | | 1 | | | |
| Harriott, James | 1 | 1 | 4 | 5 | 2 | 1 | |
| Harris, Lewis | 1 | 2 | 4 | | | | |
| Harris, William | 2 | 3 | 3 | | | | |
| Harrod, Noah | 1 | | | | | | |
| Haverlin, Michael | 1 | 1 | | | | | |
| Henderson, James | 3 | | | | | | |
| Hendricks, John | 1 | 1 | 1 | | | | |
| Herbert, Isaac | 1 | 1 | 1 | 2 | 3 | 1 | |
| Hickson, William | 1 | | | 2 | 1 | | |
| Hilburn, William | 1 | | | | | | |
| Hillburn, Hollum | 1 | | | | | | |
| Hodge, David | 1 | 2 | | | | | |
| Hodges, William | 5 | 3 | | | | | |
| Hogan, Daniel | 2 | 1 | | | | | |
| Holland, John | 1 | 1 | 3 | | | | |
| Holland, John | 1 | 1 | 1 | | | | |
| Honey, John | 1 | | | | | | |
| Honeycut, John | 2 | 4 | | | | | |
| Hopkins, John | 2 | 1 | | 1 | | | |
| Hopkins, John | 1 | 1 | 1 | 3 | 4 | | |
| Hover, Jacob | 1 | | | 6 | 3 | | |
| Howel, James | 1 | | | | | | |
| Hughes, Thomas | 1 | 1 | | | | | |
| Hume, James (esqr.) | | | | 10 | 16 | 11 | |
| Hunt, James | 1 | | | | | | |

I

|  | M. | W. | C. | M. | W. | C. |
|---|---|---|---|---|---|---|
| Ingles, Ann |  | 1 |  |  |  |  |
| Ingram, John | 3 |  |  |  |  |  |
| Ireby, Edward | 1 | 1 | 2 | 1 |  |  |
| Irvin, Robert | 2 |  |  |  |  |  |
| Islands, James | 1 | 1 | 1 | 1 | 1 |  |

J

|  | M. | W. | C. | M. | W. | C. |  |
|---|---|---|---|---|---|---|---|
| Jackson, William | 1 | 1 | 1 | 2 |  |  |  |
| Jenkins, George | 1 |  |  |  |  |  |  |
| Jenkins, Richard | 1 |  | 3 |  |  |  |  |
| Jenkins, Samuel Hunt | 1 |  |  | 4 | 5 | 2 |  |
| Johnson, Elizabeth | 3 |  |  |  |  |  |  |
| Johnson, George | 1 |  |  |  |  |  | junior |
| Johnson, George | 1 |  |  |  |  |  | senior |
| Johnson, John | 1 |  |  |  |  |  |  |
| Johnson, Rachel | 4 | 2 |  | 1 | 2 |  |  |
| Johnson, William | 1 | 2 | 1 | 2 |  |  |  |
| Johnstone, Dr. Lewis | 3 | 4 | 2 | 27 | 24 | 20 |  |
| Jollie, Martin | 3 |  |  | 31 | 13 | 11 |  |
| Jones, David | 1 |  |  |  |  |  |  |
| Jones, Inigo | 3 | 3 |  | 5 | 5 |  |  |
| Jones, James | 1 | 1 | 1 |  |  |  |  |
| Jones, John | 1 |  |  | 1 |  |  |  |
| Jones, John | 1 |  |  |  |  |  |  |

| | | | | | | |
|---|---|---|---|---|---|---|
| Jones, Samuel | 1 | | | | | |
| Jones, William | 1 | | | 15 | 14 | 16 |
| Jordan, Thomas | 1 | | | | | |

## K

| | M. | W. | C. | M. | W. | C. |
|---|---|---|---|---|---|---|
| Kelly, Joseph | 1 | 1 | 2 | | | |
| Kelly, Robert | 2 | 1 | 1 | | | |
| Kelsal, Roger | 1 | | | 15 | 18 | 7 |
| Kene, Thomas | 1 | | | | | |
| Kidd, George | 1 | | | | | |
| King, Soloman | 1 | 2 | 3 | 1 | 1 | |

## L

| | M. | W. | C. | M. | W. | C. |
|---|---|---|---|---|---|---|
| Lambert, James | 2 | 1 | | | 1 | |
| Lavinia, a mulatto | | | 1 | 2 | 1 | |
| Legate, David | 1 | | | | | |
| Leslie, Francis | 1 | | | | | |
| Leslie, James | 1 | 1 | 2 | | | |
| Leslie, Joseph | 1 | | | | | |
| Lewis, Isaac | 1 | | | | | |
| Linder, John | 2 | 1 | | 21 | 15 | 5 |
| Little, Robert | 1 | | | | | |
| Lively, Mathew | 1 | | | | | |
| Lloyd, Thomas | 1 | 1 | | | 1 | |
| Lock, Mark | 1 | | | | | 1 |
| Love, William | 1 | | | 1 | 2 | |

| | | | | | | |
|---|---|---|---|---|---|---|
| Lure, Ponsey | 1 | | | | | |
| Lyford, William | 1 | 2 | 1 | 19 | 13 | 16 |
| Lyle, James | 1 | | | | | |
| Lyle, Mathew | 1 | 1 | 2 | 2 | | |
| Lyons, Mrs. | | 1 | 3 | | | |

## M

| | M. | W. | C. | M. | W. | C. |
|---|---|---|---|---|---|---|
| Mangum, William | 2 | 2 | 2 | 4 | 2 | |
| Manlove, Boaz | 1 | | | | | |
| Manuel, Thomas | 2 | 1 | 3 | | 2 | |
| Marks, John | 1 | | | | | |
| Marron, David | 1 | 1 | 1 | 1 | 2 | 2 |
| Martin, John, esquire | 2 | 1 | 1 | 8 | 7 | 8 |
| Martin, John | 1 | | | 2 | | |
| Martin, John | 1 | | | | | |
| Martinangel, Abraham | 2 | | | | | |
| Matterson, John | 1 | 1 | 1 | 1 | 2 | 1 |
| McBride, Malcombe | 1 | 1 | 1 | 1 | | |
| McCord, John | 2 | 1 | 2 | | | |
| McDonald, Archibald | 2 | 1 | 2 | 1 | | |
| McDonald, John | 1 | | | 1 | | |
| McDonald, Patrick | 1 | | | | | |
| McDonald, William | 2 | | 1 | 1 | | |
| McGilvrey, Finlay | 1 | | | | | |
| McGirth, James | 2 | 1 | 5 | 4 | 5 | 4 |
| McGown, David | 1 | | | | | |
| McKenzie, George | 1 | | | | | |
| McLean, Alexander | 1 | | | 1 | | |
| McLeod, Donald | 2 | 2 | 1 | | 2 | |

| Name | | | | | | |
|---|---|---|---|---|---|---|
| McMinn, Thomas | 3 | | 3 | | | |
| McNiel, Archibald | 1 | | | | | |
| McPherson, Murdoch | 1 | | | | | |
| Miller, George | 1 | | | | | |
| Minsey, Abraham | 2 | 1 | 1 | | | |
| Mitchell, Elizabeth | 1 | 1 | | | | |
| Montgomerie, Samuel | 3 | | | | | |
| Moore, Arthur | 3 | 1 | | 2 | 2 | 4 |
| Moore, James | 1 | 1 | 4 | 1 | 2 | 5 |
| Moore, James | 2 | | | 1 | 2 | |
| Moore, Mathew | 1 | 1 | 1 | 1 | | |
| Moore, Samuel | 1 | | | 1 | | |
| Moore, Sarah | | 1 | | | | |
| Moore, Thomas | 1 | | | | | |
| Moore, William | 1 | 1 | 2 | 1 | | 1 |
| Morrel, Michael | 1 | 1 | | | | |
| Morrison, John | 1 | | | | | |
| Mountain, Thomas | 1 | | | | | |
| Muir, John | 4 | 2 | 2 | 1 | 1 | |
| Murray, Stephen | 1 | 2 | 3 | | | |

### N

| | M. | W. | C. | M. | W. | C. |
|---|---|---|---|---|---|---|
| Napier, John | 1 | 1 | | | | |
| Nichol, John | 2 | | | 1 | 1 | |
| Nicholson, Marcum | 2 | 1 | | | | |
| Nidray, John | 1 | 1 | | 1 | | |
| Nix, Edward | | 1 | | | | |
| Nix, James | 1 | 1 | | | | |

| | | | | | | |
|---|---|---|---|---|---|---|
| Norris, Ephraim | 1 | | | | | |
| Nowland, James | 3 | | | | | |

## O

| | M. | W. | C. | M. | W. | C. |
|---|---|---|---|---|---|---|
| Oates, William | 1 | 1 | | | | |
| Oglivie, Peter | 3 | | | 2 | 1 | |
| Oliver, Jean | | 1 | 1 | | | |
| Owen, Ann | | 1 | | | | |

## P

| | M. | W. | C. | M. | W. | C. |
|---|---|---|---|---|---|---|
| Pace, Willis | 1 | 1 | 2 | 1 | 1 | 2 |
| Peace, Darius | 1 | 1 | 1 | | 1 | |
| Perdiew, William | 2 | | | | | |
| Peters, Solomon | 1 | 2 | 1 | 1 | | |
| Phalan, Thomas | 1 | | | | | |
| Phillips, Daniel | 3 | 2 | | 1 | | |
| Phillips, George | 2 | | | 4 | 1 | |
| Phillips, John | 1 | 1 | | | | |
| Pinkley, George | 1 | | | | | |
| Pinson, Thomas R. | 1 | | | | | |
| Plummer, Robert | 1 | | | | | |
| Powell, William | 1 | | | 1 | 1 | 1 |

## R

|                      | M. | W. | C. | M. | W. | C. |
|----------------------|----|----|----|----|----|----|
| Rachley, Joel        | 1  | 2  | 1  |    |    |    |
| Rattam, Mary         | 1  | 1  |    |    |    |    |
| Rayborn, John        | 2  |    |    |    |    |    |
| Reid, Robert         | 1  |    |    | 12 | 9  | 5  |
| Reid, William        | 1  | 1  | 2  |    |    |    |
| Reynolds, Ann        | 2  | 1  | 4  |    |    |    |
| Ried, Thomas         | 1  |    |    | 1  |    |    |
| Right, John          |    |    |    | 1  |    |    |
| Roberts, Abraham     | 1  |    |    |    |    |    |
| Robertson, John      | 1  | 2  |    |    |    |    |
| Robinson, Henry      | 1  |    |    |    |    |    |
| Robinson, James      | 2  |    |    |    |    |    |
| Rogers, John         | 1  |    |    |    |    |    |
| Rogers, Joseph       | 4  | 2  | 3  |    |    |    |
| Rogers, Joseph, junior | 1 |    |    |    |    |    |
| Rollinson, George    | 2  |    | 1  | 1  | 1  | 1  |
| Ross, William        | 1  |    |    | 1  | 2  | 2  |
| Ross, William        | 2  | 1  |    | 3  |    |    |
| Rowland, John        | 1  |    |    | 1  | 1  | 1  |
| Russell, David       | 3  | 3  | 2  | 4  |    |    |
| Ryal, Samuel         | 1  |    |    | 1  |    |    |
| Rymar, Ann           |    | 2  | 2  |    |    |    |

## S

|                 | M. | W. | C. | M. | W. | C. |
|-----------------|----|----|----|----|----|----|
| Saunders, Lewis | 1  |    |    |    |    |    |

| | | | | | | | |
|---|---|---|---|---|---|---|---|
| Seymour, Rev. James | 1 | 1 | 2 | | 13 | 12 | 8 |
| Shave, Richard | 3 | 1 | | | 1 | | |
| Shaw, Francis | 1 | | | | | | |
| Shepherd, Samuel | 2 | 1 | 4 | | | | |
| Silcocke, Mary | | 1 | 3 | | | | |
| Simmonds, Willis | 1 | | | | | | |
| Sizemore, Mary | | 2 | 1 | | | | |
| Skene, Andrew | 1 | 1 | | | 1 | 2 | 2 |
| Sliterman, Elizabeth | | 1 | | | | | |
| Sloan, Samuel | 1 | 1 | 1 | | | | |
| Smallocke, Thomas | 1 | | | | | | |
| Smith, Samuel | 1 | | | | | | |
| Smith, William | 1 | 1 | | | | | |
| Smith, William, junior | 1 | | | | | | |
| Sommerlin, Henry | 3 | | 2 | | | | |
| Spence, Robert | 1 | | | | 2 | 2 | |
| Stanley, John | 1 | | | | | | |
| Steel, Hugh | 1 | | | | | | |
| Stephens, Richard | 2 | 1 | 3 | | | | |
| Stewart, Mathew | 3 | 1 | | | 11 | 5 | 1 |
| Surles, Lewis | 3 | 1 | | | 2 | 2 | |
| Swanson & McGillvrey | 2 | | | | 16 | 2 | 2 |
| Swiney, Henry | 1 | 1 | | | 1 | 1 | |
| Sykes, Margaret | | 1 | 2 | | | | |
| Sym, William | 1 | 1 | 1 | | 1 | 2 | |
| Symes, Robert | 1 | | | | | | |

T

| | M. | W. | C. | M. | W. | C. |
|---|---|---|---|---|---|---|
| Tattnall, Josiah | 1 | 2 | | 15 | 26 | 16 |

| | | | | | | | |
|---|---|---|---|---|---|---|---|
| Taylor, Charles | 1 | 1 | 1 | 5 | 4 | 3 | |
| Taylor, Mary | 1 | | | | | | |
| Taylor, Thomas | 1 | | | 1 | 1 | | |
| Taylor, Thomas | 1 | 1 | | | 2 | 4 | |
| Taylor, William | 1 | | | | | | |
| Taylor, William | 1 | | | | | | |
| Thomas, John | 2 | 1 | 3 | 1 | | | |
| Thompson, Peter | 1 | 1 | 3 | | | | |
| Thompson, Robert Campbell | 1 | | | | | | |
| Thompson, Ruelien | 1 | | | | | | |
| Thompson, William | 1 | | | | | | |
| Tibelt, Giles | 1 | | | | | | |
| Tillet, James | 1 | | | | | | |
| Tipton, Thomas | 1 | 1 | | | | | |
| Todd, John | 1 | 1 | | 1 | 1 | 2 | |
| Touchstone, Stephen | 1 | | | 1 | | | |
| Trap, Robert | 2 | 4 | | | | | |
| Travis, Aaron | 2 | | | | | | |
| Travis, Rachael | | 1 | 1 | | | | |
| Triebner, Christopher | 1 | 2 | 5 | 7 | 5 | | |
| Tullos, Elizabeth | 1 | 1 | 3 | | | | |
| Tunnis, Nehemiah | 1 | | | | | | |
| Tunnis, Thomas | 1 | | | | | | |
| Turner, Thomas | 1 | | | | | | |

U

| | M. | W. | C. | M. | W. | C. |
|---|---|---|---|---|---|---|
| Underwood, Daniel | 1 | | | | | |

75

## V

|  | M. | W. | C. | M. | W. | C. |
|---|---|---|---|---|---|---|
| Vansant, Mary | 2 | 3 |  | 3 |  |  |

## W

|  | M. | W. | C. | M. | W. | C. |
|---|---|---|---|---|---|---|
| Walker, Abraham | 2 | 2 |  | 1 |  |  |
| Walker, John | 1 |  |  | 1 |  |  |
| Wallis, James | 1 | 1 |  |  | 1 |  |
| Walsh, Nicholas | 2 | 6 | 2 | 5 |  |  |
| Walters, Thomas | 1 |  |  |  |  |  |
| Water, Sinclair | 1 | 1 | 1 | 1 | 3 | 4 |
| Watkins, Moses | 1 |  |  |  |  |  |
| Watson, Benjamin | 1 |  |  |  |  |  |
| Watson, Jacob | 1 | 1 | 4 | 6 | 1 |  |
| Watson, Nicolas | 1 |  |  |  |  |  |
| Watts, Charles | 2 | 1 | 3 | 3 | 1 |  |
| Weatherford, Martin | 2 | 2 | 4 | 8 | 3 | 3 |
| Webb, William | 1 |  |  |  |  |  |
| Weesh, George | 1 | 2 | 3 | 1 | 2 | 2 |
| Westley, James | 1 | 1 | 5 |  | 2 |  |
| White, John | 1 |  |  |  |  |  |
| Whiteman, Daniel | 1 | 1 | 1 | 2 |  |  |
| Wiles, Henry | 1 |  |  | 1 |  |  |
| Wilkins, Abraham | 1 | 1 | 3 | 1 | 1 | 2 |
| Wilkins, George | 1 |  |  |  |  |  |
| Wilkins, Rebecca | 2 | 1 |  |  |  |  |
| Wilkins, Samuel | 1 |  |  | 1 |  |  |

| | | | | | | |
|---|---|---|---|---|---|---|
| Williams, Abner | 1 | | | 2 | 2 | |
| Williams, David | 1 | | | | | |
| Wilson, John | 1 | | | | | |
| Wood, John | 1 | 1 | | 13 | 14 | 15 |
| Wood, Thomas | 1 | 1 | 1 | 1 | | 1 |
| Woodward, William | 2 | | | 4 | | |
| Wright, James | | | | 2 | 2 | |
| Wright, Thomas | 1 | 1 | | 1 | 1 | |
| Wudrup, Rose | | 1 | | | | |

## Y

| | M. | W. | C. | M. | W. | C. |
|---|---|---|---|---|---|---|
| Young, Alexander | 5 | | | 2 | | |
| Young, Henry | | | | 2 | 1 | |
| Young, John | 1 | | | 2 | | |
| Young, Nathaniel | 2 | 2 | 4 | | | |

## Z

| | M. | W. | C. | M. | W. | C. |
|---|---|---|---|---|---|---|
| Zubley, David | 2 | 1 | 2 | 16 | 12 | 4 |

|             | Whites | Blacks |
|-------------|--------|--------|
| Men         | 503    | 799    |
| Women       | 269    | 705    |
| Children    | 270    | 452    |
| TOTALS      | 1042   | 1956   |
| Grand Total |        | 2998   |

A return of refugees with their Negro's, who came to the province of East Florida in consequence of the evacuation of the province of Georgia. Received from Gentlemen, Leslie 18 July 1783.

9. Memorial and Petition of the Inhabitants of East Florida, Saint Augustine, September 11, 1783, PRO CO 5: 111

To His Excellency Patrick Tonyn Esquire, Captain General and Governor in Chief in and over His Majesty's province of East Florida, Chancellor Vice Admiral and ordinary of the same

The Memorial and Petition of the Subscribers on behalf of themselves and the other principal Inhabitants of the said province show

That your Memorialists are most sensibly affected by information that the provincial troops now stationed here, are soon to be disbanded. And beg leave to remind you Excellency of the present ungovernable and disorderly state of our Northern Frontier, of the frequent robberies, burglaries and thefts that have lately been committed in divers parts of the province, and even in the vicinity of Saint Augustine. The increase whereof is extremely to be apprehended from the extraordinary influx of idle dissolute vagrants from the northward, accustomed to subsist by plunder and rapine alone, to whom there is reason to dread the addition of many others of similar character, and these perhaps strengthened by some of the ill disposed soldiery about to be discharged. The danger is also from the unrestrained resentment of the deluded neighbouring Indians must be apparent.

Your Memorialists submit to your Excellency's consideration their doubts, whether it will be possible for the well disposed part of the Community to support the civil Government when deprived of military protection, and the probability that the Inhabitants of the Country under the prospect of being by the cession of the province, soon obliged to abandon their lands and other immoveable property, will also be stripped of their moveable effects, and reduced to the necessity of associating in Saint Augustine for mutual defence and personal safety.

Your Memorialists further request your Excellency's most serious attention in the accumulated distress which not less than ten thousand loyal Inhabitants of East Florida will be subjected to on the dissolution of our civil Government, unless supplied with shipping for the transportation of themselves and effects to other British settlements, which they conceive they are equally entitled to with their fellow Subjects of the other Colonies. And which by no other means can be procured even by the few whose circumstances may enable them to bear the charge.

Your Memorialists therefore humbly pray, that by representations to their Excellencies the Commanders in Chief, and by such other measures as to your Excellency's wisdom and experienced zeal for His Majesty's service, and the interest of the Inhabitants may seem expedient, your Excellency will be pleased to avert these impending calamities. And your Petitioners as in duty bound will every pray, etc.

Armstrong, Fleetwood

Begbie, Alexander
Bethune, Fergr

Baron, Alexander
Brown, J.
Brown, William

Browne, Archibald
Browne, J.
Browne, John
Buckley, John

Cameron, Donald
Clark, William
Clitherall, James
Courtney, Thomas

Johnson, John
Johnston, Chase
Johnston, John
Johnston, Lewis
Johnston, Lewis, Junior

Dames, Charles
Denniston, John
Deveaux, Jacob
Douglass, Jno

Kelsall, R
Kemp, Geo
Ker, George

Leslie, John

Edwards, Peter

Lord, Benjamin

Falconer, Jno

Man, Spencer

Farley, Samuel

Martin, John

McIntosh, William

Graham, Alexander
Grassell, George

McKenzie, John
McLeod, Rodk.

Haley, Jno
Holdsworth, Stephen
Holmes, John
Hume, James

McLeod, William
McMurray, James

McNair, Anthony

| | |
|---|---|
| | Scott, John |
| McQueen, Alexander | Scott, Robert |
| Michis, Charles | Sherriff, Peter |
| | Slater, William |
| | Storr, John |
| Millar, Geo. | |
| Mills, John | |
| Mitchell, John | Tattnall, John M. |
| Mobray, Joseph | |
| Morris, John | Tattnall, Josiah |
| Moss, William | Taylor, James |
| Mowbray, Jno | |
| Muir, Thomas | |
| | |
| Orr, Thomas | Taylor, Thomas |
| | |
| Panton, William | Tunno, John |
| | |
| Payne, R | Watson, William |
| Perpall, John | |
| | |
| Richardson, Jno | Westphal, George |
| Robertson, Henry | Wilson, Robert |
| Rose, John | Winniett, J |
| Rose, William | Winstanley, Thomas |
| | Wood, John |
| Ross, Malcolm | |
| Roupell, George | Yeate, David |
| | Yonge, Henry |

The Florida colonies were returned to Spain and all English ordered to evacuation the territory. Those who left East Florida, as of the 16$^{th}$ of October 1784, are given below.

## 10. Return of White and Black British Inhabitants entered [in] the books of commissioners for evacuation and who had taken out passes on the 16$^{th}$ of October 1784. PRO CO5: 546

| | |
|---|---:|
| Whites | 551 |
| Blacks | 1133 |
| | 1684 |
| Entered in the books since | 263 |
| | 1947 |
| Taken out passes since and embarked on board the William and Mary, the Polly and Elisabeth transports for Providence | 119 |
| Also Governor Graham's Negro's since embarked | 270 |
| | 389 |
| Remaining in the commission books to take out passes | 1558 |

These are exclusive of the estates of Lady Egmont, and William Egan, those under the care of Major Chase, Mr. Fatio and Colonel Young's troop with their families.

Also none of the Minorcans are in the above estimate, and several that are included in the number 1684 may have gone away privately, and still will go or remain, and many have not yet entered their names at the office.

> William Brown
> Commissioner

*Not having completed the evacuation in the stipulated time, the remaining settlers asked for an extension to complete their evacuation. They also thank the incoming Spanish governor the peace in which they were able to conduct this evacuation.*

## 11. Inhabitants of Saint Johns to Governor Zéspedes, River Saint John, January 25, 1785

To His Excellency Don Vincent Emanuel de Cespedes, Brigadier General, Governor and Commandant General of the Province of East Florida.

The Humble Address of the Inhabitants of the River Saint John and Part Adjacent, may it please your Excellency,

We the Underwritten, inhabitants of the River Saint John and part adjacent, under the Protection of His Catholic Majesty, in His Province of East Florida, take this opportunity to testify to Your Excellency our most sincere thanks and hearty acknowledgements for your Excellency's providential care of our lives and property, in having secured the persons of Daniel McGirth, William Cunningham, Stephen Mayfield and others, who in defiance of all Law have for these many years past, disturbed this province, plundered many of its inhabitants and had our lives and property instantly at their mercy, which rendered our Abode unsafe and precarious.

By having arrested the Leaders of those Robbers and Murders, we apprehend ourselves at present perfectly secure under Your Excellency's Government, and we make Bold to assure Your Excellency, that we will exert ourselves to every occasion to procure the peace and tranquility to remain undisturbed amongst us. In this Province offering to Your Excellency all the assistance that may be required at any time to pursue and arrest any person or persons that should dare to Act contrary to Your Excellency's Orders and Proclamations. And we promise to behave in every Respect becoming the duty we owe to His Catholic Majesty for His Royal Protection, while he may be pleased to permit us to remain in his Dominions. We shall continue to pray for Your Excellency's Health and Happiness and have the Honour to Subscribe ourselves with the Utmost Respect,

Your Excellency's most obedient and most Humble Servants

Ashworth, Joseph
Auston, David

Barber, Gaspar
Bishop, William
Bogan, William
Bolton, Robert
Bowdn, John
Brakor, George
Burcham, Joseph
Burnett, John
Burnett, John, Junior

Chatworth, James

Clark, Angus

Evans, William

Fatio, Lewis
Fenner, Joseph
Flicks, Henry
Fort, Drury

Godfrey, William
Goodbread, Philip
Graystock, William

Hall, Charles
Hall, Thomas

Hollingsirth, Timothy

Justin, Thomas

King, Solomon                    Mangum, William
                                 Matlet, John
Ladson, John C.                  Mitchel, William

Macdonell, A.                    Proctor, Phillip
Macdonell, Randolph
Ramey, Alex


                                 Wigengs, Joe
Scot, John                       Williams, Henry
Starlin, Frances
Stuart, Alison                   Williams, Samuel
Summerlin, Joseph                Williams, Wilson

## 12. San Augustine, February 15th, 1785, East Florida
## PRO CO 5: 561

To His Excellency, Major General Patrick Tonyn Esquire, Late British Governor of the Province of East Florida, the Address of Sundry British Subjects Resident in the Said Province

May it please Your Excellency

His Majesty's most dutiful and loyal subjects, proprietors and merchants yet resident in this province retain, as we always shall, a most grateful remembrance of the many instances here to for experienced of the unremitting attention paid by Your Excellency on all occasions as well to His Majesty's service as to the interest and welfare of the people under Your Government.

His Majesty having been graciously pleased to permit your residence amongst us, so long, for the most humane and benevolent purposes – we therefore naturally look up to Your Excellency on the occasion, presuming to hope for a continuation of your wonted favorable attention to our representations. As the period of eighteen months stipulated by the late definitive treaty of peace, for our emigrating from this province, is now at hand, it is with regret we have to mention to Your Excellency, that we have hither to failed in our utmost exertions to accomplish the disposal of our properties, and to make such other arrangement in our affairs, as are necessary previous to that event.

We are therefore desirous to benefit by that clause, in the third article of the definitive treaty, whereby His Catholic Majesty grants a prolongation of the stipulated term, encouraged thereto by the favorable disposition and equitable administration we have experienced under the protection of His Excellency Don Vincent Emanuel de Cespedes.

But as the said treaty is silent, as to the excellent conditions of the said prolongation, and as to the mode ... the same are to be ascertained; we naturally resort to Your Excellency on this occasion, entreating Your Excellency's interpretation and application in our behalf to obtain a public and official explanation of the intentions of the Spanish government on these points and how far our wishes can be complied with ... The said stipulated term until the sixteenth day of September next, with permission in the mean time to ... of our property and to settle our affairs under the protection of the Spanish government, in the same degree, and in the same manners hitherto since the commencement there of, –and finally to withdraw for any effects, and without being retained in our experience on any pretence whatsoever, during the said additional term, except for debts due to Spanish subjects, or for criminal acts.

Saint Augustine, the 15th of February 1785 (signed):

| | | |
|---|---|---|
| John Storr | | George Barnes |
| John Douglas | | William McHinnon |
| Thomas Orr | | Thomas Waters |
| John Fox | | John Johnson |
| Alexander Lorimer | | John McHenzie |
| Neil McQueen | | Thomas Tunno |
| Edward Corbell | | John Ross for eight honorables: |
| William Slater. | James Taylor. | 1. Lord Hawke |
| Thomas Rigby. | Roderick McLeod. | 2. Major General Tonyn |
| Robert Scott. | John Halvert. | 3. Henry Steackey |
| Francis Le Vole. | John McIntosh. | 4. Jacob Willinson |
| Donald Cameron | John Allen | Estate of John Willinson |
| Edward Marlin. | Charley Dames. | 5. & Himself |
| | | 6. Stephen Egan, agent for |
| | | 7. Earl Egmont & himself |
| | 8. Robert Scott, Robert Johnson, Stephen Haven, | |
| | George Kemp and John Faulamb | |

13. Saint Augustine, March 1785, East Florida. PRO CO 5: 561

To His Excellency Don Vincent Emanuel Cespedes, Brigadier General of His Catholic Majesty's forces, Governor and Commandant General of the City of Saint Augustine and province of East Florida

May it please Your Excellency,

We His Britannic Majesty's subjects resident in East Florida under the jurisdiction of the Spanish Government, previous to the expiration of the time presented by Treaty for our departure from this Country, find ourselves actuated by a high sense of gratitude, to desire leave to approach Your Excellency with our warmest acknowledgements and thanks, for the security and tranquility afforded us, under Your Excellency's wise, equitable, and mild administration; the besugnity and clemency of His Catholic Majesty, being conspicuous in his appointment of a Gentleman, equally capable and desirous to fulfill the great trusts, committed to Your Excellency, in a manner so highly honorable, to Your Sovereign, to Your tradition and to Yourself.

Authorized as we are by experience, we think it our duty to bear testimony to Your Excellency's faithful and punctual adherence, and conformity to the stipulations in our favor, in the late definitive treaty of peace; during the whole course of the Evacuation, which has been conducted with that cordiality and harmony, between Your Excellency, and our late worthy Governor, His Excellency Major General Tonyn, to be expected from, the prudence and moderation of two such distinguished characters.

The polite, liberal, and amicable deportment of the officers and gentlemen of the garrison towards us, will always be remembered with pleasure, and their attention to the discipline of the troops, whose orderly and regular behavior has been truly exemplary, demands our thankful approbation.

We cannot hear forbear to declare, the criticism concern with which have observed some publications in the Bahamas Gazette, derogatory of the Honor of the Spanish Nation; the ... benevolence and good faith which distinguish Your Excellency, will however, secure you, against such groundless aspersions, and Your Excellency may observe, that the greatest, wisest and best characters in Britain, are frequently subjected to the like unmerited abuse from the liberty of the press, which prevail throughout the dominions of Our Sovereign.

Permit us to take leave of Your Excellency with the most ardent wishes for your health and welfare, and that you may long continue in your dignified station, and instrument of the ... of Your Loyal Master's clemency and fame, and of happiness and prosperity to the people committed to your protection, the fruition of that tranquility of mind, and inward satisfaction, enjoyed only by the good and virtuous.

Saint Augustine East Florida March 1785

| | |
|---|---|
| John Leslie | William Maxwell |
| John Douglass | Robert Scott |
| John Johnson | Francis P. Fatio |
| John Mitchell | Lewis Fatio |
| John Storr | Stephen Egan |
| George Barnes | George Flymin O'Neal |
| Thomas Orr | Alexander Louinor |
| Joseph Robinson | Francis Lowell |
| Jesse Fish | David Moses |
| Simon Tushs | John Ross |
| Thomas Tunno | Joseph Peavolt |
| J. McKenzie | William Slater |
| John McIntosh | James Taylor |
| Edward Corbett | Nicolas Warrington |

Most the emigrants left for the Bahamas, Nova Scotia or the American States. Of the remainder, the largest number remained in Spanish Florida

## 14. Return of Emigrants from East Florida. March 1785.
### PRO CO 5, 561

|  | White | Black |
|---|---|---|
| To Europe | 246 | 35 |
| Nova Scotia | 725 | 155 |
| Jamaica and Spanish Main | 196 | 714 |
| Dominica | 225 | 444 |
| Bahamas | 1033 | 2214 |
| States of America | 462 | 2561 |
| Other foreign parts | 61 | 217 |
| Remain with the Spaniards | 450 | 200 |
| TOTAL | 3390 | 6540 |

At the time of the peace took place, there was supposed to be about 5000 more souls in the province, mostly back country people, who are imagined to have gone over the mountains to the States, etc.

London  2 May 1786  William Brown
                    Commissioner

# West Florida, Many Lands and Increasing People

15. West Florida 1768, Merchants Memorial. PRO CO 5. 114

Adams, Benjamin
Anderson, Alexander

Blackburn, John

Clark, Graham
Clarke, John
Codrington, Edward
Comyn, Joseph
Comyn, Stephen, junior

Donnithorne, N.
Dyer, John

Farmer, Robert

Hannay, Samuel
Hunter, Robert
Hurst, John

Johnstone, Geofrey
Johnstone, John

Mackay, Angus
Mackintosh, John
Mathers, J.

Ougston, Alexander

Payne, Edward and Rene

Yidswell, Richard, junio

Associated with this document are two others, one from the merchants of London and the other from the merchants of Liverpool, in both cases representing those individuals who are trading with West Florida. The two pages from London date from the 3$^{rd}$ of November 1768. The two pages from Liverpool has no date but appears to be from the same time frame. Both complain about being abandoned by the British soldiers. They both appear to be successful because a small garrison soon returns to Pensacola. Actually settlers, as opposed to traders, didn't appear in any number until the 1770's. The focus of their efforts would be at Natchez and Tombecbe, where the soil was fertile and the inhabitants almost completely absent. The British Lieutenant Governor, Durnford, would write (in 1769) a geographical description of the lands of West Florida.

### 16. West Florida: The Province of West Florida, Durnford. 24 July 1769, PRO CO 5: 114

The Province of West Florida is so very differently situated from any of His Majesty's other southern American colonies from its vicinity to the savages. That on a first Representation it will be found to be the interest of the government to give greater attention to this frontier province than to any of the other more internal of His Majesty's southern colonies. It is so much surrounded on every side by two numerous nations of Indians, from whom their Mother country receives yearly great advantages, by the consumption of the manufactures of Great Britain, as also from the import of skins which at present forms no small part of the advantageous trade of this Province.

I do not pretend to enumerate the great number of Indians in the Creek or Choctaw Nation, but I am convinced since part of the Management of Indian Affairs hath been taken out of the Superintendent hands, and the appointment of commissaries residing among the Indian Nations hath been abridged, that many inconveniences will arise.

The commissaries among the different Nations, in and surrounding this Province, had one salutary effect; which was that it prevented the Indians, from carrying their complaints to the towns of Pensacola, or Mobile, where their arrival is attended with considerable expense in presents and provisions, otherwise they go away dissatisfied. The commissaries by being near them immediately redressed their grievances, or took such effectual methods as saved this expense by their applications. They were also a great check on the lawless behavior of the traders, hirelings; who are generally composed of the most abandoned of mankind, and whose irregularities if not timely prevented, may be of fatal consequence to this and the neighboring provinces.

The tariff, as it is now settled, gives great satisfaction to the different tribes of Indians; but repeated complaints are made by the different Chiefs, that the traders contrary to the said tariff, sell amongst them such quantities of rum, as continually inebriates their warriors and deprives them of obtaining by their industry, those necessaries of life which they usually receive for their skins when the hunting season is over. This has been repeatedly complained of, and it requires immediate redress; therefore to show our good intentions toward them, it appears necessary to appoint two commissaries, one of which ought to reside alternately in the different towns of the Chickasaw and Choctaw Nations and the other in the Creek towns. These commissaries ought to be men of great activity, courage, integrity and good understanding; of known fidelity to His Majesty and accustomed to Indians and their manners. They should be armed with the power of Magistrates, to seize all offenders and to send them under a proper escort to the governors of those provinces where their security is lodged. They should correspond on every matter that is related to the good of His Majesty's Southern

Provinces, with the neighboring governors nearest to the place they might reside at, [so] by these means every necessary intelligence would be immediately known to all parties. They should be present at all Congresses, where they should preside next to the governors, in order to give them that consequence which is necessary amongst Indians.

It is necessary to direct townships to be laid out in the following parts of the Province of West Florida:

On the clear land reserved at the Natchez,
On the reserved land at the Iberville,
On the River Perle and on the River Mobile

In order to collect as much as possible the settlers into bodies, who are at present are greatly scattered, there is some reason to suppose that many of the French inhabitants will leave their possessions at Orleans, and settle many of them on the west part of the Province. The doubtful situation they are now in, joined to their

dread of the Spaniards return, contributes not a little; and as they have in general a number of slaves and are habituated to the country they would be a valuable acquisition.

It would also be necessary to keep up the communication with the River Mississippi by the Lakes and the River Iberville. If possible part of the Waters of the Mississippi should be turned down that channel. A port should be fixed at the entrance of Lake Maurepas as near as the situation of the ground will admit, also one at old Iberville that would be a guard to secure the carrying place when the river was low. These posts might consist of 150 men each with two row boats properly fortified and capable of carrying from twenty to forty men, which would carry ammunition, provisions, etc. between the posts, or occasionally assist the settlers. These armed boats by showing themselves on the lakes and rivers would keep the Indians in much more awe than having troops continually fixed in one Post, as they would everywhere protect the settlers by carrying a small Fortress with them.

In the same manner the settlers on the Mobile River might be protected which from the goodness of the soil will very soon be considerable in numbers. The townships on that river should be laid out on the East Side of it amidst the good lands and not too distant from Pensacola, to which place a Road should be traced. It would be very advantageous to fix a town on the east side of the Bay of Mobile nearer the entrance of the harbor as the grounds on which the Old Town stands is unhealthy and the communication with Pensacola very inconvenient. There is a spot of land on the East side of the Bay reserved for this purpose below Red Cliffs, where a post should be fixed, and which hath already been approved off by the Brigadier Generals in the Southern District. Directions were given before the troops left the province to erect a barrack for the troops appointed to do duty at Mobile, on the Red Cliffs, east side of that bay.

The Province of West Florida begins to have the appearance of a settlement, and if not checked by the violence of the savages, will in a few years become of

consequence on the continent. Many settlers from the back parts of the more northern colonies are tempted to request lands in the province. From the goodness of the soil, and the great convenience of water [storage], which from the number of navigable rivers, will be of great advantage to settlers. The banks of these rivers, being low ground, are particularly situated for rice, which may be raised in this colony in great abundance. Indigo, cotton and hemp will be the staple of the higher land. Pulse of every sort natural to warm climate grow to great perfection, particularly those of the vine species. The wild grape vine is to be seen all over the country, of which there are two sorts and may be cultivated to advantage as they grow in the most sandy barren places. Mulberry is natural to the soil and climate of this province and, with the usual attention, silk may be raised. Tobacco grows well in sandy soil, with very little care. Pitch, tar and turpentine may be produced in the greatest quantities near the seashore as these lands are sandy and produce principally the different kinds of fir, many of which are sufficiently large for Naval purposes. On the low land near the rivers and in the swamps are great quantities of Cypress, White and some Red Cedar. On the higher lands near the rivers are abundance of the different kinds of Oaks and Hickory, which will furnish the planters with great quantities of lumber for the West Indies.

Thirty or forty miles inland the face of the country is entirely changed from that near the seashore. The sand being lost in a brown loamy earth mixed with gravel interspersed with high lands often times rocky, divided by pleasant valleys having rivulets of fine water running through them which afford excellent pasturage for cattle.

Rivers which empty themselves into Pensacola Bay, do not extend too far inland as that of Mobile, and therefore have not those quantities of fine land which is found on the banks of that river and which promises to be early settled; being more convenient for transporting the produce to a proper market than the lands on the Mississippi which are equal to any in America but the navigation by Orleans is tedious. Therefore the inhabitants will labor under many disadvantages unless a communication can be made through the lakes.

## 17. Observations on Stockade Fort of Pensacola. Durnford.
## 24 July 1769, PRO CO 5: 114

The fort is situated on the North side of the Bay of that name, about three leagues from the entrance of the harbor. The stockade encloses a square of barracks besides a number of huts and houses that are occupied by troops hese barracks are covered with Cyprus bark and the sides are mostly of that material or built with posts in the ground and the intervals filled with clay which form a most miserable appearance.

The governor's house alone deserves to be called that name of all the buildings within the Fort. It is raised about ten feet above the level of the other buildings and is built with posts in the ground, the intervals filled with clay, except the north front and part of the east end, which is part brick and rubble work. But as the greatest number of posts which support this building are entirely or nearly decayed, as are the materials and west end, will fall down in a short time. Any attempt to repair it will therefore be fruitless and ill disposing of the public money.

The storehouses for ordnance stores and provisions are two temporary buildings made up of boards by order of Brigadier General Haldimand as the Old Storehouses about the time of this arrival were decayed and falling down.

The magazine has had some slight repair but is yet in bad condition and not sufficient to secure the public and merchant's powder.

The barracks, although they have undergone several repairs and a considerable expense been incurred at different times, are now if possible in as bad repair as when taken possession of by the British troops. The materials are so much decayed as to render them irreparable.

The maintaining this Post in the present state will be a considerable annual expense without the least prospect of being comfortable for His Majesty's troops or the security of the King's stores.

The New House in possession of the commanding officer, with two or three others lately built, are exceptions to what I have already mentioned respecting the buildings within the stockade.

*Elections were held to colonial assembly in 1777. Despite a lapse of several years, the assembly accomplished little and was soon disbanded by the governor. Chester, who was governor for almost ten years, preferred to rule without any interference from locals.*

18. Delegates to Council at Pensacola for British West Florida, 1777, 3rd October, PRO, CO 5, Volume 635

| Manchak | Natchez |
|---|---|
| Christie, Adam | Blommart, John |
| Flower, Samuel | Hutchins, Anthony |
| Francis, Philip | Johnson, Isaac |
| Jones, Esteban | Laitt, David |
| Poulsett, Francis | Percy, Charles |
| Stuart, Esteban | Syman, Thaddeus |
| Walker, William | Tiorn, William |
| Watts, Stephen | |

| Pensacola | Mobile |
|---|---|
| Bay, Elihu Hall | Gauet, George |
| | Grant, Michael |
| | Gordon, Willim |

Lorimer, John
Marshall, William
Miller, John
Nzie, Arthur
Strother, Arthur

McGilliavay, John
Swanson, Peter

Hdille [?]

Farmer, Robert

Indian Nation

Bethune, Tarquhar
Cameron, Alexander
McIntosh, John
McIntosh, William

*These are the delegates elected to the council in 1777 at Pensacola for British West Florida. Manchak will soon be destroyed by the Mississippi river and replaced in the next period (the Second Spanish) by Baton Rouge. It was at this time that local residents requested the establishment of burial grounds.*

## 19. Request Burial Grounds in Pensacola, 6th November 1777, PRO CO 5, 635

Bruce, James
Croyer, John
Falconer, John
Hodge, David
Gower, Benjamin
Johnston, William

Lorimer, John
Marshall, William
Neil, Arthur
Ogilvy, William
Rainsford, Andrew
Strother, Arthur

## 20. Election of the Council, June 1778
## PRO, CO 5, Volume 635

### Representatives elected for the district of Pensacola

Gauld, George           Holmes, David

Bay, Elihu Hall         Tait, Robert

### Representatives elected for town of Pensacola

Ames, James             Mitchell, John

Miller, John            Strother, Arthur

### Representatives elected for the district and town of Mobile

Chrystie, Adam

Farmer, Robert

Wegg, Edmund Rush

Ward, Daniel

At this time a faction developed in West Florida that was very much anti Chester and they requested his recall. There were many reasons given but they boil down to their lack of sympathy with his supposed views on the rebellion and his failure to divide the land among them.

21. Petition to the King of the Gentlemen, Freeholders and Inhabitants of the Province of West Florida.
1779, August 14. [Anti Chester] PRO CO 5, 580

This colony is against the rebellion in neighboring colonies but we are also against the mismanagement of Peter Chester. He exercised unwarranted powers to promote his private secretary, Phillip Livingston, whose father and numerous relatives are in rebellion. Specifically he granted lands to Peter Van Brugh Livingston, the father of Peter while he was President of the rebel Provincial Congress of New York.

He granted lands without consulting with the council. He granted lands to provincial military authorities. He granted lands to his son who never came to America. He granted lands to himself that were intended for forts and fortifications. He granted lands to people that never existed, except in the imagination of his secretary.

Chester refused to grant land, to any soldier or non commissioned officer, without fees of office. He received these fees, upward of 25 dollars per 1600 acres, for every patent.

[On other items he] paid out Indian merchandise and received money or bills of exchange, manned and equipped a vessel for public use which was used to carry blacks, clothes, provisions, etc. to his, and his secretary's, plantations. He also filled the public offices with his creatures. As chancellor he has given degrees contrary to evidence. Chester allowed James Willing and Oliver Pollock, notorious rebels, to recover money in law courts.

Chester, through kind delay and then, when too late, sent envoys to demand restitution for cargos seized in the River Mississippi. These were met with insolence and contemptuous recrimination. Chester refused to raise soldiers and, when finally he sent some, it was in very small amounts. Afterwards he refused to pay for them.

Chester refused to demand restitution of blacks and property of loyal subjects yet he, and his secretary, had all of their own blacks returned to them. Similarly his secretary, Mr. Livingston, [signed] vouchers for the use of loyal refugees but there is no instance of the refugees receiving any credit.

Therefore we request that Chester be recalled and that appointment be made of someone else who is agreeable to the people:

Aikman, George
Alexander, Jeffrey
*Allen, Benjamin
Allison, James
Amos, James
Austin, In. A.

Barnes, Jeffrey
*Baskett, Thomas
Beeks, Charles
Begbie, Alex
*Benoist, Theodore.
Bernard, James
Bethune, Ferguson
Bruner, Daniel
Bunyie, James
*Burnet, William

Caine, Anthony, junior
Cameron, Alexander

Cameron, Duncan
Campbell, John
Carney, William
*Carrier, Louis
Chrystie, Adam
Clark, William

Dallas, James
Dallas, John
Davis, James
*Dawson, John
Donalo, Robert
Duncan, William

*Ellis, John

Falconer, John
Ferguson, William
*Favre, Jean
*Fu, Favre

Frazer, James
*Frazer, William

Garden, William
Gardner, John
Gibb, Joseph
*Gilchrist, John
Gower, Benjamin
*Graham, Thomas
Grant, Charles
Grant, Humphrey
*Gretion, John
Gun, James

Harrison, Peter
*Hickinbottom, Samuel
*Hoggatt, James
Holms, David
*Horn, Benjamin

Jackson, John
James, Benjamin
Jones, Richard
Jones, Rupel

*Keal, George
*Kearney, William
Keech, Robert
*Kemp, Stephen

*Laflo, Francois
*Laflo, Claud

Laviu, T. Jean
Legg, Henry
Lewis, Francis
*Louis, Joseph
Loyal, Samuel

Mackinnon, William
Main, James
Marreu, Jacob
Marshall, Mathew
Mathews, Andrew
Mayes, Abraham
McCulloch, David
*McCurtin, Cornelius
*McGillivray, Ferguhar
McGillunay, Lachlane
*McGillivray, Findlay
McGilluray, Isaac
*McGillivray, James
*McGillivray, John
*McGillivray, Lachlan
*McGillivray, Robert
*McIntosh, Alexander
McIntosh, John
McKenzie, John
*McPherson, Donald
Mench, John
*Miller, John
Moggall, James
Montgomery, Robert

Moore, Alexander
Moore, Francis

Moore, John
Moore, Roger
Morison, John
Morris, John
*Mortimer, Daniel
Murray, James

Nowlan, George
Nicolas, Antoine
*Nicholas, Bertrand

Ogilvy, William

Parker, John
Pashley, Thomas
Perry, Mardy
Pierce, Thomas
*Pinhorn, Joseph
*Poutney, William

Randon, John
*Rees, Huberd
Reidhead, John
Richardson, Bernard
Riddle, William

Rilchie, George

*Roberts, Charles
Rochon, August

Sears, Thomas
*Schneider, Jacob
Smith, George

Smith, Peter

*Solomon, Hyam

Taylor, Edward
Thompson, William
Travis, James
Troisieus, Jean
*Turnbull, John
*Turnbull, Walter

*Walker, Charles
*Walker, Joel
Walters, Thomas
Wheeler, John
White, David
Wier, William
Wilton, William
Wood, Mark

The settlers indicated with an asterisk are also given in the petition of 1780. That petition notes the occupations of the settlers. Given the Spanish invasion in Louisiana, it is no surprise that many settlers requested the formation of a militia.

## 22. Pensacola, 10th Sept. 1779. Request formation of a Militia, PRO CO 5, 535

Alexander, Geo.
Amos, James
Arnol, Mathew

Barnard, Jas
Barnes, Geo.
Black, William
Bloomer, Laurence
Bosgrove, Joseph
Bruelsh, Puse
Burns, William
Bym, Gerald

Chastanc
Combanto, Richard
Comyiar, Thomas
Corona, Vincenzo
Cowie, Andu

Davis, John
Durcell, Joseph

Falconer, John
Farlich, James

Gould, George

Heokstall, John
Hinch, John
Hudson, John

Irving, James

Johnston, William

Laboyhu, Paul
Lee, William
Legg, Henry
Lewis, Francis

Mitchell, John

Offalh, A.
Oneil, James

Paulis, Thomas
Pimrose, Edward
Pinhorn, Joseph

| | |
|---|---|
| Richardson, Bernard | Testard, William |
| Ritchie, George | |
| | War, William |
| Shother, A. | |
| Smith, Thomas | |
| Simpson, John | Watson, George |
| | White, Isaac M. |
| | White, John |
| Tait, Robert | Winniet, Jn., junior |
| | Wisner, Leonard, junior |

23. List of ... Persons ... said to have signed a Remonstrance and Petition against ... Peter Chester, 15$^{th}$ November 1780. PRO CO 5, 580

*Following the list of names [noted in table 21], and positions [not given], the following is noted:*

Pensacola

Thomas Keston, deputy provost marshal at Natchez, being duly sworn, deposit and says that he is well acquainted with John M.Gillivray at Mobile. He, and several of his co partners, have extensive dealings in this province and are largely involved in the Indian trade. They have a great deal of influence among the Indian countrymen and the poor people in the town and district of Mobile on account of the large credit they give. And this deponent further says that he knows that the said John M.Gillivray and his copartners and dependents were very busy in and about Mobile in the later end of the year 1778 and beginning of 1779 in carrying about a paper for people to sign against Governor Chester. And deponent has heard and believes that by their influence and persuasion they got many poor needy persons and others to sign said paper. And this deponent says that he has heard that the persons whose names are in the foregoing list signed said paper, that he, the deponent, knows them well. That many of the said supposed signers are persons in mean low circumstances and so illiterate as not to be able ... to write their names. And that others of them are dependant on said house and their connections. And this deponent also says that the foregoing list of said signors names are as they stand marked and distinguished. There is, to the belief of this deponents knowledge and belief, just and true, and that the said lists justly represent the characters and situation of said signers.

    Thomas Keston

4$^{th}$ of July
W. Clifton

    This is a true copy of the original and was examined there with this 15$^{th}$ day of November 1780

    E. Wegg
    E. B. Bay

*In February 1780 a census was taken of the inhabitants of Pensacola.*

## 24. Names of Inhabitants of town of Pensacola, February 1780. PRO CO 5, 635

Aird, James, artificer
Alexander, George, merchant
Amar, John, artificer
Amos, James, member of Assembly
Arnold, Mathew, artificer

Atkins, Edward, merchant

Ballantine, Hugh, merchant
Band, James, member of
    Council
Barker, Thomas, merchant
Barnes, George, merchant
Batholimieau, Busly, artificer
Bay, Elihu Hall, member of
    Assembly
Bay, John
Beaumont, Henry, merchant
Black, John, merchant
Black, William, of the ordinance
Blias, Cluk
Bosgrove, Joseph, artificer
Brasher, John, artificer
Bruce, James,
    member of Council
Bryan, John O., artificer
Bunyu, James, merchant
Byane, Gerald, artificer

Cameron, Captain,
    superintendent
Car, Richard, merchant
Carter, John Coleman,
    merchant
Chester, Governor
Christie, Adam, member of
    Assembly
Clarke, William, merchant

Clifton, William, member of
    Council
Combest, Simon, artificer
Cook, John, artificer
Corona, Vincent, merchant
Cowie, Andrew, artificer

Davis, Eran, artificer
Davis, Evan, merchant
Davis, John, artificer
Dennis, Robert, clerk of
    superintendent
Donald, Robert, merchant
Dun, William, artificer
Duncan, William, merchant
Durnford,
    Lieutenant Governor
Duryer, Jacob, merchant

Faith, Robert, member of
    Assembly
Falconer, John, merchant
Farley, James, merchant
Fontinille, Doctor, of the
    staff
Fooly, Robert, merchant
Frazer, William

Gannaway, Josiah, artificer
Gauld, George, member of
    Assembly
Gayton, James, merchant

Giorgust, Philip, merchant
Glover, John, artificer
Gordon, William, in King's
    employment
Grant, Charles, artificer

Hallacourt, Westly, merchant
Hamaman, James, merchant
Hannah, John, merchant
Hickstate, John, artificer
Hodge, David, member of
    Council
Holmes, David, member of
    Assembly


Irving, James, artificer


Johnstone, Captain, of the
    Council


Lorimer, Doctor, of the staff

Kennedy, William, artificer
Kippir, William, artificer
Kirk, James, merchant

Macutlagh, Alexander, D.P.M.
Martin, John Allen,
    comptroller
Marshall, William, LB
McClarty, artificer

McKinnon, William, merchant
Meller, John, member of Assembly
Miller, Behr, artificer
Mitchell, John, member of
    Assembly
Mitchell, John, junior
    merchant
Montgomery, Thomas
    merchant
Moore, John, merchant
Mouson, John

Newland, George, merchant
Niel, Arthur, of the ordinance
Noonoy, James, in King's
    employment


Offutt, Alex, merchant
Ogden, Doctor, of the staff
Ogilvy, William, merchant
Oliver, John, artificer
O'Neil, James, merchant

Parker, Joshua, artificer
Pashly, Thomas, merchant
Payne, Henry, artificer
Philippi, Philip, artificer
Poui, John, merchant
Primron, Edward, merchant
Primrose, Joseph, merchant
Purcell, Joseph, merchant

Rainsford, Captain, of the Council
Rayon, John, artificer
Richardson, Bernard, artificer
Richie, John, merchant
Ritson, John, merchant
Ross, Robert, merchant

Seamark, Richard, merchant
Simpson, John, merchant
Skegg, Richard, artificer
Smith, Thomas, artificer
Stephen, Phinix, artificer
Stephenson, John, member of Council
Stiel, Lieutenant Colonel, of the Council
Stokes, John, merchant
Strother, Arthur, member of Assembly

Tims, John, merchant
Tistard, William, artificer
Tonis, John, artificer
Tuby, John, naval officer

Underwood, Thomas, merchant

Vinderwid, Conrad, merchant

Waly, James, merchant
Wallington, Timothy, merchant

Government Council, General Assembly and Officials of Government, 23
Merchants and others not employed in the King's Service, 67

Watson, George, merchant
Wegg, E. R., member of Assembly
Wennett, John, merchant
Westland, Thomas, artificer
Whistle, William, of the ordinance
White, Isaac, merchant
White, John, merchant
Wies, William, merchant
Wilton, William,
Wisner, Leonard, merchant

Military gentlemen, Artificers employed in the service of the government, 40

TOTAL, 130

## 25. Inhabitants of Pensacola, Satisfied with Chester Administration. 1781, 21st February. PRO CO 5: 580

Amer, John

Bey, Elihu Hall
Bosgrove, Joseph

Clifton, William
Combauld, Richard, paymaster royal artillery

Fairlic, James
Firby, John

Glover, John
Grant, W.

Irving, James

Johnstone, William

Kirk, James

Lyman, Thaddeus

Macullagh, Alexander
Marshall, William
Martin, J. D., comptroller customs
Miller, Peter
Mitchell, John

Ogden, John, surgeon

Primrose, Edward
Rilson, J.

Simpson, John
Stephenson, James
Stokes, John

Tait, Robert
Tims, John

Underwood, Thomas

Wegg, E. R.
Wenniet, John
Wesner, Leonard
Williams, William

26. Pensacola, Householders at Time of Capitulation,
May 1781, AGI Cuba 2353

Amer, John. Ordnance
Amos, James. Officer of Ordnance
Arnold, Mathew. Bricklayer
Besley, Barkin. Carpenter
Bay, Elihu Hall. Provisional Secretary
and Judge Admiralty
Bell, Mrs. Widow
Brashier, Jesse. Yeoman
Bruce, James. Counselor
Burns, William. Pilot
Carr, Richard. Planter
Clifton, William. Chief Justice
Corona, Vincent. Retailer of Liquor
Crozer, Mary. Widow
Donald, Robert. Merchant
Duncan, William. Court Crier
Fairlie, James. Merchant
Falconer, John. Merchant
Farmer, Mrs. Widow
Finley, John. Schoolmaster
Garden, William. Commissary
Gauld, George. Magistrate
Glover, John. Master Carpenter
Griest, James. Pilot
Halley, David. Military House Keeper
Hannay, John. Taylor
Hodge, David. Counselor
Irving, James. Carpenter

Johnson, William. Pilot
Johnstone, Captain. Military gentleman of the council
Kiar, James. Planter
Kirton, Thomas. Jailer
Legg, Henry. Carpenter
Lorimer, John. Magistrate
Macullagh, Alexander. Provisional Marshal
Marshall, William. Magistrate
Martin, Allen. Comptroller
Martyn, John. Attorney at Law
Mitchell, John. Magistrate
Moore, Alexander. Planter
Moore, John. Barman
Murray, James. General Clerk
Neil, Arthur. Officer of Ordnance
Oneil, James. Shopkeeper
Pashley, Thomas. Taylor
Purcell, Joseph. Surveyor General
Rainsford, Captain. Military gentleman of the council
Richardson, Barnard. Carpenter
Safold, Isham. Deputy Surveyor
Seamark, Richard. Shopkeeper
Shakespear, Stephen. Shopkeeper
Simpson, John. Keeper
Stephens, Phentz. Constable
Stephenson, John. Counselor
Stokes, John. Baker
Strachan, Patrick. Planter
Strother, Arthur. Magistrate
Swanson, Peter. Merchant
Tait, Robert. Magistrate

Travis, James. Carpenter
Underwood, Thomas. House Keeper
Walters, William. Yeoman
Watson, George. Ship Carpenter
Wegver, Leonard. Blacksmith
Wegg, Edmund Rush. Attorney General
White, Isaac. Taylor
White, John. Carpenter
Whiteside, William. Blacksmith
Wilton, William. Officer of Ordnance
Wisner, Leonard. Blacksmith

27. Natchez, 17th January 1779, Anti Indian
PRO. CO5: 580

Thanks to Chester for support and never fail to assemble when called upon by Jeffrey Hutchins. Thanks to Colonel Stuart for aid of his Loyal Refugees under Captain Jackson's command who have been very useful to us and for the Company under the command of Captain William McIntosh lately arrived and hope they will be of no less service. They do not want the Indians, [as] reported by Captain McIntosh, to be sent to us for most are too well acquainted with the Indians to feel least confidence in them. What they can do is destroy the provisions that ought to support and sustain this Post and keep us in bodily fear. They are the reason that many fled and another visitation by them will add to the desolation.

Absheir, John A.
Alexander, Isaac
Allen, Charles
Alston, Philip
Andias, Joseph
Atheison, Thomas

Bingaman, C.
Bingaman, Lewis L. B.
Boyd, Alexander
Brabazon, Anthony

Carrol, Benjamin
Carlos, Edward
Canedine, Parker
Carrel, John
Carter, Jesse
Carter, Nehemiah
Carter, Thomas
Choly, John
Clayton, James
Clemons, Patt
Cobean, Jacob
Coplen, James
Cory, Job.
Crane, Silas
Crungetten, James

Dalba, Stephen
Douglas, Earl
Dun, Richard
Dunbar, Robert

Dwight, Senno E.
Dyeen, Thomas
Dyevo, Joseph
Dyson, Clement, senior
Dyson, Clement, junior
Dyson, John

Ellis, Hardy
Ellis, John, senior
Ellis, William
Ellis, William, senior

Felt, John
Flever, Joseph
Flower, Elisha
Frazer, Samuel

Gardner, Daniel
Gardner, John
Gawett, Ebenezer
Gayle, John
Gibson, Samuel
Goble, Ephraim
Guise, Christopher, senior
Guise, Christopher, junior
Guise, David
Guise, John
Guise, Manuel

Hallmon, David, junior
Hallmon, Solomon
Hamberston, Anthony H.
Hannon, James
Harmon, Hezekiah
Harmon, Jacob
Harmon, Roger
Harmon, Thomas
Haybraker, John
Hayes, Bosman
Hayes, William
Heady, Samuel
Hide, John
Holford, Joseph
Holmes, Thomas
Holsten, John
Holsten, Stephen
Holt, David
Holt, Dibdall
Holts, John
Hooper, Absalom
Horton, Abraham
Horsler, John F. H.
Hotchkiss, Timothy
Howard, Josheau
Hulbard, William

Ive, Nathaniel

James, Thomas
Johnson, Isaac
Johnson, Nathaniel
Jordan, Thomas
Jourdens, Stephen
Joyner, William

Kenard, Cephas
Kesmissons, Nath
King, Caleb
King, Justees
King, Richard

Le Floe, James
Leonard, Elijah
Lewis, Samuel
Llewellyn, Abednego
Love, Thomas
Lyman, Oliver
Lyman, Thaddeus

Madden, Immanuel
Mathias, Israel
Mayes, Stephen
Maygatt, Daniel
McCoy Alston, John
Meek, Francis
Meaks, William

Nair, Christopher

Ogg, John
Oglesby, James
Oglesby, William
Osborn, Samuel

Paul, Jacob
Perry, James
Phelps, M.
Phipps, Samuel
Platna, Henry C.

Ratleff, William
Reed, William
Routh, Jeremiah
Rucker, Coleby
Ryan, John

Schofield, Joseph
Sexton, Luke
Sheldon, Isaac
Shunks, John
Simmons, Charles
Simmons, James
Smith, John

Smith, William
Spain, Francis
Spell, Sterling
Stampley, George
Stampley, Henry
Stampley, Jacob
Stampley, Peter
Standlie, Joseph
Staybraker, John
Swayze, Elijah
Swayze, Nathan
Swayze Ogden, Justus
Swayze, Richard, junior
Swayze, Samuel
Swayze, Stephen

Tally, John
Terry, John
Thily, Mathias
Thornell, Ephraim
Truly, James

Weber, William W.
Weed, Joel
Wetmore, Ira
Wilson, James

## 28. Natchez inhabitants, October 4, 1779,
## PRO CO 5: 397

*Message from Alexander Dickson (Lieutenant Colonel of the 16th Regiment of Foot), and Oliver Pollock (agent of the Continental Congress and Virginia), ordered the surrender of the garrison at Fort Panmure. The subsequent letter from the inhabitants of Natchez provides the names of fifty-nine inhabitants of that town. PRO CO 5:597 has the same list for the same date with two minor changes in spelling.*

Alston, John

Bingham, C.
Bisland, John
Blommant, J.                        Eason, Will
Boles, Geofrey                      Ellis, Hardress

Carradine, Parker                   Farrell, Francis
Carson, Walter                      Ferguson, Wile
Carter, Thomas                      Foley, Patrick
Case, William                       Forney, George
Coble, Jeremiah
Collins, John                       Gelison, James
Collins, Luke                       Green, Rodolphus
Collins, Luke, Junior               Gregson [Gregorie], James
Collins, Theops. [Theo.]
Collins, William                    Hansborough, Caleb
                                    Harmon, Jacob
Devall, Richard                     Hartley, John
Dey, Benjamin
Douglass, Earl
                                    Mayer, Stephen

McIntosh, Alexander
McIntosh, William
McPherson, Donald
Mulkey, Philip
Murray, Alexander


Heyes, William
Hold, Dibbal
Homes, Joseph
Hooper, Absalom
Horn, William [W. Hiorn]
Hotchkiss, Timothy


Kennede, John


Jordan, Stephen



Leonard, Elijah
Lyman, Thaddeus

Nelson, Peter


Orcherroird, Cesar


Pearis, George
Percy, Charles
Pountney, William


Row, John




Spell, Sterling
Strain, Francis


Truly, James


Vousdan, William


Wells, Sam.
Whitfield, Andrew

## 29. Mobile [1770] inhabitants of, PRO CO 5:587

Bowles, Thomas
Brown, Jeffrey

Campbell, James
Coulson, Fran.

Dalrympie, Robert
Downnison, Francis
Durade, James

Gauld, George
Gazzow, Joseph
Gerard, Francois
Gordon, William
Gurin, Fran

Lizars, Henri
Llorimer

Marshall, William
McPherion, A.
Moore, Alexander

Pemberton

Ross, David

Southwell, John
Struthers, Arthur
Struthers, William
Swanson, Pet

Taith, David

Vincent, P.

Ward, Ben
Wegg, E. R.

30. Letter to the colonial assembly from the Principal Inhabitants of
Mobile on enfranchisement,
November 1778  (Hamilton 1910:306)

| | |
|---|---|
| | Lavall, |
| Austin, John A. | Lusser, Jean Bapt$^e$ |
| | Lusser, Louis |
| Baskett, Thomas | |
| Benoist, Thre | |
| | Maroteau, Jean Louis |
| | Maroteau, L. |
| Carriere, L. | McCleish, David |
| Colburt, James | McCurtin, Cornelius |
| | McGillivray, James |
| Dallas, James | McIntosh, John |
| Dow, George | McIntosh, John, junior |
| | Mortimer, Daniel |
| Ellis, William Cocke | |
| | Nicolas, Bertrand |
| Favre, Jean | |
| Fieury, Francois | Pittman, Buckner |
| | |
| Gordon, William | Roberts, Francis |
| Grelot, Barthelemy | |
| Guilliory, Pierre | Strother, Thomas |
| | Struthers, William |
| Hay, Gilbert | Swanson, Peter |
| Hood, Walter | |
| | Troup, George |

31. Tombecbec under English (left 21 October 1779, PRO CO 5: 635) and Spanish (right AGI Cuba 1359)

|  |  |
|---|---|
|  | Abrams, Robert |
| Arrish, William |  |
| Avny, In. |  |
|  | Banks, Sutton |
| Basketh, Thomas | Baskett, Thomas |
|  | Basset, Thomas |
| Beson, Biler |  |
| Bird, Abraham | Bird, Abraham |
|  | Bradey, John |
| Bradley, Henry | Bradley, Henry |
|  | Brown, John |
| Brouna, Thomas | Brown, Thomas |
|  | Chaurt, Richard |
|  | Collins, William |
| Coplan, Jaz |  |
| Cooper, Jaz. | Cooper, James |
| Cooper, Samuel | Cooper, Samuel |
| Dawson, In. |  |
|  | Dawson, John |
| Farley, John |  |
| Farrow, Alexander |  |
| Folsome, Abenezer |  |
| Folsome, Israel, |  |
| Fordice, Jaz |  |

Fuller, Mordecai M.

                Girould, David
                Greed, John W.
                Guger, John
Gray, Jaz.                        Gray, James
                          Gretian, John
              Haggeth, Jaz
            Haggath, Welsfoard
Hancock, John              Hancock, John
              Harrison, Bilu
                        Harrison, Peter
                        Hickman, John
                        Hood, Walter
              Hufman, Adam
              Hull, Daniel
              Hyker, Garland

              Jackson, In.
                        Jackson, John
           Jackson, senior, William
           Jackson, junior, William

              Lavis, Joseph
                        Lemon, Gilbert
                        Little, Abraham
Little, Thomas              Little, Thomas
                        Lord, Gershom
              Loth, Absalom
              Loth, In.
              Loth, Mark

|  |  |  |
|---|---|---|
| | Loth, Nathan | |
| | Loth, William | |
| | | Lott, John |
| | Low, In. | |
| | | |
| | | Marcelas, Peter |
| | Mathews, In. | |
| | Mays, Abraham | |
| | | McCurtin, Cornelius |
| | | |
| | McGillivray, Finley | |
| | McGillivray, James, merchant | |
| | McGillivray, Laughlin | |
| | McGlaughlin, James | |
| | McGlaughlin, John | |
| | McMillan, Jaz | |
| | Moore, Arthur | |
| | Moore, Roger | |
| | Murray, John | |
| | | |
| | Norial, Joseph | |
| | | |
| | Oneil, William | |
| | | |
| | Redground, David | |
| | | Reese, [Huberd] |
| Ruth, Benjamin | | Ruth, Benjamin |
| Ruth, Francis | | |
| | | Smith, John |
| | | Solomon, Hyam |
| | | Spires, William |
| | | Stephens, William |

Sterns, Joel
                    Taylor, Thomas
    Thires, Ino.
                    Troup, George, Esqr.
    Tucher, Junior, Thomas
                    Turnbull, John
                    Turnbull, Walter
                    Twidale, William
        Walker, Joel
        Wall, Jese
        Wall, William
                    Whitehead, John
                    Williams, John

## 32. Tensa and Mobile under Spanish. 1780. AGI Cuba 2359

Alby, John, tensa

        Higinbottom, Samuel, tensa

Baily, Thomas, tensa

Burnett, William, tensa    *Keston, Thomas, tensa

Christie, Captain John, mobile  Mather, Alexander, tensa

Cordrey, Thomas, tensa    McIntire, John, tensa

Craig, Robert, tensa

Deforge, Peter, tensa    Oats, Jeremiah, tensa

Gordon, William, tensa    Oats, William, tensa

Grant, Michael, mobile

        Poor, Patrick, tensa

        Strachan, Patrick, tensa

        Strother, Thomas, mobile

## 33. List of the Inhabitants of Mobile District who swore neutrality, 16th of May 1780. AGI Cuba 2359

Alby, John
Allen, Charles
Atkison, Thomas
Azbel, John

Bailey, Richard
Baird, John
Baley, Thomas
Banks, Sutton
Baskett, Thomas
Bassett, Thomas
Biesson, Peter
Billings, Ichebod
Bird, Abraham
Booth, John
Bradley, Henry
Brady, John
Brazeal, Eliza
Brown, James
Brown, John
Brown, Thomas
Burnett, William

Chaot, Richard
Clark, John
Clark, John
Collins, William
Cooper, James

Cooper, Samuel
Corck, Richard
Cowen, Robert
Craige, Robert
Crery, John

Dawson, John
Deforge, Peter
Dyer, John
Dyson, Edward

English, John
Evans, John

Farley, John
Farrow, Alexander
Fogel, John
Fooy, Benjamin
Fordice, James
Fuller, Mordicai
Fulsom, Israel

Gallehan, Patrick
Garner, John
Georgius, Philip
Gilehrist, Nimrod
Gillies, David

Giroud, David
Gordon, William
Gow, Alexander
Gray, James
Gray, Robert
Gretion, John

Hall, Henry
Harnest, John
Harrel, Jacob
Hickman, John
Higkebottom, James
Hincock, William
Hoggatt, James
Holmes, Thomas
Hood, Walter
Hooper, Absalom
Hoplon, Abner
Horne, Benjamin
Hubbard, Stephen
Hull, Daniel

Jackson, James
Jackson, Joseph
Jackson, William
Jacttion, John
Johnston, John
Jones, Russell
Joyner, William

Keil, George

Kemp, William
Keston, Thomas

Latto, Henry
Lavis, Joseph
Lemmon, Gilbert
Littell, Abraham
Llewellynn, Abednego
Lord, Gershom
Lott, Absalom
Lott, John
Love, Thomas
Loyd, Samuel

Man, George
Marseles, Peter
Mather, Alexander
Mathews, Andrew
Mathews, John
Matteair, Ezehel
Mayes, Abraham
McClendon, Joel
McCullogh, John
McCurtin, Cornelius
McGillivray, Fendly
McGillivray, James
McGillivray, Lachlan
McGlauon, Edmond
McGlauon, James
McGrew, John
McIntosh, John
McIntyre, Peter

Medows, Edward
Megochan, John
Mitchel, James
Mitchel, William
Moore, Arthur
Moore, Roger
Mortimer, Daniel
Munford, James
Murray, John

Nell, James
Nobles, Joshua

Oats, William

Pigg, John
Poplin, James
Price, John

Rainsford, John
Ratliff, William
Read, Hardy
Root, Francis
Routh, Benjamin

Safold, Isham
Safold, Joshua
Sawer, Ephraim
Smith, John

Snell, Christopher
Speirs, William
Stacey, Joshua
Steel, John
Stevens, William
Strachan, Patrick
Stuart, Charles
Sulivan, Cornelus

Tollow, Daniel
Troup, George
Tucker, Charles
Turnbull, Walter
Twidale, William

Vansant, George
Vanzant, Stephen

Walker, Joel
Wall, Jesse
Ward, Daniel
Whitehead, Amos
Whitehead, John
Williams, Thomas
Winn, Joseph

# Annotated Bibliography of Spanish/English war
# West Florida campaign (1779-1781)

It was originally my intention to do a history of the Spanish/English war of 1779/1784 but after examining the published material on the subject, I decided that the topic had been "beaten to death." There have now been several books and various articles written on this topic. What I have provided, instead, has been an annotated bibliography of the sources relating to this topic. The published material, the articles and books, date largely from the 1970's and 1980's. There is little subsequent material on this topic. The manuscript material is another story.

The British material mostly comes from the Public Record Office (PRO) in the London area. It consists of original documents from the West and East Florida colonies. They were copied for the Manuscript Division of the Library of Congress in the late '20's and early '30's of the last century. I was working with photostats and transcripts of this material. My emphasis was census and census like material. Because of my focus on the events leading up to the Hispanic/English war and the war itself, material dates largely from the last ten years of English rule. However, because settlement was relatively late in both West and East Florida, I would not expect to find much earlier material. This data is given in the previous sections.

There are references in documents of the United States but, because they did not take a direct part in the Hispanic/English war, the citations are minor. They come, largely, from Letters of Delegates (1774-1789) of the Library of Congress.

The Spanish documents, while very interesting, date largely from the period of Spanish conquest and control and so are largely beyond the prevue of this paper. Only documents from the actual period of transition are noted here. For further information on the Second Spanish period (1784/1821), one should see Feldman (1991) and (1998). The records of the Second Spanish period (Saint Augustine) for East Florida are curated at the Library of Congress while the West Florida material is largely at the Archivo General de Indias (AGI) in Seville Spain.

The actual military campaigns that resulted in the conquest of West Florida are reported on by Galvez (1781) and, for the conquest of Pensacola by Eelking (1863), log book of the British ship Mentor (Deans as given in Rea and Serves 1982), the Journal of the siege of Pensacola (Farmer 1781). Eelking, which is a nineteenth century abstract of eighteenth century events, is less useful than Galvez, Farmer or Deans There are also journals kept by various Spaniards who took part in the siege (e.g. Miranda *in* Worcester 1951) but these, which seldom give the detail of the English texts, are less useful. Finally, as noted below, I have provided the manuscript references to the actual events of the English/Spanish war. These are mostly from the English sources (mostly PRO documents), since I don't currently have access to the Spanish equivalent.

## Manuscripts (listed chronically)

**Author**: Campbell, John
**Title**: Campbell to Germain, December 26
**Location**: PRO CO 5: 597
**Date**: 1778
**Section**: Jamaica
**Abstract**: Force on way to Pensacola includes- Regiment of Waldeck (613 soldiers), Pennsylvania Loyalists (149 soldiers) and Maryland Loyalists (265 soldiers).

**Author**: Eelking (1977)

**Title**: "The German allies, 1776-1783, in the North American wars for liberation"

**Date**: 31 December 1778

**Section**: Saint Augustine

**Abstract**: On this day the flotilla put out to sea and passed between the coast of Cuba and the wide Gulf of Mexico.

**Author**: Eelking (1977)

**Title**: "The German allies, 1776-1783, in the North American wars for liberation"

**Date**: 20$^{th}$ of January to 2$^{nd}$ of February 1779

**Section**: Pensacola

**Abstract**: On the 29$^{th}$ of January 1779 the crew and all a board disembarked from the three ships. The crew of the BRITTANIA, which was composed of two companies, landed on February 2$^{nd}$.

**Author**: Campbell, John
**Title**: Campbell to Germain, February 20th
**Location**: PRO CO 5: 597
**Date**: 1779
**Section**: Pensacola, Mobile
**Abstract**: Require that be built at Pensacola the offices of the Commanding Officer, Bake House, wharf. Barracks, roof of all public buildings, barrack at brick kilns, Central Hospital, battery at Red Cliffs, block houses, work on Rose Island for defense of harbor, block house at Tartar point.

**Author**: Campbell, John
**Title**: Campbell to Germain, March 2nd
**Location**: PRO CO 5: 597
**Date**: 1779
**Section**: Pensacola, Natchez
**Abstract**: Conflict between Colonels Allen and Chalmers of provincial corps of Pennsylvania and Maryland regarding who is senior. Great confusion in Indian department due to the expected death of Colonel Stuart while the situation in fort at Natchez is reported to be good.

**Author**: Campbell, John
**Title**: Campbell to Germain, March 21st
**Location**: PRO CO 5: 597
**Date**: 1779
**Section**: Pensacola
**Abstract**: One sergeant, 2 corporals, and 4 privates who were Maryland loyalists deserted in a body with arms and 100 pounds of ammunition per man. Their intention seems to escape through the Indian nations and return to their own province.

**Author**: Campbell, John
**Title**: Campbell to Germain, 22$^{nd}$ March
**Location**: PRO CO 5: 597
**Date**: 1779
**Section**: Pensacola
**Abstract**: No shipping available other than one vessel, the West Florida

**Author**: Galvez, Bernardo de
**Title**: Expedición contra Los Establecimientos Ingleses sobre el Misisipí, 1 Mayo [1779] – 28 Marzo [1780]
**Location**: AGI Santo Domingo 2598
**Date**: 1779 – 1780
**Section**: Natchez
**Abstract**: 82 letters on this topic

**Author**: Campbell, John
**Title**: Campbell to Henry Clinton, 31st May
**Location**: PRO CO 5: 597
**Date**: 1779
**Section**: Natchez
**Abstract**: Because of rise of Mississippi, except for Captain Miller's company and a small detachment of the 16th regiment, this fort [of Manchac] was abandoned on the 16th of April and the troops retreated to Baton Rouge which is about 11 miles higher up the bank of the river. Colonel Dickson wrote, that at time of their leaving Manchac, 14 inches of water were in the barracks and storehouses. Left stores needed to be deposited in the upper apartments.

**Author**: Campbell, John
**Title**: Campbell to Bernardo de Galvez, 31st May
**Location**: PRO CO 5: 597
**Date**: 1779
**Section**: Pensacola/New Orleans
**Abstract**: Received report that Choctaws were invited to New Orleans; this is allowed by British King but not reception of his rebellious subjects.

**Author**: Campbell, John
**Title**: Campbell to Lieutenant Colonel William Stiell (3$^{rd}$ battalion of 60$^{th}$ regiment of foot), 22$^{nd}$ of June
**Location**: PRO CO 5: 597
**Date**: 1779
**Section**: Pensacola
**Abstract**: Stiell is to inspect the accounts of William McIntosh Captain of company of loyal refugees.

**Author**: Galvez, Bernardo de
**Title**: Bernardo de Galvez to Joseph de Galvez, 3$^{rd}$ of July
**Location**: AGI Santo Domingo 2656
**Date**: 1779
**Section**: New Orleans
**Abstract**: As of June 9$^{th}$ last year, there were 1000 men (both white and Indian) by the English post of Natchez and 200 in Manchak. This year arrived 225 more at the said post and 400 men at Manchak of the regiment of Waldeck. The forces that I have at my disposal are 200 men from Havana and 300 from a local Battalion. The remaining 300 come from various posts in the Antilles and Mexico.

**Author**: Campbell, John
**Title**: John Campbell to Lord George Germain, 15$^{th}$ of July
**Location**: (?) PRO CO 5: 597
**Date**: 1779
**Section**: Pensacola, Mobile, Natchez
**Abstract**: Captain McIntosh on verge of being seized for payment of credit so ordered payment made from government funds. Galvez is encouraging the seduction of the Choctaws. Campbell ordered barracks at Mobile to be repaired. Because of the threat of invasion, I have ordered reinforced Colonel Dickson with the grenadiers of the Regiment of Waldeck. The Natchez district on the Mississippi is most deserving of protection and encouragement.

**Author**: Dickson, Lieutenant Colonel
**Title**: Dickson to Brigadier General Campbell, 18<sup>th</sup> of July
**Location**: (?) PRO CO 5: 597
**Date**: 1779
**Section**: Natchez
**Abstract**: Received visit from M. Macent, Colonel of militia in Louisiana, regarding about 600 Americans near Illinois (English side) who are said to be preparing an expedition to "Detroit." However I thought that the expedition may be to "West Florida."

**Author**: Dickson, Lt. Col. Alexander
**Title**: Dickson to Campbell, 30 July
**Location**: PRO CO 5: 597
**Date**: 1779
**Section**: Natchez
**Abstract**: Situation of Manchac unanimously condemned and Fort considered indefensible against cannon [...accordingly moved to Baton Rouge where cleared ground...]

**Author**: Chester, Peter
Title: Chester to Germain, 17<sup>th</sup> August
Location: PR) CO 5: 622
Date: 1779
Section: Pensacola
Abstract: Mail from Pensacola goes to Saint Augustine and not to Jamaica. Mail to Pensacola goes to Jamaica and then Havana.

**Author**: Campbell, James
**Title**: James Campbell to Captain Le Monkeus (commanding sloop Storm), 5$^{th}$ of September
**Location**: PRO CO 5: 597
**Date**: 1779
**Section**: Pensacola
**Abstract**: The cargo of provisions in the Charlotte transport sloop, for Manchac, should have a convoy

**Author**: Campbell, James
**Title**: James Campbell to Lieut. Col. Dickson, 9$^{th}$ of September
**Location**: PRO CO 5: 597
**Date**: 1779
**Section**: Natchez
**Abstract**: Notification of Declaration of War and request to cut a channel between the Mississippi and Iberville rivers. Should the Spaniards begin hostilities then most take possession of the posts at Galveztown and Fort Gabriel. James Campbell also wishes to learn the state of the garrison of New Orleans both in regard to troops and fortifications.

**Author**: Campbell, James
**Title**: James Campbell to Captain Anthony Forster [Natchez], 9$^{th}$ of September
**Location**: PRO CO 5: 597
**Date**: 1779
**Section**: Natchez
**Abstract**: Request that hold oneself ready to join Colonel Dickson at Manchac with your company and volunteers.

**Author**: Campbell, James
**Title**: James Campbell to Charles Stuart, Superintendent of Indian Affairs, 9th September
**Location**: PRO CO 5: 597
**Date**: 1779
**Section**: Pensacola
**Abstract**: Pleased to confirm Sir Henry Clinton's appointment of Captain Cameron as Superintendent of Indian Affairs.

**Author**: Campbell, John
**Title**: John Campbell to Governor Chester, 9th of September
**Location**: PRO CO 5: 597
**Date**: 1779
**Section**: Pensacola
**Abstract**: An embargo should be placed upon all vessels and crafts going to sea from Pensacola and Mobile.

**Author**: Campbell, James
**Title**: James Campbell to Captain F. Montreis, 10th September
**Location**: PRO CO 5: 597
**Date**: 1779
**Section**: Pensacola
**Abstract**: Requires that Spaniards be kept ignorant of state of war and that Colonel Dickson be informed expeditiously as possible of the rupture between the two crowns.

**Author**: Montreis, Captain F.
**Title**: F. Montreis to James Campbell, 10th of September
**Location**: PRO CO 5: 597
**Date**: 1779
**Section**: Pensacola
**Abstract**: No boats available to send to Manchak. Island of Jamaica is in critical situation with 26 ships of the line, 10 or 12 frigates, 17,000 regulars and 4 or 5 thousand enemy militia destined for Jamaica. When the fight is over, then we will send considerable forces to Pensacola.

**Author**: Campbell, John
**Title**: John Campbell to Governor Chester, 10th September
**Location**: PRO CO 5: 597
**Date**: 1779
**Section**: Pensacola
**Abstract**: Request that compel inhabitants to carry arms in their own defense and to declare martial law within the province of West Florida.

**Author**: Chester, Governor
**Title**: Governor Chester to John Campbell, 10th of September
**Location**: PRO CO 5: 597
**Date**: 1779
**Section**: Pensacola
**Abstract**: An embargo has been placed upon all vessels.

**Author**: Board
**Title**: Board to Governor Peter Chester, 11th of September
**Location**: PRO CO 5: 597
**Date**: 1779
**Section**: British West Florida
**Abstract**: Advise that martial law is illegal and unconstitutional but advise instead that inhabitants give oath of allegiance, enroll their names in the militia and nominate officers. They should do this in the east side of the Bay of Mobile, Tensa, Brier Creek, Tombeckly settlements to Pensacola. They should also do it in the west side of the Bay of Mobile, Manchac, and Natchez.

**Author**: Chester, Peter
**Title**: Peter Chester to Major General Campbell, 11th of September
**Location**: PRO CO 5: 597
**Date**: 1779
**Section**: British West Florida
**Abstract**: I have laid before the members of His Majesty's Council your request for martial law and am submitting the response. I would also request that you give orders to the officers commanding at Mobile, Manchac and Natchez for carrying out the proclamation.

**Author**: Chester Peter
**Title**: Proclamation of the Governor of West Florida, 11th of September
**Location**: ANC, fondos Florida
**Date**: 1779
**Section**: British West Florida
**Abstract**: Calls upon the inhabitants to enlist in the militia for the defense of the province.

**Author**: Campbell, Major General John
**Title**: Major General John Campbell to the Public, 12$^{th}$ of September
**Location**: PRO CO 5: 597
**Date**: 1779
**Section**: British West Florida
**Abstract**: Request that every inhabitant enroll under officers of their own choice to serve wherever the exigency of His Majesty's service may require.

**Author**: Campbell, John
**Title**: Campbell to Germain, 14th September
**Location**: PRO CO 5: 597
**Date**: 1779
**Section**: Pensacola
**Abstract**: Received notice of War against Spain. He mentions returning from Manchac to Baton Rouge. The West Florida, an armed ship on the lake that carried 3 and 4 pounders, must fall prey to superior force.

**Author**: Dickson, Lt. Col. Alexander
**Title**: Dickson to Campbell, 21 September
**Location**: PRO CO 5: 597
**Date**: 1779
**Section**: Baton Rouge
**Abstract**: Reasons for Colonel Dickson on remaining in Baton Rouge with list of members of garrison.

**Author**: Eelking (1977)

**Title**: "The German allies, 1776-1783, in the North American wars for liberation"

**Date**: 20th of October 1779

**Section**: Pensacola

**Abstract**: A courier brought the news of Dixon's surrender to people of Pensacola.

**Author**: Dickson, Lt. Col. Alexander
**Title**: Dickson to Campbell, 4 October
**Location**: PRO CO 597
**Date**: 1779
**Section**: Natchez
**Abstract**: Redoubt of Baton Rouge invested on 12 September. Early in morning of 21st battery of heavy cannon was opened against it and forcing it to yield after 3 hours.

**Author**: Chester, Peter
**Title**: Chester to Germain, 8th November
**Location**: PRO CO 622
**Date**: 1779
**Section**: Pensacola
**Abstract**: Spain began hostilities, capturing the towns of Manchac and Natchez. "Chachan" Indians have joined the Spaniards. Would have recommended that Campbell send a force to Natchez but Campbell never asked Chester. No fortifications of any importance carried out by Campbell in Pensacola or Mobile. The inhabitants of Pensacola, Tensa and Tombighby set up volunteer companies.

**Author**: Dickson, Lt. Col. Alexander
**Title**: Dickson to Campbell, 15th of December
**Location**: PRO CO 5: 597
**Date**: 1779
**Section**: Pensacola
**Abstract**: Return of different detachments of His Majesty's troops including Regular Artillery, 16th Regiment, 60th Regiment, Waldeck Regiment, independent company, garrison staff plus how many officers, etc., in each unit. They were at Baton Rouge, Manchek, Thompson Creek on the Mississippi river, and on the Lakes.

**Author**: "Generales y Comandantes"
**Title**: Comunicaciones y Noticias ... sobre la Expedicion a Panzacola
**Location**: AGI Santo Domingo 2543
**Date**: 1779-1780
**Section**: Pensacola

**Author**: Governor of Havana
**Title**: Governor of Havana to Galvez, 2nd of January
**Location**: AGI Papeles de Cuba 1291
**Date**: 1780
**Section**: Havana
**Abstract**: On the 5th of November the expedition against Pensacola was turned into one against Mobile and supplied with 7 heavy batteries, ships and 1200 soldiers. On the 6th of December, the frigate O, and then on the 20th the Saint John and the Saint Dorothea arrived in Havana damaged by a storm and so delaying the attack against Mobile.

**Author**: Governor of Havana
**Title**: Governor of Havana to Galvez, 5$^{th}$ of January
**Location**: AGI Papeles de Cuba 1291
**Date**: 1780
**Section**: Havana
**Abstract**: The Governor of Havana provides a report on the state of the forces, transport ships, and other forces for the expedition against Mobile.


**Author**: Eelking (1977)

**Title**: "The German allies, 1776-1783, in the North American wars for liberation"

**Date**: 6$^{th}$ of February 1780

**Section**: Pensacola

**Abstract**: There was an earthquake shock so severe that in the barracks the weapons fell off the walls and furniture was overthrown in the rooms. Chimneys fell down and there was danger of fire from the open kitchen fireplaces. Houses had tumbled down and people buried underneath were crying for help.


**Author**: Peabody, Nathaniel
**Title**: Nathaniel Peabody to William Whipple, 7$^{th}$ of February
**Location**: New Hampshire Historical Society (Langdon-Elwyn Family Papers), Concord
**Date**: 1780
**Section**: Natchez
**Abstract**: By letters from General Lincoln we learn that the Spaniards are warmly engaged in reducing the British Settlements upon the River Mississippi, have taken 900 prisoners, etc.

**Author**: Ellsworth, Oliver
**Title**: Oliver Ellsworth to Jonathan Trumbull, Sr., 8th of February
**Location**: Connecticut State Library, Hartford (Trumbull Papers)
**Date**: 1780
**Section**: Natchez
**Abstract**: [General Lincoln wrote] "that the Spaniards had been up the Mississippi & taken possession of the British settlements & made 900 prisoners. And that a considerable Naval force with 4,000 Troops on board, sailed from the Havana ... for Pensacola ... There is every reason to believe, Sir, that Spain will make a serious diversion in the Florida's: to which perhaps we can have no objection, provided she does not extend her views on the Mississippi beyond the Latitude of 31, nor an exclusive navigation of that river."

**Author**: Campbell, John
**Title**: Campbell to Germain, 12th February
**Location**: PRO CO 597
**Date**: 1780
**Section**: Pensacola
**Abstract**: Eleven ships and vessels of the enemy arrived on the 10th. It is expected that Fort Charlotte would be immediately invested... They will be joined in Mobile Bay by the force of ... Galvez....

**Author**: William Ellery
**Title**: Rhode Island Delegates to William Greene, 15th February
**Location**: Rhode Island State archives [published in Letters of Delegates, 1774-1789, Volume 14, Library of Congress, Washington DC, 1987]
**Date**: 1780
**Section**: Mobile, Pensacola, St. Augustine
**Abstract**: "...The 60th Regiment was order'd to St. Augustine. The enemy seems to be alarmed at the movements of the Spaniards. We do not know yet the fate of Mobile or of Pensacola. There is some reason to believe that they are both in the hands of the Spaniards. ... This is undoubtedly the report in Savannah ...".

**Author**: Campbell, John
**Title**: Campbell to Durnford at Mobile, 19th February
**Location**: PRO CO 597
**Date**: 1780
**Section**: Pensacola
**Abstract**: Can't pay for blacks employed for defense of Mobile but British government will pay and will concur in an application for restitution of costs.

**Author**: Durnford, Elias
**Title**: Durnford to Galvez, 2nd March
**Location**: PRO CO 597
**Date**: 1780
**Section**: Mobile
**Abstract**: [Refusal to surrender to Galvez]

**Author**: Eelking (1977)
**Title**: "The German allies, 1776–1783, in the North American wars for liberation"
**Date**: 5th of March 1780
**Section**: Pensacola
**Abstract**: The 60th regiment, and on the 6th the rest of the Waldecker Regiments, left for Mobile as reinforcements. On the 11th the General himself followed with the Pennsylvanians and one detachment of artillery.

**Author**: Durnford, Elias
**Title**: Durnford to Galvez, 14th March
**Location**: PRO CO 597
**Date**: 1780
**Section**: Mobile
**Abstract**: [Surrender to Galvez]

**Author**: Campbell, John
**Title**: Campbell to Germain, 21st March
**Location**: PRO CO 597
**Date**: 1780
**Section**: Pensacola
**Abstract**: Fort Charlotte of Mobile surrendered on 14th instant by capitulation... I made a movement to Tensa, about 30 miles above Mobile and 72 miles from Pensacola, with some Indians from the Creek nation... Taking a 5 inch howitzer and two field pieces (3 pounders) over the river Perdido I arrived at Tensa on the 10th and constructed rafts to go down Tensa about 3 miles and then through creek to Mobile river and thence to Fort Charlotte... Firing between besiegers and besieged ceased on evening of the 12th and, then about 10 o'clock on the Tuesday morning, Spanish colors were displayed on Fort Charlotte... I therefore returned to this place [Pensacola] on the 18th and 19th. By the above event... West Florida ... reduced to the District of Pensacola...

**Author**: Campbell, John
**Title**: Campbell to Germain, 28th March
**Location**: PRO CO 597
**Date**: 1780
**Section**: Pensacola
**Abstract**: [Sighted hostile fleet outside harbour]

**Author**: Eelking (1977)

**Title**: "The German allies, 1776-1783, in the North American wars for liberation"

**Date**: 27th of March to 30th of March 1780

**Section**: Pensacola

**Abstract**: On March 27th the Spanish flotilla came in sight. On the following day the twenty-one ships could be seen clearly, and they anchored in the harbor of Pensacola. Everyone was alarmed. The city was evacuated and the cannon in the batteries were rendered useless. The Regiment of Waldeck retreated to a place near Fort George and encamped. Campbell hurried with the rest of the troops to Gage Hill. There was great surprise on the morning of the 30th when it was seen that the flotilla had vanished.


**Author**: Eelking (1977)

**Title**: "The German allies, 1776-1783, in the North American wars for liberation"

**Date**: 1st of April 1780

**Section**: Pensacola

**Abstract**: On April 1st two companies of the Marylanders united with the Waldeckers by Fort George. Over these troops Colonel von Hanxleden was in command.

**Author**: Eelking (1977)

**Title**: "The German allies, 1776–1783, in the North American wars for liberation"

**Date**: 9th of April 1780

**Section**: Pensacola

**Abstract**: Lieutenant Colonel von Horn came ashore with his two sons. He came from Waldeck and brought a transport of recruits, consisting of one sergeant and nineteen men. They had been one full year on the way.

**Title**: Remite la Muesta deL Tanaco de Natchez nuevamento conquicado, 12 abr.
**Location**: AGI Santo Domingo 2609, no. 8
**Date**: 1780
**Section**: Natchez

**Author**: Eelking (1977)

**Title**: "The German allies, 1776–1783, in the North American wars for liberation"

**Date**: 20th of April 1780

**Section**: Pensacola

**Abstract**: A new line of trenches and breastworks had been constructed behind Fort George and was called Waldeck. All the ships were waiting before the harbor. On the land there was only the Perdido (River) between the opposing troops. The outposts were on opposite banks of the rivers. So far everything was quiet on both shores. On the 20th the Spanish crossed over, drove back the outpost guards, and took some horses back across the Perdido. At once Campbell sent out 200 Choctaws and Chickasaws and cleared the surrounding country of the enemy again.

**Author**: Navarro, Diego Jose
**Title**: Navarro to Jose Galvez, 23$^{rd}$ April
**Location**: AGI Santo Domingo 80-1-16
**Date**: 1780
**Section**: Havana
**Abstract**: On the 10$^{th}$ of March a hurricane dispersed the Spanish fleet and the frigate Santa Marta was grounded off the coast of Yucatan. Subsequently another storm scattered the Spanish ships remaining by Mobile.

**Author**: Navarro, Diego Jose
**Title**: Navarro to Jose Galvez, 23$^{rd}$ April
**Location**: AGI Santo Domingo 80-1-16
**Date**: 1780
**Section**: Havana
**Abstract**: On the 14$^{th}$ of March the fortress of Mobile surrendered and Galvez captured the garrison.

**Author**: Campbell, John
**Title**: Campbell to Germain, 13th May
**Location**: PRO CO 597
**Date**: 1780
**Section**: Pensacola
**Abstract**: Spanish captured Mobile on the 14th of March. Could have taken the harbor of Pensacola but weather prevented it.

**Author**: Chester, Peter
**Title**: Chester to Germain, 17$^{th}$ May
**Location**: PRO CO 622
**Date**: 1780
**Section**: Pensacola
**Abstract**: The capitulation of Mobile made by Lieutenant Governor Dunford.

**Author**: Deans, Robert
**Title**: May 19th 1780 log book entry
**Location**: University of West Florida, John C. Pace Library, Special Collections Group 75-15
**Date**: 1780
**Section**: Pensacola
**Abstract**: At 6, saw 2 large ships & a brig to the eastward, standing to the westward. Made the signal for all captains. Made the private signal but they did not answer it. Sent two 12 pounders ashore on west end Rose Island. The ships hoisted Spanish King's colors & made sail the southward.

**Title**: Siete cartas ... de la expedición de la Mobila, 31 Mayo a 12 Juno
**Location**: AGI Santo Domingo 2572
**Date**: 1780
**Section**: Mobile

**Author**: Gayarre, Juan Antonio
**Title**: Juan Antonio Gayarre a don Jose de Galvez, 31 Mayo
**Location**: AGI Santo Domingo 2572
**Date**: 1780
**Section**: Mobile
**Abstract**: Da cuenta de su empleo en el ejercito y una relacion subcinta de la campaña [Mobile & Pensacola]

**Author**: Houston, William Churchill
**Title**: William Churchill Houston to William Livingston, 5th of June
**Location**: New York Public Library, New York
**Date**: 1780
**Section**: Mobile
**Abstract**: Dispatches from General Bernardo de Galvez dated at Mobile on the 8th and announce reduction of the Fort. The Captain's information is that the Garrison consisted of 800 Regulars besides Militia...

**Author**: Fell, John
**Title**: Diary, 6$^{th}$ of June
**Location**: Massachusetts Historical Society, Beverly
**Date**: 1780
**Section**: Mobile
**Abstract**: Letters by Capt Pickles from Mr Polock at New Orleans advising of the taking of Mobile by the Spaniards.

**Author**: Navarro, Jose de
**Title**: Governor of Havana gives an account of the conquest of Mobile., 10$^{th}$ of June
**Location**: AGI Audiencia de Santo Domingo 80-1-16
**Date**: 1780
**Section**: Havana
**Abstract**: On the 22$^{nd}$ of March, being 70 leagues from this bay, the auditor of Marine (Ignacio Ponce) asked me to increase the number of cannon, bombs, balls and other supplies. On the 20$^{th}$ I returned to this port asking that the commanding general of this convoy ask Bernard Galvez to end the expedition against Pensacola and leave in Mobile a garrison of 800 men under the command of the Colonel of the Regiment of Infantry of Navarre, Jose Ezpeleta.

**Author**: Jose Galvez
**Title**: Response of His Majesty to the events at Mobile, 22$^{nd}$ of June
**Location**: AGI Papeles de Cuba 175
**Date**: 1780
**Section**: Madrid
**Abstract**: The taking of the fort of Mobile, so well fortified and defended with vigor, is an act to be applauded especially given the small number of soldiers (recently saved from two shipwrecks) at the disposal of the invaders. The King is very satisfied with the result and concedes the title of Brigader to the Colonel of the Regiment of the Prince, Don Gerono Giron and that of Lieutenant of the Regiment of Spain with the grade of Captain to the mentioned Manuel Gonzalez.

**Author**: Governor of Havana
**Title**: English prisoners who arrived at this fortification from the 23$^{rd}$ of April, [23$^{rd}$ June]
**Location**: AGI Santo Domingo 80-1-16
**Date**: 1780
**Section**: Havana
**Abstract**: From the Loyal Regiment of Pennsylvania captured 1 sergeant, 2 corporals, and 2 soldiers. From the Regiment 60 captured 1 lieutenant, 1 sergeant, 6 corporals, 3 drummers, 33 soldiers (including one from Campeche). From the Loyal Regiment of Maryland captured 3 soldiers. From the body of artillery captured 2 soldiers. From Embarcaciones captured two captains, 1 pilot, and 53 sailors. Taking part in this squadron were John Bautista (French), Francisco Luis (Portuguese), Henry Lain, Pedro Doren (Pardo), Thomas Smuh, Robert May and Daniel Carnelius (Moreno). From the Urca Saint Mary Saint Thomas, captured from the English in Mobile, were from the 60$^{th}$ Regiment its captain Jaime Wirch, sergeant Marcos McRins, Maria (his wife) and Ana (his daughter). From the Balandra Saint Mary the Terrible, which returned with the expedition of Mobile, were the sailors William Redli and Samuel Novvler.

**Author**: Rendon, Francisco
**Title**: Account of the Investigations done with regard to the English, 4$^{th}$ of July
**Location**: AGI Indiferente General 146-3-11
**Date**: 1780
**Section**: Philadelphia
**Abstract**: When the Goletilla Buckskin arrived at this port I received a letter sent to my dead chief John Murallos dated May 26$^{th}$ on the expedition sent to attack Pensacola. I note that the provinces of Virginia and North Carolina have sent 15,000 troops and others of militia to blockade the English in Charlestown. These troops were the command of General Gates.

**Author**: Deans, Robert
**Date**: July 24th 1780 log book entry
**Location**: University of West Florida, John C. Pace Library, Special Collections
Group 75-15
**Date**: 1780
**Section**: Pensacola
**Abstract**: Made the signal for a petty officer from the Port Royal to assist the vessel coming in, a sloop, under Spanish flag of truce from New Orleans.

**Author**: Deans, Robert
**Date**: July 29th 1780 log book entry
**Location**: University of West Florida, John C. Pace Library, Special Collections
Group 75-15
**Date**: 1780
**Section**: Pensacola
**Abstract**: Sailed, the sloop flag of truce for [New] Orleans

**Author**: Piernal, Pedro
**Title**: Acting governor to Bernardo de Galvez giving an account of the destruction wrought by the hurricane of August 24
**Location**: ANC-Fondos Floridas
**Date**: 1780
**Section**: New Orleans

**Author**: Campbell, John
**Title**: Campbell to Germain, 26th August
**Location**: PRO CO 597
**Date**: 1780
**Section**: Pensacola/Mobile
**Abstract**: Return of the killed, wounded and prisoners of the garrison of Fort Charlotte including 4th battalion of 60th regiment (90), united Provisional Corps of Pennsylvania and Maryland loyalists (16), seamen (61), inhabitant volunteers (57), officers (21), blacks (52.

**Author**: Campbell, John
**Title**: John Campbell to Joseph Ezpeleta, 30th August
**Location**: PRO CO 597
**Date**: 1780
**Section**: Pensacola/Mobile
**Abstract**: Ready to send flag of truce to conduct two officers clothing, only waiting response in order to learn if you will send ship or expect me to send them to Mobile.

**Author**: Ezpeleta, Joseph
**Title**: Joseph Ezpeleta to General Campbell
**Location**: PRO CO 597
**Date**: 1780
**Section**: Mobile
**Abstract**: Vessel will come to Pensacola as soon as receive passport for truce purpose.

**Author**: Campbell, John
**Title**: Campbell to Germain, 29$^{th}$ September
**Location**: PRO CO 597
**Date**: 1780
**Section**: Pensacola
**Abstract**: Great preparation for an attack on Pensacola with intention to attack without any reinforcements from Cuba. However four vessels from Cuba for New Orleans were seen, a fortnight ago, from the east end of Rose Island.

**Author**: Madison, James
**Title**: James Madison to Edmond Pendleton, 3$^{rd}$ of October
**Location**: Library of Congress, DC
**Date**: 1780
**Section**: Pensacola
**Abstract**: If any foreign operations are undertaken on the continent it will probably be against the Floridas by the Spaniards. A Spanish Gentleman who resides in this City has received information from the Governor of Cuba that an armament would pass from Havana to Pensacola toward the end of last month, and that 10 or 12 ships of the line and as many thousand troops would soon be in readiness for an expedition against Saint Augustine.

**Author**: Mayorga (Viceroy of New Spain)
**Title**: The Virrey of New Spain provides the reasons for conducting to Havana the English prisoners who were sent to Veracruz by the Governor of Lousiana, 4$^{th}$ of October.
**Location**: AGI Indiferente General 146-2-7
**Date**: 1780
**Section**: Mexico City
**Abstract**: The governor of Louisiana sent to Veracruz 330 English prisoners. They being inconvenient to keep here, and having consulted with the Inspector Pascual Cisneros, I sent these prisoners, on the 26$^{th}$ of August, to Havana.

**Author**: Ezpeleta, Joseph
**Title**: News of Mobile, 6th of October
**Location**: AGI Santo Domingo 80-1-16
**Date**: 1780
**Section**: Mobile
**Abstract**: Campbell, general of Pensacola, sent a Parliamentarian who noted that the inhabitants are prohibited from crossing the river. Joseph Ezpeleta received help from the Indians who provided fresh meat for the troops who came to attack Penzacola. I sent a sergeant and four men to accompany an English sergeant who brought the paper of Pensacola to Mobile. Upon their return they encountered a group of Choctaw who served the English. They had orders to kill whatever Spaniards they encountered to which the sergeant responded that he did not want to offend nor could he offend those who came under a flag of truce. Nevertheless when they returned the Spanish sergeant and two soldiers were killed, the third wounded and the fourth arrived wounded at Mobile.

**Author**: Navarro
**Title**: Governor of Havana decides to suspend the expedition against Pensacola, 18th of October
**Location**: AGI Santo Domingo 80-1-16
**Date**: 1780
**Section**: Havana
**Abstract**: An epidemic attacks the entire squadron, being more than 2000 ill in the Hospital, and causing the dispersal of the Squadron.

**Author**: Navarro, James Joseph
**Title**: Navarro to Joseph Galvez, 7th of November
**Location**: AGI Santo Domingo 80-1-16
**Date**: 1780
**Section**: Havana
**Abstract**: The forces of Bernard Galvez experienced a storm for three days convincing them that they could continue their voyage and disarmed several boats. Subsequently supplies were sent to Mobile. The supplies included 400 quintals of gunpowder, 100,000 cartuchos of Fusil with ball, 10,000 flints, 50 quintals of balls, 25 respas of paper and artificial lights. The extraordinary rains that followed prevented a more satisfactory response.

**Author**: Eelking (1977)
**Title**: "The German allies, 1776-1783, in the North American wars for liberation"
**Date**: 15th of November 1780
**Section**: Pensacola
**Abstract**: When the soldiers had the trenches and breastworks behind Fort George almost finished, the British general decided to make the earthworks almost the same. He decided it would be more necessary to have earthworks on the cliffs as it would give more range to the guns in covering the entrance to the harbor. For this reason he had the largest guns brought from Fort George to the cliffs, the 32 pounders, on the 15th of November.

**Author**: Eelking (1977)

**Title**: "The German allies, 1776-1783, in the North American wars for liberation"

**Date**: 19$^{th}$ of November 1780

**Section**: Pensacola

**Abstract**: On the 19$^{th}$ of November, Major Pentzel got an order to go with fifty Waldeckers to the cliffs that they had just fortified. The steep cliffs were those facing the waterside. Traveling over land this way, which was very hazardous, they had to travel through swamps and stagnant waters and then a small narrow strip of land they had to travel over to the cliffs. On both sides of the strip the water was very deep.

**Author**: Navarro, James Joseph
**Title**: Navarro to Joseph Galvez, 28$^{th}$ of November
**Location**: AGI Santo Domingo 80-1-16
**Date**: 1780
**Section**: Havana
**Abstract**: Number of troops of the Expedition to Pensacola that arrived at the Port of Campeche as a result of the Hurricane.

**Author**: Eelking (1977)

**Title**: "The German allies, 1776–1783, in the North American wars for liberation"

**Date**: 3$^{rd}$ of January 1781

**Section:** Pensacola

**Abstract**: Colonel von Hanxleden was ordered to march with one hundred men, Infantry of the 60$^{th}$ Regiment, eleven on horseback, Provincials, 300 Indians, and sixty men of his own regiment and to travel to the French village, a settlement of the Mississippi, to drive out the Spanish from their fortifications. The command of Waldeckers consisted of Captain von Baumbach, the Lieutenants von Wilmosky and Stirlin, the standard Bearer Ursal, six under officers, two musicians, and forty-seven privates.

**Author**: John Campbell to George Germain, 5 January
**Location**: PRO CO 597
**Date**: 1781
**Section**: Mobile
**Abstract**: Storm defeated Spanish intentions on Pensacola. British will attack Mobile with troops and Mentor.

**Author**: John Campbell to George Germain, 5 January
**Location**: PRO CO 597
**Date**: 1781
**Section**: Mobile/Pensacola
**Abstract**: Repulse of detachment that attacked Mobile and killing of Colonel De Hanxleben.

**Author**: Robert Farmer, January 7th
**Location**: Journal Siege Pensacola, Library of Congress microfilm
**Date**: 1781
**Section**: Pensacola
**Abstract**: Attacked the village about daybreak and was defeated because Waldeck not supporting the 60th and Provincials. Colonel de Hantbaden and Lieutenant Sterling of the Waldeck Regiment and Lieutenant Gordon of the 60th were killed. Lieutenant Bayartun and Lieutenant Pinkorn of Provincials wounded, 15 privates killed and 19 wounded. Reckoned killed and wounded of the enemy in the redoubt 25 of the former and 34 of the latter among which there are several officers.

**Author**: Eelking (1977)

**Title**: "The German allies, 1776-1783, in the North American wars for liberation"

**Date**: 7th to 9th of January 1781

**Section**: Mobile

**Abstract**: With so many wild tribes (Indians) and such a mixture of men, it was no easy task for Colonel von Hanxleden. Hanxleden arrived on the morning of the seventh and tried to storm the Spanish forts that resisted strongly. Several times the Germans tried to storm the forts with their bayonets, but their forces were very weak and the Indians were no help in this matter. All efforts were useless, and they had to retreat with heavy losses after they had lost their commander or fuehrer of their division, Colonel von Hanxleden, Lieutenant Stirlin, and the English Lieutenant Gordon died on this spot. Lieutenant von Baumbach and one officer of the Provincials were wounded. But the Spanish also had heavy losses, and one of their powder magazines was burned.

They buried the body of Colonel von Hanxleden in haste, this grave later was fenced by the Spaniards who honored him as a brave man. The place that they selected for the grave was under a very large tree. The rest of the unlucky expedition came back on the 9th of January to their place of encampment.

**Author**: John Campbell to George Germain, 11 January
**Location**: PRO CO 597
**Date**: 1781
**Section**: Mobile/Pensacola
**Abstract**: Attacked village in two columns but with death of De Hanxleben the soldiers retreated. Mentor and Gerind got into Mobile Bay in the afternoon but contrary winds prevented them from proceeding with land forces. Captured prisoners and afterwards a detachment of marines and seamen landed on Dauphin island to destroy a log house. The remainder of the enemy fled to the mainland.

**Author**: Navarro, James Joseph
**Title**: Governor of Havana to Jose Galvez, 15$^{th}$ of January
**Location**: AGI Papeles de Cuba 1291
**Date**: 1781
**Section**: Saint Augustine
**Abstract**: State of Saint Augustine Florida, providing the fortress and the guns [for this fortress].

**Author**: Navarro, James Joseph
**Title**: Account of the English attack upon Mobile, 17$^{th}$ of January
**Location**: AGI Santo Domingo 87-1-19
**Date**: 1781
**Section**: Mobile
**Abstract**: Attack upon a village, 3 leagues from Mobile, by an English troop commanded by the Count of Hanxleden. The attack was defeated and the Count killed by the Spaniards.

**Author**: Ezpeleta, Joseph de
**Title**: Remite circunstanciada copia de la Relacion. No. 35. 17th January
**Location**: AGI Santo Domingo 2609
**Date**: 1781
**Section**: Mobile
**Abstract**: del ataque executado por las tropas inglesas mandadas por el Coronel del Reximiento de Infanteria de Waldeck Conde de Hanxleden al puesto avanzado de la Aldea el 7 de Enero el 7 de Enero de este año.

**Author**: David Yeats
**Title**: David Yeats to James Grant of Ballindalloch, 3rd February
**Location**: Papers of James Grant at Ballindallich Castle, Box 26, Manuscript division, Library of Congress
**Date**: 1781
**Section**: Saint Augustine
**Abstract**: ... Have noted great hopes of success if these cursed Spaniards don't distract us, but we have very threatening accounts from the Havana by a cartel vessel which went from here and is lately returned from that place we have undoubted intelligence that the Spaniards after failing in two attempts against Pensacola have not been disheartened and are preparing a third. ... For some time past they have been sending small bodies of troops to Mobile and Don Galvez, the present Governor of New Orleans, who commands the expedition is said to sail from Havana the 12th ultimo with two ships of the Line, some frigates and transports with the remainder of the troops, and to form an army of five thousand men ... in order to besiege Pensacola. Confident of success this province next to be attacked and four ships of the line three frigates and twelve new galleys, each carrying a twenty four pounder and calculated for our shallow navigation are prepared and ,,, thought would be ready to sail in March with six Regiments and irregulars in all composing a body of about four thousand men ...

**Author**: Galvez, Joseph
**Title**: Joseph Galvez to Bernard Galvez, 9th February
**Location**: AGI Papeles de Cuba 175
**Date**: 1781
**Section**: New Orleans
**Abstract**: The principal objective of the land and sea forces is the capture of Pensacola for as long as it is under British control there is no security for Spanish possessions in the Gulf of Mexico. Secondly, you need to ask Havana for supplies and soldiers. Third, after obtaining the surrender of Pensacola you need to place it under competent officers and soldiers. Fourthly, after the conquest of Pensacola and Mobile you will need to consider the recovery of Omoa and launching another expedition against Saint Augustine of Florida.

**Author**: Galvez, Joseph
**Title**: Galvez to Governor of Havana, 12th of February
**Location**: AGI Papeles de Cuba 1330
**Date**: 1781
**Section**: Madrid
**Abstract**: The principal objective is the capture of Pensacola. The second objective is the siege of Pensacola. After the conquest troops and officials need to be sent to prevent their reconquest by the English. Fourth, supplies must be sent to the posts of Pensacola and Mobile. As a fifth objective, Havana should dislodge the English from their establishments in the Gulf of Honduras and on the San Juan river. Sixth, you need to defend Cartagena and Portobelo in order to protect the cargos of Anil that derive from these ports...

**Author**: John Campbell to George Germain, 15th February
**Location**: PRO CO 597
**Date**: 1781
**Section**: Pensacola
**Abstract**: No hope of military support but Peter Parker promised Naval aid. Major Campbell named as Deputy Paymaster. Shipment of clothing for provincial troops lost so need another shipment.

**Author**: John Campbell to George Germain, 23$^{rd}$ February
**Location**: PRO CO 597
**Date**: 1781
**Section**: Pensacola
**Abstract**: Return of Lieutenant Colonel Stiel of 3$^{rd}$ Battalion of the 60$^{th}$ Regiment will provide details. Presenting letter of Captain James of Sloop of War who will be able to answer questions regarding Naval department.

**Author**: Robert Farmer, March 9th
**Location**: Journal Siege Pensacola, Library of Congress microfilm
**Date**: 1781
**Section**: Pensacola
**Abstract**: Appeared in sight a Spanish fleet consisting of 32 sail of vessels the same night. They landed a number of men on Santa Rosa. About 12 o'clock midnight chiders brig got safe out bound for Jamaica.

**Author**: Deans, Robert
**Date**: March 9$^{th}$ log book entry
**Location**: University of West Florida, John C. Pace Library, Special Collections Group 75-15
**Date**: 1781
**Section**: Pensacola
**Abstract**: At 7 AM, discovered a fleet of ships to the SE. At 8, fired alarm guns; sent a shore to acquaint the commanding officer at the Royal Navy Redoubt that the above fleet was on the coast. Sailed, His Majesty's Brig Childers for Jamaica with information of said fleet. At Noon, the fleet in the SE; saw 34 sail from the masthead.

**Author**: Eelking (1977)

**Title**: "The German allies, 1776–1783, in the North American wars for liberation"

**Date**: 9$^{th}$ of March 1781

**Section**: Pensacola

**Abstract**: On the 9$^{th}$ of March 1781 the Spaniards appeared before Pensacola where they had been expected. The only armed ship that was in the harbor, the MENTOR, signaled with seven shots the arrival of the flotilla of the enemy... In the morning, at 9:00 o'clock, the flotilla was so close that thirty-eight ships could be distinguished. They traveled from the east on the coast of Rose Island. The ships cruised in the bay during the day, and later in the evening they left for Rose Island to land the troops and the guns.

The troops, which were at present under General Campbell's command, were not quite a thousand men. The rest consisted of two very weak Provincial regiments, and some quickly got-up militia. The very cautious Spanish general, Bernardo de Galvez, commanded a force six times as strong, and was prepared with all the artillery and ammunition necessary for the siege. During the night Campbell sent a ship, which had arrived the day before, to Jamaica to report the arrival of the Spanish. He asked for reinforcements from Jamaica, and immediately began preparations for defense and was aided in this [defense] by his small but courageous force.

**Author**: Robert Farmer, March 10

**Location**: Journal Siege Pensacola, Library of Congress microfilm
**Date**: 1781
**Section**: Pensacola
**Abstract**: The Spaniards took the Port Royal boat and crew of 9 men who went onshore at Rose Island for their stock. Captain Roberts arrived this afternoon in a schooner that he took on Wednesday night last near Round Isle.

**Author**: Deans, Robert

**Date**: March 10th log book entry

**Location**: University of West Florida, John C. Pace Library, Special Collections Group 75-15

**Date**: 1781

**Section**: Pensacola

**Abstract**: PM, at 1 pm, the brig Childers anchored near us, the flood hindered her getting over the bar. Sent the Lieutenant of the Port Royal and some men ashore to the Navy Redoubt. Sent prison ship up to town. The Spanish fleet anchored opposite without Rose Island. At 7 PM, saw a great many soldiers at the signal house on Rose Island. Fired several broadsides at them. At 10, saw a great many soldiers the outside Rose Island Point near Port Royal. Fired several shot at them. Sailed in the night, brig Childers for Jamaica.

**Author**: Eelking (1977)

**Title**: "The German allies, 1776-1783, in the North American wars for liberation"

**Date**: 10th of March 1781

**Section**: Pensacola

**Abstract**: On the tenth the flotilla again appeared in the harbor and set up a blockade. At the same time the troops from the landside surrounded Pensacola to begin an organized and earnest siege of the town.

In the afternoon a ship, which had been sent by the MENTOR, brought in a Spanish *schaluppe*, which they had captured near Mobile. The *schaluppe* had on board baggage and stores for a Spanish lord, who was well fortified against the deprivations incident to travel in the American wilderness. On board were found 20,000 thalers (dollars) in cash, beautiful silver, excellent wines, all kinds of utensils for a good kitchen, and many other things.

**Author**: Robert Farmer, March 11th
**Location**: Journal Siege Pensacola, Library of Congress microfilm
**Date**: 1781
**Section**: Pensacola
**Abstract**: The enemy erected batteries on Rose Island that obliged the Mentor and Port Royal to quit their stations. Some of their vessels attempted to come over the bar but put back one of their men of war struck as she was coming over, but got off again in about 20 minutes.

**Author**: Deans, Robert
**Date**: March 11th log book entry
**Location**: University of West Florida, John C. Pace Library, Special Collections Group 75-15
**Date**: 1781
**Section**: Pensacola
**Abstract**: Arrived, the launch from reconnoitering, with 6 prisoners. Saw a schooner to the westward, her prize. One of the enemys brigs gave chase. Fired several broadsides at the schooner. At 3 PM, came in the schooner. Sent the schooner & launch to town. At 7 AM, cut the bouy from the Childer's anchor which she slipt in getting under way.

**Author**: Eelking (1977)

**Title**: "The German allies, 1776-1783, in the North American wars for liberation"

**Date**: 11th of March 1781

**Section**: Pensacola

**Abstract**: On March 11 the Spaniards began firing from one of their fortifications on Rose Island. They first directed their fire at the MENTOR, who answered back, but had to retreat after she was hit twenty-eight times by 24-pounders. She drew away close to the town docks.

**Author**: Robert Farmer, March 12th
**Location**: Journal Siege Pensacola, Library of Congress microfilm
**Date**: 1781
**Section**: Pensacola
**Abstract**: From the fort at the cliff they fired three shots at those who were erecting a battery on Rose island obligating them to quit.

**Author**: Deans, Robert
**Date**: March 12$^{th}$ log book entry
**Location**: University of West Florida, John C. Pace Library, Special Collections Group 75-15
**Date**: 1781
**Section**: Pensacola
**Abstract**: PM, ½ past, observed the Spanish fleet heaving up [and] at 1 PM, the greatest part of their square rigged vessels under sail, standing down for the bar. Hove up and made sail down towards the bar to dispute their coming over. At 2, a row galley from the back of Rose Island Point fired several shot at us but none of them took place. At ½ past, the Spanish fleet put about and stretched off to the SE. At 3, the Spanish fleet having all stretched to the SE, we bore away to come up above Tartar Point clear of their batteries. At ½ past 3, they opened two batteries upon us from Rose Island, from which they hull'd us several times. Two of their shot lodged between decks, each of which weighed 26 ¾ pounds. At ½ past 5, came to anchor in 5 ½ fathom water above Tartar Point. AM, observed the Spaniards heaving up an entrenchment on Rose Island Point [and] the fort at the Cliffs fired several shot at them. Loosed sails to dry [and] the Galvez brig under way.

**Author**: Deans, Robert
**Date**: March 13th log book entry
**Location**: University of West Florida, John C. Pace Library, Special Collections Group 75-15
**Date**: 1781
**Section**: Pensacola
**Abstract**: PM, boats employed carrying shot to the Cliffs.

**Author**: Robert Farmer, March 14th
**Location**: Journal Siege Pensacola, Library of Congress microfilm
**Date**: 1781
**Section**: Pensacola
**Abstract**: The enemy ships toward the night made a manuevre to the southwards.

**Author**: Deans, Robert
**Date**: March 14th log book entry
**Location**: University of West Florida, John C. Pace Library, Special Collections Group 75-15
**Date**: 1781
**Section**: Pensacola
**Abstract**: AM, Sent some casks ashore to the redoubt.

**Author**: Deans, Robert
**Date**: March 16th log book entry
**Location**: University of West Florida, John C. Pace Library, Special Collections Group 75-15
**Date**: 1781
**Section**: Pensacola
**Abstract**: Came down from town the Love & Unity's Increase. Came on board Mr. Davis, ship carpenter, & 3 more seamen as volunteers during the siege. Sent 2 of

our 12 pounders on board the Love & Unity's Increase, with 2 barrels powder & materials for the guns. Read the Articles of War.

**Author**: Robert Farmer, March 17th
**Location**: Journal Siege Pensacola, Library of Congress microfilm
**Date**: 1781
**Section**: Pensacola
**Abstract**: The enemy attempted to land at the mouth of Perdido under cover of two row galleries. The number of Indians in sight prevented them. Three row galleries sent [over] the bar . . . at which the fort fired some shot.

**Author**: Deans, Robert
**Date**: March 17th log book entry
**Location**: University of West Florida, John C. Pace Library, Special Collections Group 75-15
**Date**: 1781
**Section**: Pensacola
**Abstract**: At 10 A.M., the Diligence, packet, anchored here from town. Rowed guard. Employed watering.

**Author**: Robert Farmer, March 18th
**Location**: Journal Siege Pensacola, Library of Congress microfilm
**Date**: 1781
**Section**: Pensacola
**Abstract**: The Mentor, Port Royal and other vessels came up from their stations abreast of the town. The Galvez brig and three row galleries passed the fort on the cliff and anchored under their batteries of Rose island.

**Author**: Deans, Robert
**Date**: March 18th log book entry
**Location**: University of West Florida, John C. Pace Library, Special Collections
Group 75-15
**Date**: 1781
**Section**: Pensacola
**Abstract**: At 2 PM, the Navy Redoubt fired at one of the enemy's row galleys under Rose Island Point. The galleys returned the fire and a slow cannonading ensued till sunset, when the galleys retreated more under Rose Island Point. Employed sending powder & shot on board the packet to carry up to Fort George. At 7, got under way in company with the Port Royal & the Love & Unity's Increase, a transport, to go up to town to land the guns, ammunition & stores, &c., for the forts. At ½ past 11, calm; came too. At 4 AM, warped up abreast of Sutton's Lagoon; came in 3½ fathoms of water. Employed getting the stores to hand.

**Author**: Eelking (1977)
**Title**: "The German allies, 1776-1783, in the North American wars for liberation"
**Date**: 18th of March 1781
**Section**: Pensacola
**Abstract**: Until the 18th the flotilla had been very quiet, but on this day at one o'clock in the afternoon, Don Galvez suddenly arrived in the harbor with a brig and two galleons and took a position where the guns could not reach him. So they could not be occupied, Campbell burnt the houses close to the harbor.

**Author**: Robert Farmer, March 19th
**Location**: Journal Siege Pensacola, Library of Congress microfilm
**Date**: 1781
**Section**: Pensacola
**Abstract**: About 2 o'clock P.M. 22 ships of the enemy came over the bar and passed the fort at the cliffs without receiving any damage.

**Author**: Deans, Robert

**Date**: March 19th log book entry

**Location**: University of West Florida, John C. Pace Library, Special Collections Group 75-15

**Date**: 1781

**Section**: Pensacola

**Abstract**: Employed getting out the guns & stores to send to Fort George. AM, ditto weather. Employed as before


**Author**: Eelking (1977)

**Title**: "The German allies, 1776-1783, in the North American wars for liberation"

**Date**: 19th of March 1781

**Section:** Pensacola

**Abstract**: On the 19th under favorable wind, the Spanish flotilla entered the harbor, in spite of heavy firing from the forts and batteries, which lasted for two hours.

**Author**: Robert Farmer, March 20th
**Location**: Journal Siege Pensacola, Library of Congress microfilm
**Date**: 1781
**Section**: Pensacola
**Abstract**: Captain Stevens arrived with a party of Indians who told us that yesterday they fell in with an enemy boat and crew consisting of eleven men, 10 of which were killed, and one brought at prisoner who informs us that on their passage from Havana they saw an English fleet which was the one that sailed from here on the 25th for England. They, being much too the windward, could not catch them after a 24 hour chase.

About 5 0'clock P.M. General Galvez sent a flag of truce to General Campbell to the same purpose as Lord Albermarle sent at the siege of Havana that was not to burn the shipping, King's building or town. [He] threatened very much for Campbell's answer to that was the threats of an enemy was not to be minded. About 8 o'clock at night the blockhouse on Tartar Point was set on fire by our own people as a signal of the enemy attempting to land.

**Author**: Deans, Robert
**Date**: March 20th log book entry
**Location**: University of West Florida, John C. Pace Library, Special Collections
Group 75-15
**Date**: 1781
**Section**: Pensacola
**Abstract**: At 3 PM the enemy's fleet forced the harbor and came to an anchor inside of Rose Island. One of their transports got a ground going up toward Rosey Bay. Sent all the people ashore to Fort George except 12 men who is to carry the Mentor up Middle River. Sailed, the Mentor up the river.

**Author**: Robert Farmer, March 21[th]
**Location**: Journal Siege Pensacola, Library of Congress microfilm
**Date**: 1781
**Section**: Pensacola
**Abstract**: About 10 O'clock A.M. General Campbell sent Colonel Dickson of the 18th regiment, Lieutenant Gordon, and De Camp as flag of truce to Galvez. After 3 O'clock P.M. 2 brigs and 3 row galleries harried the fort at the cliffs. [At] 9 O'clock at night the blockhouse and the Blue Stone at the cliffs was set on fire by our people.

**Author**: Deans, Robert
**Date**: March 21[th] log book entry
**Location**: University of West Florida, John C. Pace Library, Special Collections Group 75-15
**Date**: 1781
**Section**: Pensacola
**Abstract**: The enemy sent in a flag of truce. Our troops set fire to the blockhouse on Tartar Point. The enemy fired a great many guns.

**Author**: Robert Farmer, March 22nd
**Location**: Journal Siege Pensacola, Library of Congress microfilm
**Date**: 1781
**Section**: Pensacola
**Abstract**: The enemy landed on Tartar Point under cover of the Galvez brig and two row galleries. About noon General Galvez sent a flag of truce to General Campbell. 4 O'clock P.M. 2 polacres and 3 small vessels harried the fort at the cliffs.

**Author**: Deans, Robert
**Date**: March 22$^{nd}$
**Location**: log book entry, University of West Florida, John C. Pace Library, Special Collections Group 75-15
**Date**: 1781
**Section**: Pensacola
**Abstract**: Four sail came from the westward; 2 anchored in the harbor, the other 2 stood out to sea. AM, a party that was at the Cliffs came in, the Spaniards having landed at Tartar Point from Rose Island, and some troops and horse from the Perdido set down before the Navy Redoubt. The block houses & houses at the Cliffs was set fire to by our people. This day a flag of truce went to the fleet and returned. Mustered the ship's company. Prize money was paid for the Spanish schooner Santo Servanto and her cargo.

**Author**: Robert Farmer, March 23$^{rd}$
**Location**: Journal Siege Pensacola, Library of Congress microfilm
**Date**: 1781
**Section**: Pensacola
**Abstract**: One o'clock P.M. a sloop came over the bar. 4 o'clock 16 vessels passed the fort at the cliffs. About 6.30 evacuated the town of Pensacola and took stations at the two redoubts, the 16$^{th}$ the advanced and the 60$^{th}$ the center one.

**Author**: Deans, Robert
**Date**: March 23$^{rd}$ log book entry
**Location**: University of West Florida, John C. Pace Library, Special Collections Group 75-15
**Date**: 1781
**Section**: Pensacola
**Abstract**: PM. People employed carrying sails up for tents and water casks to the fort. AM. Appointed a lieutenant & for men to the advanced redoubt, and an officer & 35 [men] from the Port Royal to the middle redoubt.

**Author**: Eelking (1977)

**Title**: "The German allies, 1776–1783, in the North American wars for liberation"

**Date**: 23$^{rd}$ of March 1781

**Section**: Pensacola

**Abstract**: Don Galvez knew he was so much superior in strength, to those who opposed him, yet he asked for reinforcements, and sixteen ships arrived from Havana on the 23$^{rd}$. The Indians tried to prevent their landing, but were compelled to retreat. They returned, however, with two cannon and some troops. The Spanish were compelled to reembark in such haste that several men were drowned.

**Author**: Robert Farmer, March 24$^{th}$
**Location**: Journal Siege Pensacola, Library of Congress microfilm
**Date**: 1781
**Section**: Pensacola
**Abstract**: 9 0'clock A.M. the Spanish admiral got under way and stood to the eastward. Mr. Stephenson went [with] a flag of truce from the Governor regarding the town women and children. A large transport of the enemy struck on the bank as he was coming in.

**Author**: Deans, Robert
**Date**: March 24th log book entry
**Location**: University of West Florida, John C. Pace Library, Special Collections Group 75-15
**Date**: 1781
**Section**: Pensacola
**Abstract**: PM. Saw a fleet to the eastward standing to the westward. 18 sail forced the harbor and joined the other fleet. The Navy Redoubt on the Cliffs kept up a brisk fire when they [the Spaniards] attempted to come round Rose Island Point. Sent the officer & men to the redoubt. People employed in sundries. AM. One of the fleet, the two decked ship that lay outside of Rose Island, got under way and stood to the eastward. At 10 a flag of truce went down to the fleet. Mustered the people. John Roberts, seaman, ran from the Navy Redoubt.

**Author**: Robert Farmer, March 25th
**Location**: Journal Siege Pensacola, Library of Congress microfilm
**Date**: 1781
**Section**: Pensacola
**Abstract**: 9 0'clock A.M. the Indians brought in 23 horses belonging to the enemy and 2 scalps.

**Author**: Deans, Robert
**Date**: March 25th log book entry
**Location**: University of West Florida, John C. Pace Library, Special Collections Group 75-15
**Date**: 1781
**Section**: Pensacola
**Abstract**: The Navy Redoubt and the fleet fired great guns; also heard vollies of small arms. AM. People employed rolling full water casks to the advanced redoubt. Mustered the people.

**Author**: Robert Farmer, March 26th
**Location**: Journal Siege Pensacola, Library of Congress microfilm
**Date**: 1781
**Section**: Pensacola
**Abstract**: 4 O'clock P.M. the enemy fleet weighted anchor and took their stations between Moore and Sutton lagoons. We, imagining that they meant to land, sent out a detachment of a hundred men under the command of Captain Byrd who was joined by two hundred and fifty Indians under Captain Cameron.

**Author**: Deans, Robert
**Date**: March 26th log book entry
**Location**: University of West Florida, John C. Pace Library, Special Collections Group 75-15
**Date**: 1781
**Section**: Pensacola
**Abstract**: PM. The pilot & boatswain & 6 men returned from the Mentor, she having overset in a squall going up Middle River. AM. Mustered the people; sent the prisoners on board the Port Royal.

**Author**: Robert Farmer, March 27th
**Location**: Journal Siege Pensacola, Library of Congress microfilm
**Date**: 1781
**Section**: Pensacola
**Abstract**: 7 o'clock A.M. three of the Indians came from the mouth of Sutton's Lagoon who say that they saw a few of the enemy land there. Upon which the whole of the Indians went down to Neil's house where five boats of the enemy were attempting to land but upon the Indians firing they returned to their shipping. 42 sails of the Spanish fleet took their station between the Moor and Neil houses.

**Author**: Deans, Robert
**Date**: March 27th log book entry
**Location**: University of West Florida, John C. Pace Library, Special Collections
Group 75-15
**Date**: 1781
**Section**: Pensacola
**Abstract**: AM. 28 of the fleet got under way and three men of war & the row galleys anchored off Sutton's Lagoon. A party of the light infantry went down to oppose their landing the troops. Heard several vollies of small arms. AM. A flag of truce came up from the fleet. Mustered the people & exercised great guns in Fort George. Employed rolling water casks up to the redoubt. Sail makers employed making tents.

**Author**: Robert Farmer, March 28th
**Location**: Journal Siege Pensacola, Library of Congress microfilm
**Date**: 1781
**Section**: Pensacola
**Abstract**: Arrived an express from the cliffs informing us that a schooner came from the westward and attempting to pass the fort she received a shot in her hull which caused her running aground on Rose island.

**Author**: Deans, Robert
**Date**: March 28th log book entry
**Location**: University of West Florida, John C. Pace Library, Special Collections
Group 75-15
**Date**: 1781
**Section**: Pensacola
**Abstract**: PM. People employed as before. Spaniards at 5 P.M., landed their troops betwixt Moor's Lagoon and Sutton's. Heard some firing in the night from the Indians. All the seamen employed getting water into the redoubts.

**Author**: Robert Farmer, March 29th
**Location**: Journal Siege Pensacola, Library of Congress microfilm
**Date**: 1781
**Section**: Pensacola
**Abstract**: About 9 o'clock a.m. some of the Indians came in and say that they had a brush yesterday afternoon the other side of Suttons Lagoon with the enemy and drove in the picket three times upon which their grenadiers turned out and fired twice at them and retired. 4 of the Indians are wounded, one of which is wounded in the neck with small shot. The Indians report that they killed and wounded a number of the enemy but could not get their to aim on account of the enemy's troops turning out with a number of dragoons.

Mr. Roberts went to the cliffs in a boat in case an English fleet appeared off to pilot them as had every reason to expect reinforcement with a strong convoy under Admiral Rowley.

**Author**: Deans, Robert
**Date**: March 29th log book entry
**Location**: University of West Florida, John C. Pace Library, Special Collections Group 75-15
**Date**: 1781
**Section**: Pensacola
**Abstract**: AM. William Morgan returned from the Mentor. His musquet went off by accident, blowed his left thumb off and wounded in the arm. Carpenters & blacksmiths employed at the works.

**Author**: Robert Farmer, March 30$^{th}$
**Location**: Journal Siege Pensacola, Library of Congress microfilm
**Date**: 1781
**Section**: Pensacola
**Abstract**: About 9 o'clock an advanced paquet under the command of Captain Kennedy of the Maryland Loyalists was obligated to retreat as the enemy was marching down upon them and began to fire their field pieces. 10 o'clock Captain Kennedy's party marched down to Niel Meadows about a mile and a quarter from our works. About 2 o'clock the Indians went there also and attacked the main body of the enemy and kept up a very heavy fire until 5 o'clock being supported by Captain Johnstone with two field pieces, 1 howitzer [and] also by 50 negroes. Lieutenant Meggs went with 25 men of the 60$^{th}$ to cover the field pieces. On account of the heavy fire they received from Captain Johnstone, the Indians and Negro's, they retired under cover of their shipping and galleys. ½ after 5 o'clock captain Johnstone and lieutenant Meggs returned. The Indians came in and brought with them 4 of the enemy's drums, one head and a number of scalps. The inhabitants of the town say that they saw a shell from the howitzer fall in the midst of 15 boats full of men coming ashore, that made them return again to their ships. We have one Indian killed and 2 slightly wounded and one Negro wounded in the foot.

**Author**: Deans, Robert
**Date**: March 30$^{th}$ log book entry
**Location**: University of West Florida, John C. Pace Library, Special Collections Group 75-15
**Date**: 1781
**Section**: Pensacola
**Abstract**: PM. At 10, sent the pilot and a boat down to the Cliffs; carpenters & blacksmiths as before.

**Author**: Robert Farmer, March 31st
**Location**: Journal Siege Pensacola, Library of Congress microfilm
**Date**: 1781
**Section**: Pensacola
**Abstract**: The enemy encamped in Neil's Meadow.

**Author**: Deans, Robert
**Date**: March 31th log book entry
**Location**: University of West Florida, John C. Pace Library, Special Collections Group 75-15
**Date**: 1781
**Section**: Pensacola
**Abstract**: PM. Several parties of the enemy appeared near Neill's house. The out pickets retreated nearer the fort. A party of Indians was sent out to support the pickets with field pieces; stop the enemy's advancing and drove them back to their boats. At 8 AM, their men of war & ships advanced nearer the shore to cover their men throwing up entrenchments at Neil's house. Their encampment extends to the heights above the house; carpenters, armorers, & blacksmiths as before.

**Author**: Robert Farmer, April 1st
**Location**: Journal Siege Pensacola, Library of Congress microfilm
**Date**: 1781
**Section**: Pensacola
**Abstract**: The enemy was seen reconnoitering all around us. Mr. Roberts returned from the cliffs having seen nothing.

**Author**: Deans, Robert
**Date**: April 1st log book entry
**Location**: University of West Florida, John C. Pace Library, Special Collections
Group 75-15
**Date**: 1781
**Section**: Pensacola
**Abstract**: PM. The pilot returned from the Cliffs; left the boat and hands there. Enemy employed landing their troops and artillery. Some soldiers deserted from the Waldecks and Americans.

**Author**: Robert Farmer, April 2nd
**Location**: Journal Siege Pensacola, Library of Congress microfilm
**Date**: 1781
**Section**: Pensacola
**Abstract**: Found one our officer's dead who was killed by the enemy on the 30th of March last that we imagined had deserted. The enemy this evening embarked all their troops.

**Author**: Deans, Robert
**Date**: April 2nd log book entry
**Location**: University of West Florida, John C. Pace Library, Special Collections
Group 75-15
**Date**: 1781
**Section**: Pensacola
**Abstract**: A polacre and a brig anchored without the bar. Employed preparing the guns for an attack, which was laid aside.

**Author**: Robert Farmer, April 3rd
**Location**: Journal Siege Pensacola, Library of Congress microfilm
**Date**: 1781
**Section**: Pensacola
**Abstract**: About 2 o'clock p m the enemy disembarked their grenadiers and dragoons. The Galvez brig went up the Bay.

**Author**: Deans, Robert
**Date**: April 3rd log book entry
**Location**: University of West Florida, John C. Pace Library, Special Collections Group 75-15
**Date**: 1781
**Section**: Pensacola
**Abstract**: PM. ... A strong reconnoitering party of the enemy on the heights to the southward of Fort George [which] In the night they moved their encampment from Neil's house. Above the town the enemy took a schooner. AM, two of the frigates went down to Rose Island. At Noon, the large ship at Rose Island came to an anchor above the fleet near the town. Several troops landing at Sutton's Lagoon at the head of which the enemy has encamped. At Noon, the Galvez brig and several boats went up the river above the town.

**Author**: Robert Farmer, April 4th
**Location**: Journal Siege Pensacola, Library of Congress microfilm
**Date**: 1781
**Section**: Pensacola
**Abstract**: Last night the enemy took possession of the Port Royal that had on board about 100 Spanish prisoners.

**Author**: Deans, Robert
**Date**: April 1st log book entry
**Location**: University of West Florida, John C. Pace Library, Special Collections
Group 75-15
**Date**: 1781
**Section**: Pensacola
**Abstract**: PM, read the Articles of War to the officers & seamen. At 10, was alarmed with firing of musketry. Found the enemy were taking possession of the Port Royal with all the prisoners, and towed her off to the fleet with two transports and one merchant vessel. A flag of truce went off to the ships. Seamen employed making wadds; the carpenters and armourers employed.

**Author**: Saavedra, Francisco
**Title**: Saavedra to Joseph Galvez, 4th of April
**Location**: AGI Indiferente General 146-2-3
**Date**: 1781
**Section**: Pensacola
**Abstract**: On the 9th of March arrived the convoy near the beach of the Rose Island that is situated in the mouth of the Port of Pensacola. This same night it disembarked 1,300 men who advancing companies of grenadiers. On the 10th they unloaded supplies and mounted two cannons of 24 that fired on the two frigates forcing them to retreat into the interior of the bay. On the 11th the General tried to force the Bay that was defended by 5 cannon of 32 and some smaller pieces from Red Canyons. The ship San Ramon attempted to enter the Bay but grounded in the channel and was forced to retreat. On the 18th the General embarked on a small brig, flying his flag and passed by the Fort that shot 27 thick caliber pieces at him but without hitting anything. On the 19th the frigates and the convoy entered the port and while 145 shots were fired at them, none of them caused any damage. On the 20th, after a difficult march, arrived from Mobile 905 men. On the 24th enter the Port another convoy with 16 ships from New Orleans that carried 1348 men. On the 25th the Army, composed of 3553 men, reunited on the main land.

**Author**: Robert Farmer, April 5th
**Location**: Journal Siege Pensacola, Library of Congress microfilm
**Date**: 1781
**Section**: Pensacola
**Abstract**: A schooner passed the fort at the cliffs and joined the enemy fleet. By some work that came from up the bay, we are informed that the Galvez brig has taken the polacre that was taken by the Hunter sometime ago.

Mr. Stephenson, who came from the Spanish camp, told us that [the Spanish camp] is along Sutton Lagoon, having the Lagoon up the rear and an entrenchment in front. The Indians at night attacked both wings of the enemy's camp and kept them under arms the whole night.

**Author**: Deans, Robert
**Date**: April 5th log book entry
**Location**: University of West Florida, John C. Pace Library, Special Collections Group 75-15
**Date**: 1781
**Section**: Pensacola
**Abstract**: The enemy quiet in their encampment and on board their ships. The Galvez brig took a polacre up the bay with some boats belong to the inhabitants. AM, a schooner passed along the south side of Rose Island toward the bar. A flag of truce went out to the enemy's camp. Seamen employed making wadds, &c.; carpenters and armours as before.

**Author**: Deans, Robert
Date: April 6<sup>th</sup> log book entry
Location: University of West Florida, John C. Pace Library, Special Collections
Group 75-15
Date: 1781
Section: Pensacola
Abstract: PM. The enemy encamped upon the side of the Lagoon. The flag of truce returned. The Indians attacked the enemy's out posts in the night; several vollies were heard from both sides and the Indians retreated. Several of the enemy's craft were cruising about the harbor. People employed as before. One Waldeck soldier deserted to the enemy.

**Author**: Deans, Robert
Date: April 7<sup>th</sup> log book entry
Location: University of West Florida, John C. Pace Library, Special Collections
Group 75-15
Date: 1781
Section: Pensacola
Abstract: PM. At 4, one of the enemy's boats went up the bay. Heard some guns fired to the eastward & northeastward, supposed the first to have been at sea & the 2d to have been the Galvez brig up the bay. Cut away the buoys from the Port Royal's anchors. Several vollies of small arms fired in the night by the Indians on the Spanish encampment.

**Author**: Robert Farmer, April 8<sup>th</sup>
Location: Journal Siege Pensacola, Library of Congress microfilm
Date: 1781
Section: Pensacola
Abstract: Mr. Stephenson went as a flag to the Dons.

**Author**: Deans, Robert
**Date**: April 8th log book entry
**Location**: University of West Florida, John C. Pace Library, Special Collections
Group 75-15
**Date**: 1781
**Section**: Pensacola
**Abstract**: PM. One of the enemy's galley's went up the Yamasa, supposed to be bound up Middle River. An express set out for the Cliffs. The enemy's fleet making various signals. People employed as before. AM, hauled the launch up.

**Author**: Robert Farmer, April 9th
**Location**: Journal Siege Pensacola, Library of Congress microfilm
**Date**: 1781
**Section**: Pensacola
**Abstract**: As the artillery was firing, one of the 24 pounders burst but did not hurt anyone. About 5 o'clock pm a brig passed the fort at the cliffs... John and Alex McGilliverey came in with 70 Creek along with them.

**Author**: Deans, Robert
**Date**: April 9th log book entry
**Location**: University of West Florida, John C. Pace Library, Special Collections
Group 75-15
**Date**: 1781
**Section**: Pensacola
**Abstract**: The seamen employed in removing into the fort. Armors & carpenters employed as before. The morning gun burst in firing, supposed to have been occasioned by over loading her. Went down a flag of truce to General Galvez. Came in about 60 Creek Indians. The enemy was sounding in their boats towards the west end of the town. Sent an express to Georgia by land.

**Author**: Robert Farmer, April 10th
**Location**: Journal Siege Pensacola, Library of Congress microfilm
**Date**: 1781
**Section**: Pensacola
**Abstract**: One of the Waldecks who was taken at Baton Rouge and had enlisted in the Regiment of Louisiana deserted and came and ... his regiment. He says that the enemy are here bad off for provincials 8 men only get 1 pound of meat per day.

**Author**: Deans, Robert
**Date**: April 10th log book entry
**Location**: University of West Florida, John C. Pace Library, Special Collections Group 75-15
**Date**: 1781
**Section**: Pensacola
**Abstract**: The flag of truce returned from General Galvez. About 5 PM, a brig came over the bar and joined the fleet. Observed the Royal Navy Redoubt to fire many guns at her. AM, a sloop joined the fleet from the westward. Seamen employed with the artillery; armourers and carpenters as before. A Waldeck deserter came in from the Spanish camp.

**Author**: Deans, Robert
**Date**: April 11th log book entry
**Location**: University of West Florida, John C. Pace Library, Special Collections
Group 75-15
**Date**: 1781
**Section**: Pensacola
**Abstract**: PM, the Galvez brig lying in the mouth of Scamby apparently aground on Indian Point. [I] spied several boats from the enemy cruising in the bay. A flag of truce came up to town for the prisoners' baggage, which the Indians fired upon. In the morning the Galvez brig still lying a ground and the enemy [is] in their encampment on the edge of Sutton's Lagooon. Seamen employed making wads; armourers & carpenters as before.

**Author**: Robert Farmer, April 12th
**Location**: Journal Siege Pensacola, Library of Congress microfilm
**Date**: 1781
**Section**: Pensacola
**Abstract**: The enemy was seen checking the opposite hills. A few Indians went out and had a skirmish with them. As Lieutenant Pinkorn was going out, he received a shot in the head. They fired several shots at the enemy from the fort and the advanced redoubt. A grape shot from the fort killed one of the Waldeck sentries and wounded a sergeant. The Indians brought in a couple of Spanish muskets. One of the frigates and a snow went down and landed abreast Rose island and at 8 o'clock p.m. Lieutenant Pinkorn died of his wound.

**Author**: Deans, Robert
**Date**: April 12$^{th}$ log book entry
**Location**: University of West Florida, John C. Pace Library, Special Collections
Group 75-15
**Date**: 1781
**Section**: Pensacola
**Abstract**: PM, one of the enemy's galleys came down Yamasa with a schooner & sloop, supposed to be the Poder de Dios & Dilligence packet, taken from Middle River. AM, the Galvez brig as before, with several boats round her: the galley lying behind Englishman's Head. Two of the enemy's frigates went down the harbor & came to an anchor abreast the signal house on Rose Island. An express came in from the Cliffs. Enemy encamped as before. Seaman belonging to the Port Royal was killed loading a gun at the Navy Redoubt

**Author**: Robert Farmer, April 13$^{th}$
**Location**: Journal Siege Pensacola, Library of Congress microfilm
**Date**: 1781
**Section**: Pensacola
**Abstract**: The enemy encamped upon the opposite hills and [was] seen throwing a breastwork before their camp. The frigate came up again. A Polacre passed the fort at the cliffs and joined the enemy fleet.

**Author**: Deans, Robert
**Date**: April 13th log book entry
**Location**: University of West Florida, John C. Pace Library, Special Collections Group 75-15
**Date**: 1781
**Section**: Pensacola
**Abstract**: PM, the enemy made their appearance on a height to the WNW, upon which several guns were fired from Fort George & the redoubts among them which apparently dispersed them. Soon after they made their appearance again, the Royal Foresters & a party of Indians were ordered out to attack them. A brisk firing soon ensued and the enemy retreated under cover of their field pieces. The skirmishing continued till dark. Our loss consisted in one officer of the Royal Foresters wounded, who died in a few hours. One Waldeck killed by accident from one of our guns. AM, observed the enemy to have thrown up some works on the side of a rising ground to the north of their encampment.

**Author**: Deans, Robert
**Date**: April 14th log book entry
**Location**: University of West Florida, John C. Pace Library, Special Collections Group 75-15
**Date**: 1781
**Section**: Pensacola
**Abstract**: Two of the enemy's frigates got under way from abreast of the signal house on Rose Island and came up the left wing of the fleet. At 2, a polacre came over the bar and joined the fleet. The Royal Navy Redoubt fired several guns. At 6, several vollies of small arms were heard from the enemy upon a party of Indians, which they returned & retreated. AM, the Galvez brig still aground and the seamen making wadds; carpenters & armourers as before. Received information that the three men left in charge of the Mentor had set fire to her & gone in the country on the approach of the Spaniards who pursued them.

**Author**: Robert Farmer, April 15th
**Location**: Journal Siege Pensacola, Library of Congress microfilm
**Date**: 1781
**Section**: Pensacola
**Abstract**: A very heavy rain fell last night that washed in a great quantity of sand from the barrier and ditch of the fort and the redoubt. The enemy threw up a work in a place about ½ miles from hence. Supposed as a cover for naval convoys of artillery and provisions. Lieutenant Jones and A. Frazer arrive with about 90 Choctaw.

**Author**: Deans, Robert
**Date**: April 15th log book entry
**Location**: University of West Florida, John C. Pace Library, Special Collections Group 75-15
**Date**: 1781
**Section**: Pensacola
**Abstract**: The first part, blowing fresh with hard rain. At 10 PM, the rain increased as to lay the ground works of the fort and redoubts under water. The rain continued till day light, during which time the works received considerable damage. From 1/2 past 4, drizzling rain until 9, the latter part, fair and black to the SE. 100 Chacta Indians came in while the enemy encampt as before.

**Author**: Deans, Robert
**Date**: April 16th log book entry
**Location**: University of West Florida, John C. Pace Library, Special Collections Group 75-15
**Date**: 1781
**Section**: Pensacola
**Abstract**: PM. Deserted one Waldecker. 4 seamen came in from the Royal Navy Redoubt, one of which belonged the Mentor, the other three to the Port Royal. Several boats passed from Scambie to town. Seamen did what they did before while the carpenters & armours employed at the works.

**Author**: Robert Farmer, April 17th
**Location**: Journal Siege Pensacola, Library of Congress microfilm
**Date**: 1781
**Section**: Pensacola
**Abstract**:  Last night about eight o'clock a sergeant of the regiment of Flanders deserted from the enemy who confirms all that the words of the Waldeck: that the enemy is very bad off for provisions and that Galvez got slightly wounded on Thursday last.

11 o'clock a. m. an express arrived from Saint Augustine with duplicate of the letters that were received some time ago informing us that Lord Cornwallis had an engagement with the Rebels at Hillsbourgh North Carolina and had killed 3000 of the Rebels. A party of Creeks, who came with the express, took a boat belonging to the enemy at Deer Point. They killed 3 of the enemy and took one prisoner.

This afternoon five Negroes took a Spaniard at Gulf Point.

**Author**: Deans, Robert
**Date**: April 17th log book entry
**Location**: University of West Florida, John C. Pace Library, Special Collections
Group 75-15
**Date**: 1781
**Section**: Pensacola
**Abstract**: A deserter came in from General Galvez. AM. Several boats came down from Middle River, brought a confirmation of the Mentor's being burnt. The Galvez brig and several other small craft [are] lying in Yamasa Bay [with] seamen, carpenters, & armourers [continuing] as before.

**Author**: Robert Farmer, April 18th
**Location**: Journal Siege Pensacola, Library of Congress microfilm
**Date**: 1781
**Section**: Pensacola
**Abstract**: Yesterday evening the inhabitants took a Spaniard up Mr. Stephenson's wharf. About 9 o'clock a polacre came from the eastward and a brig from the westward passed the brig at the cliffs and joined the enemy fleet and about 5 o'clock the enemy began to fire... Early this morning began to erect a mortar battery inside the abbatus at the advanced redoubt.

**Author**: Deans, Robert
**Date**: April 18th log book entry
**Location**: University of West Florida, John C. Pace Library, Special Collections Group 75-15
**Date**: 1781
**Section**: Pensacola
**Abstract**: PM. Hauled the pinnace up. Quartered the men to the guns in Fort George. AM. Two Spanish prisoners brought in. The enemy's fleet and army continued as before. Carpenters, armourers & seamen continued as before.

**Author**: Robert Farmer, April 19th
**Location**: Journal Siege Pensacola, Library of Congress microfilm
**Date**: 1781
**Section**: Pensacola
**Abstract**: Mesidaver and a party of Indians went and laid close to the enemy camp and this morning they had a skirmish with the ... The Indians brought in with them a scalp [and] one of the Indians got wounded in the thigh. This morning about 3 o'clock the Creeks brought the prisoners that they took in the boat at Deer Point. About 11 o'clock there appeared in the off... 7 vessels. The largest ship of which got aground but got off again. They fired several guns, hoisted signals and ... off and on consist... of six ships and a brig.

**Author**: Deans, Robert
**Date**: April 19th log book entry
**Location**: University of West Florida, John C. Pace Library, Special Collections Group 75-15
**Date**: 1781
**Section**: Pensacola
**Abstract**: PM, one of the enemy's sloops stretched in close with the town and about 5 [took place] a general salute of cannon from their fleet and redoubts. A polacre arrived. AM, various signals from their shipping. Several sail hove in sight. A prisoner brought in from Rose Island by the Creek Indians.

**Author**: Robert Farmer, April 20th
**Location**: Journal Siege Pensacola, Library of Congress microfilm
**Date**: 1781
**Section**: Pensacola
**Abstract**: About 4.30 the brig ... on the bar. At 5 o'clock, three row galleys went down and anchored at Rose island, the brig stood to the eastward.

**Author**: Deans, Robert
**Date**: April 20th log book entry
**Location**: University of West Florida, John C. Pace Library, Special Collections Group 75-15
**Date**: 1781
**Section**: Pensacola
**Abstract**: PM. 5 sail in sight, supposed to be enemy's. At 3, one of them got aground on the easterly part of the bar... made a number of signals. The shipping inside got up yards & topmasts, unmoored their ships, and seemed to be in confusion. A flag of truce came in from Galvez. Heard several guns fired in the night. Died, James Manson, a. b. AM, several guns fired at daybreak; seamen [were] at their quarters in Fort George [with] carpenters and armourers. The enemy's ship got off the bar in the night after heaving many things overboard.

**Author**: Robert Farmer, April 21st
**Location**: Journal Siege Pensacola, Library of Congress microfilm
**Date**: 1781
**Section**: Pensacola
**Abstract**: Early this morning three row galleries arrived at the bar and stood eastward by Rose island. About eleven o'clock one of the galleries came over the bar. 1 o'clock four vessels seen... About 4 o'clock Mr. Colbert arrived and informs us that the vessels consist of 7 line of battle ships, 9 frigates, and a few brigs and sloops. ...The ship that ... arrived yesterday afternoon was obligated to throw her grain overboard. Upon examining two of the carriages and casks that came ashore by the cliffs, they proved to be either French or Spanish. 4 o'clock a sloop came over the bar from the fleet outside and joined the enemy fleet.

**Author**: Deans, Robert
**Date**: April 21th log book entry
**Location**: University of West Florida, John C. Pace Library, Special Collections Group 75-15
**Date**: 1781
**Section**: Pensacola
**Abstract**: PM, a brig lying outside Rose Island. The galleys got under way & went down to the Island. A boat from Sutton's Lagoon went down to the Island. A boat from Sutton's Lagoon went out to the brig that soon after got under way and stood to the eastward. At ½ past 5 AM, observed the galleys outside of Rose Island. At ½ past 10, they came round Rose Island Point and stood up along the Island inside. Observed the cliffs to fire two guns at them when coming in. An express arrived from the Cliffs with an account that a fleet of Spanish & French men of war appeared off the bar, in all 22 sail. A deserter came in from came in from the Spanish camp.

**Author**: Robert Farmer, April 22nd
**Location**: Journal Siege Pensacola, Library of Congress microfilm
**Date**: 1781
**Section**: Pensacola
**Abstract**: About 6 o'clock a.m. a deserter came from the enemy who say that they are very bad off for provisions. A man only gets three ounces of beans per day. About 12 o'clock we observed about 5 or 600 of the enemy on a hill within the distance of 300 yards from the Advanced Redoubt and fired five guns at them. They then retreated. There was immediately some ... Indians pursued them; also a detachment from the 60th, provincials and the command of the 134 regiment who when they got upon the ground found that the enemy had retired to their camp. As Mr. Gordon was aide de camp to General Campbell, he immediately got the plan of the enemy works and the manner that they mean to attack us. The advance redoubt is their chief objective. The [Spanish] engineer, during this engagement was killed by one of the cannon shot as the tree that he stood by was struck and near it a great quantity of blood. About 4 o'clock some small vessels passed the Cliffs and joined the Spanish fleet. The enemy was seen disembarking several hundred men at Sutton Lagoon. The Indians killed four Waldecks as they were cutting branches of trees.

**Author**: Deans, Robert
**Date**: April 22nd log book entry
**Location**: University of West Florida, John C. Pace Library, Special Collections Group 75-15
**Date**: 1781
**Section**: Pensacola
**Abstract**: PM, the enemy's boats passing & repassing betwixt the fleet, the outside of the harbor; the Cliffs annoying them as they passed. At 3 AM, heard several guns fired from the sea. A cutter came in over the bar under French colors & joined the fleet in the harbor. The enemy's shipping outside consisting of 19 sail.

**Author**: Eelking (1977)

**Title**: "The German allies, 1776-1783, in the North American wars for liberation"

**Date**: 22nd of April 1781

**Section**: Pensacola

**Abstract**: On the 22nd of April, the rest of the Spanish were disembarked and went to a camp near Pensacola.

**Author**: Robert Farmer, April 23rd
**Location**: Journal Siege Pensacola, Library of Congress microfilm
**Date**: 1781
**Section**: Pensacola
**Abstract**: 12 o'clock midnight 40 rank and file of the 60th under the command of Captain Byrd and 100 Indians went in front of the advanced redoubts advanced 300 yards.

**Author**: Deans, Robert
**Date**: April 23rd log book entry
**Location**: University of West Florida, John C. Pace Library, Special Collections Group 75-15
**Date**: 1781
**Section**: Pensacola
**Abstract**: PM, a body of the enemy appeared in the valley to the NW of the advanced redoubt. The redoubt fired several shot amongst them which put them to the route. The Indians, with some of the light troops, pursued them and fired several vollies upon them. Took the engineer's plan of the works & supposed the engineer to have been wounded as a good deal of blood was seen where the plan was found. At 3 AM, an express came in from the advanced redoubt of the enemy moving towards our works. Several boats landing troops. A brig came in over the bar and joined the fleet that [was] in sight outside.

**Author**: Robert Farmer, April 24th
**Location**: Journal Siege Pensacola, Library of Congress microfilm
**Date**: 1781
**Section**: Pensacola
**Abstract**: Between 7 and 8 o'clock a body of about 300 enemy soldiers advanced upon the Indians with their fire making the Indians return [to our lines]. Then Captain Byrd with the 60th advanced within 70 yards and gave them a volley that caused them to rapidly retreat. [At] 8 o'clock Captain Kearney with 50 provincials and Captain Johnstone with 2 howitzers and 2 field pieces went to his support. At 8.30 Captain Byrd with his party and the artillery came in. 2 o'clock p. m. a brig came between the Neil and Christe houses and fired two guns at the fort at which the fort and Waldeck and provincial redoubts fired several shots. 3 o'clock Captain Johnstone with one howitzer and a party of the Waldecks went upon the beach and began to fire from the howitzer upon which the brig retired. About 5 o'clock Captain Kearney with his party had a brush with the enemy who was endeavoring to gain the height but they retired. He took one prisoner belonging to the Irish brigade. Davies arrived from Carolina who brings word that Lord Cornwallis had totally defeated the rebels at Guildford, killed 2000 of them and taken a number of cannon, stores and prisoners upon the news of which, at 8 o'clock we fired a feu de joy.

**Author**: Deans, Robert
**Date**: April 24th log book entry
**Location**: University of West Florida, John C. Pace Library, Special Collections
Group 75-15
**Date**: 1781
**Section**: Pensacola
**Abstract**: PM, observed the enemy carrying fachines to the back of a hill to the westward. A flag of truce came in with some of the inhabitants who told of two regiments, one French and one Dutch, landed from the fleet. Their fleet consisted of 9 sail of line of battle & 6 frigates. At 6, the picket guard attacked a party of the enemy in the valley, drove them with the loss of one private of the 60th Regiment wounded.

**Author**: Eelking (1977)
**Title**: "The German allies, 1776-1783, in the North American wars for liberation"
**Date**: 24th of April 1781
**Section**: Pensacola
**Abstract**: On the 24th news of the taking of Charlestown had reached Pensacola, and the troops had a celebration with the firing of salutes. [The text would indicate there were also bonfires.]

**Author**: Robert Farmer, April 25th
**Location**: Journal Siege Pensacola, Library of Congress microfilm
**Date**: 1781
**Section**: Pensacola
**Abstract**: About 7 o'clock a. m. the advanced piquet had a skirmish with the enemy and beat them off. We had one of the provincials dangerously wounded.

**Author**: Deans, Robert

**Date**: April 25<sup>th</sup> log book entry

**Location**: University of West Florida, John C. Pace Library, Special Collections Group 75-15

**Date**: 1781

**Section**: Pensacola

**Abstract**: PM, one of the enemy brigs came up abreast the west end of the town & fired at her. Found the two shot, one by the covered way and one in the Waldeck encampment. They were 24 pounders. At 2, the howiseteers went down to the beach abreast of the brig, covered by a party of the Waldecks. Fired several shot at her and sent her off. A flag of truce came up to town from the enemy. At 5, the enemy attacked our picket by the upper redoubt, were beat back with the loss of one prisoner taken. ½ past 7, fired a fire de joy from the fort & redoubts on account of an express arriving from Georgia & North Carolina. AM at 6, our picket attacked again by the enemy; were beat off with the loss of two men wounded on our side; the carpenters and armourers [continued] as before.


**Author**: Eelking (1977)

**Title**: "The German allies, 1776-1783, in the North American wars for liberation"

**Date**: 25<sup>th</sup> of April 1781

**Section**: Pensacola

**Abstract**: On the 25<sup>th</sup> Campbell tried to attack the Spanish, but several deserters carried the plans to the enemy, one being a Catholic corporal of the Waldeckers. The Spanish then removed their camp to another place.

Campbell started an attack on another Spanish position. He had English, Waldeckers, and some Indians with him in this second attack. The Spanish were driven from their fortifications; some prisoners were taken, of whom several were officers. The fortifications taken from the Spaniards were hastily demolished.

**Author**: Robert Farmer, April 26th
**Location**: Journal Siege Pensacola, Library of Congress microfilm
**Date**: 1781
**Section**: Pensacola
**Abstract**: We are informed by Mr. Stephenson, who went as a flag of truce yesterday from the governor to General Galvez, the fleet on the outside consists of 11 Spanish and 4 French line of battle ships and a few frigates. Early this morning two field pieces and 50 men of the 16th and 60th regiments went out as an advanced picket under the command of lieutenants Carrique and Ward. About 4 o'clock p.m. the enemy advanced with their field pieces but was driven back by the picket. The advanced redoubt fired several shot at them and the center fired one. [We] finished the counter battery on the left wing and began another one on the right wing of the advanced battery.

**Author**: Deans, Robert
**Date**: April 26th log book entry
**Location**: University of West Florida, John C. Pace Library, Special Collections Group 75-15
**Date**: 1781
**Section**: Pensacola
**Abstract**: PM, a schooner flag of truce came up to town and returned immediately. A schooner cam in from the fleet outside Rose Island and joined the fleet in the harbor. A hermophridte brig went out of the harbor and stood o the eastward. At 5, two of their men of war got under way and stretched to the offing. The flag of truce sent by Governor Chester returned from General Galvez. A sloop passed from Yamasa, supposed to be the Diligence packet taken by the Spaniards up Middle River. AM, the enemy's fleet as before. Seamen employed in sundries. An express arrived from the Cliffs brings account of ships of the line, French and Spaniards, off the bar. By some things driven on shore from the frigate that was aground to the eastward of the bar, it appears she is called the Andromahce, French frigate of 32 guns.

**Author**: Robert Farmer, April 27th
**Location**: Journal Siege Pensacola, Library of Congress microfilm
**Date**: 1781
**Section**: Pensacola
**Abstract**: Captain Kearney went with 52 Provincials, relieved Le Carrique at 2 o'clock. The enemy was seen advancing, at 11 o'clock, with their field pieces. Some of the Indians got away. Upon their back, we began to fire our field pieces until 2 o'clock including several howitzers and shot from the advanced redoubt. The Indians came about 2 o'clock (Colbert had arrived with 54 Chickasaws) and brought a great number of scalps, firelocks and bayonets. One of the interpreters says that 5 shells from the howitzer burst in the center of a column and that the enemy had a party of men to carry off the dead and wounded.

**Author**: Deans, Robert
**Date**: April 27th log book entry
**Location**: University of West Florida, John C. Pace Library, Special Collections Group 75-15
**Date**: 1781
**Section**: Pensacola
**Abstract**: PM, several of the fleet outside the bar under sail. Some skirmishing on the rising ground in front of the advanced redoubt. At 7 AM, the enemy's advance attacked our picket in the advance of the outer redoubt. Several guns were fired at them. Two of the Marylanders deserted. Enlarged the works at the outer redoubt & making a morter bed.

**Author**: Eelking (1977)

**Title**: "The German allies, 1776–1783, in the North American wars for liberation"

**Date**: 27$^{th}$ of April to May 7$^{th}$ 1781

**Section**: Pensacola

**Abstract**: On the morning of the 27$^{th}$ the beleaguered citizens found opposite their main redoubt a battery being placed by the enemy. They began firing at those working, with balls and bombs, but the enemy had dug themselves in so deeply that the firing did less harm than was hoped to inflict. And the firing was returned with vigor. The firing back and forth went on until April 30$^{th}$. Only about from the first to the second of May was the firing from the side of the Waldeckers stopped long enough to repair damages. There were so few men that those who manned the guns had to be taken to aid in the repairs. From the second to the seventh, the firing went on without ceasing.

The little fort could have held out much longer had it not been for the work of spies. One of the Provincial officers, whose conduct and character had proved bad, had been paid off and thrown out of the fort. In revenge he went into the service of the Spanish, and since he knew the plans of the fort, he pointed out the weakest spots, and the Spanish directed their fire to those.

**Author**: Robert Farmer, April 28th
**Location**: Journal Siege Pensacola, Library of Congress microfilm
**Date**: 1781
**Section**: Pensacola
**Abstract**: Last night two deserters from the Irish brigade who inform us that the enemy had in the engagement yesterday 100 men killed or wounded. About 11:30 three deserters came from the enemy. One of them belonged to the 16th and one to the Provincials who informed the general that great numbers of them would desert if the general would forgive and agree upon a signal that was to fire three guns at 12 o'clock that was complied with. 5 o'clock two vessels appeared off toward the eastward upon which some of the ships on the outside were given anchor and stood toward them. At sunset Colbert went with a party of Chickasaw with ammunition to the cliffs.

**Author**: Deans, Robert
**Date**: April 28th log book entry
**Location**: University of West Florida, John C. Pace Library, Special Collections Group 75-15
**Date**: 1781
**Section**: Pensacola
**Abstract**: PM, the enemy still skirmishing with the Indians. Fired several shot at them from the outer redoubt that entirely dispersed the enemy. Brought in three scalps & 3 dead bodies were found on the field. At midnight, two deserters came in from the enemy. At 9 AM, the outer redoubt fired several shot at the enemy straggling in the bush. At 10, fired a gun from the fort at the enemy's party which dispersed them; also, three deserters came in from the enemy. Seamen continued as before with carpenters caulking the plate forms in the fort.

**Author**: Robert Farmer, April 29th
**Location**: Journal Siege Pensacola, Library of Congress microfilm
**Date**: 1781
**Section**: Pensacola
**Abstract**: The enemy early this morning was seen throwing up an entrenchment that they had begun last night. It is the length about 2 miles. About 1 o'clock our advanced picket was obliged to retire near the advanced redoubt as the enemy had got some 9 and 12 pounders upon their flanks fired from the last and the two redoubts several shot and shells during the day and night at the enemy's ...

**Author**: Deans, Robert
**Date**: April 29th log book entry
**Location**: University of West Florida, John C. Pace Library, Special Collections Group 75-15
**Date**: 1781
**Section**: Pensacola
**Abstract**: PM, the enemy skirmishing in front of the outer redoubt with the Indians. A French frigate came in over the bar & joined the enemy in the harbor. Two deserters went off to the enemy. At 5, observed the enemy throwing up works in two places in front of the advanced redoubt. Brought the heavy guns to bear upon them. Kept annoying them from the fort and redoubts.

**Author**: Robert Farmer, April 30th
**Location**: Journal Siege Pensacola, Library of Congress microfilm
**Date**: 1781
**Section**: Pensacola
**Abstract**: About 2 o'clock this morning the enemy drove in our advanced guard. 8 o'clock a.m. the Indians brought in a prisoner that they took close to the enemy work. It was with great difficulty they gave him up. A French frigate came over the bar and joined the enemy fleet inside.

**Author**: Deans, Robert
**Date**: April 30th log book entry
**Location**: University of West Florida, John C. Pace Library, Special Collections Group 75-15
**Date**: 1781
**Section**: Pensacola
**Abstract**: PM, five sail of the enemy's vessels stood in from sea to their fleet; two polacres came to anchor and the other three sail stood off to the eastward. After making a private signal, the Spanish frigates in the harbor struck yards & topmasts. The French frigate hoisted a broad pendant from the main topmast head. Kept throwing shells and shot at the enemy's works to annoy them in the night. AM, the Indians brought in a Spanish prisoner. Seamen making wads; carpenters as before. Issued tobacco to the ship's company. Joseph Martin, belonging to the Port Royal, deserted.

**Author**: Robert Farmer, May 1st
**Location**: Journal Siege Pensacola, Library of Congress microfilm
**Date**: 1781
**Section**: Pensacola
**Abstract**: Kept up a fire from the fort and the two redoubts during the day and night at the enemy works. They cut out 7 embrasures and had 3 guns mounted.

**Author**: Deans, Robert
**Date**: May 1st log book entry
**Location**: University of West Florida, John C. Pace Library, Special Collections Group 75-15
**Date**: 1781
**Section**: Pensacola
**Abstract**: PM, one of the polacres at anchor outside of Rose Island came over the bvar and joined the fleet in the harbor. The enemy throwing up works in front of the redoubts to the westward. AM, at broad day, observed their works considerably enlarged. Several ambusurs formed. At 7, observed them dragging up cannon and mounting them on their works. An officer & 10 men from the middle redoubt were sent to reinforce the advanced redoubt. Carpenters as before.

**Author**: Robert Farmer, May 2nd
**Location**: Journal Siege Pensacola, Library of Congress microfilm
**Date**: 1781
**Section**: Pensacola
**Abstract**: About 9 o'clock this morning the enemy hoisted their flag and opened batteries of 6 ... and 2 mortars. They killed and wounded five but did no other material damage. Toward night the enemy weakened considerably. At night we repaired the damage they did and made another ... at the advanced redoubt. Our people picked up a number of the enemy shot [of] 24 pounders and some shells that did not burst.

**Author**: Deans, Robert
**Date**: May 2$^{nd}$ log book entry
**Location**: University of West Florida, John C. Pace Library, Special Collections Group 75-15
**Date**: 1781
**Section**: Pensacola
**Abstract**: PM, at 4, one of the enemy's frigates got aground in attempting to come in over the bar and joined their fleet in the harbor. At 9 the enemy opened their battery on the outer redoubt. 3 of their frigates came up abreast of the west end of the town and made every preparation as if they were going to cannonade the fort or the lines, the enemy constantly throwing shot & shells from their battery. At the advanced redoubt a corporal of the 16$^{th}$ Regiment was killed and three men belonging to the Port Royal were wounded.

**Author**: Robert Farmer, May 3$^{rd}$
**Location**: Journal Siege Pensacola, Library of Congress microfilm
**Date**: 1781
**Section**: Pensacola
**Abstract**: Last night the enemy was heard working in the front of the advanced redoubt. About the distance of ½ mile this morning we fired at them now and then but could not hurt as they were behind a hill. The enemy fired during the day 534 shot and 186 shells. They killed one man of the 16$^{th}$ and wounded one of the seamen belonging to the Port Royal, and one man of the 16$^{th}$ but did very little damage otherwise. At night we repaired the work at the advanced redoubt and worked at the counter battery on the right wing. Our people picked up today about 400 shot some of which we returned ... Five row galley's came and laid opposite the west end of the town.

**Author**: Deans, Robert
Date: May 3rd log book entry
Location: University of West Florida, John C. Pace Library, Special Collections Group 75-15
Date: 1781
Section: Pensacola
Abstract: PM, the enemy keeping a heavy cannonade upon the advanced redoubt from their battery. Picked up a number of their shot and several of their shells. At 11, the enemy advanced in a large body towards our outer works and took possession of a rising ground in front of the advanced redoubt. AM, the enemy throwing up works on ditto. The advanced redoubt and SE battery continually cannonading each other [with] several shells thrown from the enemy's bomb battery into the lines of Fort George [and] seamen making wads. Carpenters are with the engineer, armourers with the ordnance [and] gunner's crew making cartridges. Three seamen deserted who belonged to the merchantmen.

**Author**: Robert Farmer, May 4th
Location: Journal Siege Pensacola, Library of Congress microfilm
Date: 1781
Section: Pensacola
Abstract: About 4 o'clock we began to fire upon the enemy from the advanced redoubt and at their battery and the people at work in front. [At] 12 o'clock 94 Provincials under the command of Major McEvenald, and Waldecks under the command of Lieutenant Colonel De Horn supported them, stormed the works in front of the advanced redoubt and spiked 6 pieces of cannon plus 874 rounds. The enemy had a great many killed, wounded and taken prisoner among which there are: 1 captain, 1 lieutenant of the Irish brigade, 1 lieutenant of the regiment of Majorca and 4 privates. We had one sergeant of the Provincials killed and one man of the Light Horse wounded. The Provincials brought in 1 drum, a number of muskets and 5 swords. Ensign Ursel of the Waldeck was killed by a cannon ball and one private wounded. The enemy fired 171 shot and 37 shells during the day. The Lieutenant of the Irish Brigade died of his wounds and was buried with the honors of war. His name was O. Dunn.

**Author**: Deans, Robert
**Date**: May 4th log book entry
**Location**: University of West Florida, John C. Pace Library, Special Collections Group 75-15
**Date**: 1781
**Section**: Pensacola
**Abstract**: PM, the enemy keeping up a heavy cannonade on the advanced redoubt, throwing shells at Fort George. Two row galleys lying abreast of the west end of the town and three frigates; the enemy throwing up works on the side of the hill in front of the advanced redoubt. One of the Port Royal's men got his leg shot off and a soldier of the 16th Regiment wounded in the arm. AM, the enemy still continuing the approaches in front of the advanced redoubt and a heavy cannonade from their battery. The man belonging to the Port Royal who was wounded has since died.

**Author**: Robert Farmer, May 5th
**Location**: Journal Siege Pensacola, Library of Congress microfilm
**Date**: 1781
**Section**: Pensacola
**Abstract**: Enemy ships on the outside of Rose island left about 6 o'clock. Two deserters from French train of artillery came in who informed us that enemy loss yesterday amounted to 30 killed among which is a major of the Catalan Volunteers and that on Wednesday we dismounted one of their 24 pounders. The deserters have agreed to act with the artillery. The enemy fired during the day 85 shot and 43 shells. We had nobody hurt [and] kept firing from the advanced redoubt during the night. [The] shells and grape shot at the enemy working in their front. The enemy threw a few shells during the night. One of prisoners died of his wounds.

**Author**: Deans, Robert
**Date**: May 5th log book entry
**Location**: University of West Florida, John C. Pace Library, Special Collections
Group 75-15
**Date**: 1781
**Section**: Pensacola
**Abstract**: PM, the Provincials and Waldeckers under the command of Lieutenant Colonel De Horn and Major McDonald went out to the enemy's advanced redoubt where up to 300 men were throwing up works. Ninety of the Provincials entered the works, killed and wounded upward of 30 of the enemy, spiked up four of their cannon, brought off a captain, lieutenant and three other prisoners with the loss of one sergeant of the Provincials killed and one of the Royal Forresters wounded. A lieutenant of the Waldecks was killed and a sergeant wounded in the advanced redoubt. AM, the enemy shipping fired several guns in the night, apparently signal guns of distress. Two deserters came in from the enemy. Lieutenant A. Duly, brought in prisoner at PM, isince dead, while seamen, carpenters and armourers, continued as before. Numbers of enemy's shot and shells brought in by the soldiers and Indians, some of their shells upwards of 13 inch. Mounted a new 24 gun carriage.

**Author**: Robert Farmer, May 6th
**Location**: Journal Siege Pensacola, Library of Congress microfilm
**Date**: 1781
**Section**: Pensacola
**Abstract**: Two ships of the enemy fleet appeared outside [the bar] and came to an anchor. Last night fell a very heavy rain that washed some of the sand from the barme of the fort and the redoubt. About a ½ hour after 9 o'clock the enemy began to fire from two mortars they had in their works in the front of the advanced redoubt. The shot and shell fired from the enemy during the day amounted to 563 shot and 206 shells. We have one Waldeck, the bombardier and one sailor wounded by a shell. As one of the seamen belonging to the Port Royal was picking up the shot fired by the enemy, a 24 inch ball buried itself in his flesh. He lived for about five hours.

The enemy kept up a very heavy fire that hurt our advanced redoubt very much and dismounted three pieces of cannon, 12 and 9 pounders. The works were repaired at night and shot up two embrasures fronting the enemy flank battery.

**Author**: Deans, Robert
**Date**: May 6$^{th}$ log book entry
**Location**: University of West Florida, John C. Pace Library, Special Collections
Group 75-15
**Date**: 1781
**Section**: Pensacola
**Abstract**: PM, the enemy keeping up a heavy cannonade on our works and throwing shells in the night. AM, heavy rain which continued till ½ past 4, during which time it swept great quantity of sand from covered way into the ditch and underminded the fort in several places, sweeping away the bricks from under the foundation. About sunrise observed one of enemy's ships and two schooners ashore by mouth of Sutton's Lagoon, and only two of their ships of the line riding at anchor outside Rose Island. The rest supposed to have been obliged to put to sea by stress of weather. The enemy mounted a mortar on their most advanced work and threw several shells into our advanced redoubt. Two seamen at the advanced redoubt wounded by bursting of a shell on the plate form. Mounted a new 24 gun carriage [with] seamen, carpenters & armourers as before. Pork served the seamen instead of beef.

**Author**: Robert Farmer, May 7th
**Location**: Journal Siege Pensacola, Library of Congress microfilm
**Date**: 1781
**Section**: Pensacola
**Abstract**: About 6 o'clock a shell from enemy flank battery fell in a tent at advanced redoubt where some men of the artillery were making fuses for shells. A number of loaded shells and loose pounder blew a box of powder and burst a shell that killed one man of the Waldeck train and wounded another of the Royal Artillery, and three seamen, were wounded by that shell. A deserter came in from the enemy. He is a German and belonged to the Regiment of Flanders. He informs us that the Dons are very bad off for provisions and Colonel Galvez, and French general do not agree. He told Galvez that if we did not surrender on the $2^{nd}$ instant that he would withdraw his troops and vessels and go upon the expedition he was destined for. Further he says that a shell from us yesterday killed one Captain, one Lieutenant and 2 privates from Catalan volunteers. Yesterday one of Pennsylvania loyalists attempted to desert but was taken and brought back by the Indians. He received 500 lashes and today about 12 noon he was drummed out of the regiment with his hands tied behind him and a large label pinned to his breast ... He was taken close to the Spanish lines and left to his fate but he soon returned.

The whole of the Indians went out about ½ past 12 o'clock to get to the rear of the enemy's encampment. They would not suffer a white man to go with them. They returned in a short time with ten scalps. About 2 o'clock p.m. a shell from the enemies flank battery came in at a window of one of advanced redoubt barrack that killed Lieutenant Carroll and wounded Captain Forster of the $16^{th}$ Regiment. Our fire from advanced redoubt did the enemy a great deal of damage to their works in our front.

6 o'clock p. m., we imagine that their mortar beds in their front battery were hurt as they have not thrown any shells since 2 o'clock. About 8 o'clock Captain Kearney with sixty of Pennsylvania Loyalists took command at advanced redoubt and $16^{th}$ regiment took possession of their camp.

**Author**: Deans, Robert
**Date**: May 7th log book entry
**Location**: University of West Florida, John C. Pace Library, Special Collections
Group 75-15
**Date**: 1781
**Section**: Pensacola
**Abstract**: Keeping up a continual fire upon our advanced redoubt [with] several people wounded by bursting of shells. The artillery cart was blown up by a shell from the enemy but did little damage.

**Author**: John Campbell to George Germain, 7th May
**Location**: PRO CO 597
**Date**: 1781
**Section**: Pensacola
**Abstract**: Besieged by Naval force consisting of 15 ships of the line, 5 heavy frigates, a 24 gun ship, two King's snows, armored brigs, and land forces of 7000 men. Besiegers landed on Rose Island while British ships retired to Pensacola. On 22nd troops from Mobile marched unopposed on coast. The next day seventeen vessels, with troops from New Orleans, joined them in the harbor. On the 28th they were discovered to have formed a regular encampment. The forces encamped on high grounds to the west of Fort George. By light of the 29th they had thrown up trenches close to a mile in length and next morning a large battery was seen. On the 2nd of May a battery of two 13 inch and two inch mortars and six of 24 pounders against the advanced redoubt. We attacked with 120 provincial troops on flank and 80 men of Waldeck regiment. The troops got within 40 yards of the redoubt before discovered. Pushing into the redoubt with bayonets, captured three officers, spiked 8 pounders, two 4 pounders and retired upon the approach of a large body of enemy.

**Author**: Robert Farmer, May 8th
**Location**: Journal Siege Pensacola, Library of Congress microfilm
**Date**: 1781
**Section**: Pensacola
**Abstract**: About 9 o'clock a.m. a shell from the enemy front battery was thrown at door of the magazine and the advanced redoubt. As the men were receiving powder which blew it up and killed forty seamen belonging to the H. M. Ship Mentor and the Port Royal and forty five men of the Pennsylvania Loyalists were killed by the same explosion. There were a number of men wounded besides. Captain Byrd with seventy men of the 60th regiment immediately went up to the advanced redoubt and brought off 2 field pieces and one howitzer and a number of the wounded men but was obliged to retire as a great quantity of shell was laying about filled.

10 o'clock, the enemy took possession of the remains of the advanced redoubt and sent up from it a very heavy fire of small arms and cannon from their flank battery upon the center redoubt that wounded Lieutenant Nard and 18 men of the 60th regiment and 12 seamen; a number of whom died of their wounds as they were mostly wounded in the head.

About 2 o'clock hoisted a flag of truce from Fort George and offered to surrender upon capitulation. Lieutenant Meggs of the 60th Regiment went as a hostage from us and we received Lieutenant Kenny of the Regiment of Hibernia from the enemy.

**Author**: Deans, Robert
**Date**: May 8th log book entry
**Location**: University of West Florida, John C. Pace Library, Special Collections
Group 75-15
**Date**: 1781
**Section**: Pensacola
**Abstract**: PM, a captain of the 16th Regiment was wounded and a lieutenant of the ditto Regiment killed by the bursting of a shell from the enemy. The provincials relieved the 16th Regiment in the advanced redoubt. At 9 AM the magazine was blown up by a shell from the enemy advanced works and the magazine adjoining the barracks carried the conflagration through the whole redoubt. Near a hundred seamen & soldiers were either blown up or buried in the ruins, amongst were a midshipman & 16 seamen killed and 10 wounded belonging to His Majesty's Ship Mentor. Immediately after the explosion, the enemy advanced which obliged the few remaining to retreat after spiking up the cannon & bringing off two field pieces. The enemy appeared in a large body on the right of the advanced redoubt but soon withdrew under cover of the ruins [with] the middle redoubt firing upon them. The enemy kept up a brisk fire from their musquetry and two field pieces upon the middle redoubt that was reinforced from Fort George with an officer & 12 seamen. 13 killed & 8 wounded in the advanced redoubt belonging to His Majesty's Sloop Port Royal.

**Author**: Eelking (1977)

**Title**: "The German allies, 1776-1783, in the North American wars for liberation"

**Date**: May 8th 1781

**Section**: Pensacola

**Abstract**: Through his information they directed their fire at a powder magazine of one of the outer batteries, and on the morning of May 8th, reached their mark, and it exploded, doing terrific damage: fifty-two men were killed by the explosion, many were wounded, and the works were destroyed in a short time. The Spaniards took advantage of the confusion and started an attack, coming in such masses and with such force that the small garrison could not withstand it.

Campbell had the still useful guns loaded with *kartaschen* and sent word to Don Galvez that if the surrender was refused, he would defend the fort to the last man. This brought results. And the adjutant came back with Don Galvez's terms.

These were, under the circumstances, moderate enough and were as follows: the garrison was to march out to music and flying colors; each soldier could keep six rounds of ammunition in his pocket. Five hundred paces from the fort they were to stack their guns, and the officers were to keep their side arms. All troops were supposed to be put on board a ship, at the expense of the Spanish, to be brought to a British port, which was to be designated by the commanding officer. They were not to take arms again against the Spanish until prisoners equal in number and rank could be exchanged from Great Britain. The wounded and the sick would be cared for, and as soon as recovered would be sent after the group to the same place. Privates and officers could keep their belongings. Campbell had asked to be sent to the Port of New York.

**Author**: Robert Farmer, May 9th
**Location**: Journal Siege Pensacola, Library of Congress microfilm
**Date**: 1781
**Section**: Pensacola
**Abstract**: Spent all day setting terms.

**Author**: Deans, Robert
**Date**: May 9th log book entry
**Location**: University of West Florida, John C. Pace Library, Special Collections
Group 75-15
**Date**: 1781
**Section**: Pensacola
**Abstract**: At 2 PM, a flag of truce was hung out at Fort George upon which hostilities ceased and a capitulation proposed. One of the Mentor's seamen wounded yesterday died.

**Author**: Galvez, May 9th
**Title**: Articles of Capitulation of West Florida
**Location**: ANC, Fondos Floridas
**Date**: 1781
**Section**: Pensacola
**Abstract**: Articulos de Capitulacion convenidos y acordados entre el Senor don Bernardo de Galvez y los Excmos. Senores Don Pedro Chester y Don Juan Campbell. 28 articulos.

**Author**: Eelking (1977)

**Title**: "The German allies, 1776-1783, in the North American wars for liberation"

**Date**: May 9th 1781

**Section**: Pensacola

**Abstract**: The articles of surrender were signed May 9, 1781 by Don Bernardo de Galvez, in military camp near Pensacola, and by Governor Peter Chester and by Major General John Campbell at Fort George.

**Author**: Robert Farmer, May 10th
**Location**: Journal Siege Pensacola, Library of Congress microfilm
**Date**: 1781
**Section**: Pensacola
**Abstract**: About 5 o'clock p.m. we surrendered to the arms of Spain. The Spanish grenadiers under the command of Don Bernardo de Galvez took possession of Fort George and the sixty trench chasseurs of the center redoubt.

**Author**: Deans, Robert
**Date**: May 10th log book entry
**Location**: University of West Florida, John C. Pace Library, Special Collections Group 75-15
**Date**: 1781
**Section**: Pensacola
**Abstract**: The Spaniards made their entry in the town of Pensacola.

**Author**: Robert Farmer, May 11th
**Location**: Journal Siege Pensacola, Library of Congress microfilm
**Date**: 1781
**Section**: Pensacola
**Abstract**: The corps under the command of Lieutenant General Campbell camped on the east side of the town.

**Author**: Deans, Robert
**Date**: May 11th log book entry
**Location**: University of West Florida, John C. Pace Library, Special Collections Group 75-15
**Date**: 1781
**Section**: Pensacola
**Abstract**: At 5 PM, the garrison of Fort George marched out of the lines with honors of war to the distance of 400 yards and grounded their arms. The garrison was immediately delivered up to the Spanish General, who struck the English colors and hoisted those of Spain.

**Author**: Campbell, John
**Title**: Campbell to George Germain, 12th May
**Location**: PRO CO 597
**Date**: 1781
**Section**: Pensacola
**Abstract**: On morning of the 8th a shell burst by the door of the magazine of the advanced redoubt killing 48 military, 27 seamen and one black plus wounding 24 men. ...There was a necessity of abandoning these works after first spiking up pieces of artillery in the flank works... [capitulation of the English].

**Author**: Deans, Robert
**Date**: May 12th log book entry
**Location**: University of West Florida, John C. Pace Library, Special Collections Group 75-15
**Date**: 1781
**Section**: Pensacola
**Abstract**: At 7 PM, Lieutenant Hargood arrived from the Cliffs with seamen under his command who had been in garrison. At 8 AM, the seamen shifted their encampment from the lines of Fort George to the east end of the town of Pensacola.

**Author**: Deans, Robert
**Date**: May 13th log book entry
**Location**: University of West Florida, John C. Pace Library, Special Collections Group 75-15
**Date**: 1781
**Section**: Pensacola
**Abstract**: Two of the enemy ships appeared off the bar.

**Author**: Deans, Robert
**Date**: May 14th log book entry
**Location**: University of West Florida, John C. Pace Library, Special Collections Group 75-15
**Date**: 1781
**Section**: Pensacola
**Abstract**: A barrel of Pork, a barrel of flour and 200 weight [of] bread was served to the seamen [with] Doctor attending the hospital.

**Author**: Galvez, Bernardo de
**Title**: Account and estimated value of the Forts, Public Buildings, Storehouses, etc. of Pensacola, May 15th
**Location**: ANC, fondos Floridas
**Date**: 1781
**Section**: Pensacola
**Abstract**: Relacion de los Fortificaciones Provisionales, cuarteles, pavellones, casa de gobierno politico, almacenes y demas edificios que pertenecen al Rey con la estimacíon prudencial de cada uno según el actual estado. 3 pages.

**Author**: Deans, Robert
**Date**: May 15th log book entry
**Location**: University of West Florida, John C. Pace Library, Special Collections
Group 75-15
**Date**: 1781
**Section**: Pensacola
**Abstract**: The seamen in their encampment [with] Doctor as before. Provisions issued to the people at short allowance.

**Author**: Deans, Robert
**Date**: May 16th log book entry
**Location**: University of West Florida, John C. Pace Library, Special Collections
Group 75-15
**Date**: 1781
**Section**: Pensacola
**Abstract**: Seamen in their encampment at the east end of the town [with] Doctor as before.

**Author**: Deans, Robert
**Date**: May 17th log book entry
**Location**: University of West Florida, John C. Pace Library, Special Collections
Group 75-15
**Date**: 1781
**Section**: Pensacola
**Abstract**: Seamen as before [with] Doctor at the hospital.

**Title**: Declaraciones tomadas á varios Ingléses sobre la Rebelión de Natchez, 24th and 26th May
**Location**: ANC, fondos Florida
**Date**: 1781
**Section**: Natchez
**Abstract**: 16 pages

**Title**: Da Parte de haber rendido a las armas de S.M. la Plaza y fuertes de Pansacola, 26th May
**Location**: AGI Santo Domingo 2548, No. 23
**Date**: 1781
**Section**: Pensacola
**Abstract**: incluye el diario, relactiones de los muertos y heridos, la capitulacion, inventario de artilleria, estado de los prisoners y evaluo hecho por los ingenieros del valor de los fuertes que tenian los ingleses en ella y relacionada las demas circunstancias dignas de la noticia de su Magestad

**Title**: Solicita el grado y sueldo de Teniente. 27th May
**Location**: AGI Santo Domingo 2548, No. 38
**Date**: 1781
**Section**: Pensacola
**Abstract**: Para Mr. Cannon official yngles del Reximiento de Maryland que durante el sitio de esta plaza se paso a nuestro campo expone los motivos que dichos official tubo para ello y la utilidad que sera para el real servicio su admission en nuestros tropes por el conocimiento que del local de estos paises tiene y del modo de hacer la Guerra a los indios.

**Author**: Captain-General of Cuba, May 28th
**Title**: Letter of the Captain-General of Cuba to the Secretary of the Indies
**Location**: ANC, fondos Florida, legajo 1, No. 22
**Date**: 1781
**Section**: Pensacola
**Abstract**: Providing an account of the capture of Pensacola

**Author**: Robert Farmer, June 1st
**Location**: Journal Siege Pensacola, Library of Congress microfilm
**Date**: 1781
**Section**: Pensacola
**Abstract**: Embarked on board the Spanish troop ports.

**Author**: Robert Farmer, June 4th
**Location**: Journal Siege Pensacola, Library of Congress microfilm
**Date**: 1781
**Section**: Pensacola
**Abstract**: sailed from Pensacola.

**Author**: Eelking (1977)
**Title**: "The German allies, 1776-1783, in the North American wars for liberation"
**Date**: June 4th 1781
**Section**: Pensacola
**Abstract**: The captives were placed on ship to be sent to Domingo and Havana.

**Title**: Felicita a su Excelencia, 25 Jun.
**Location**: AGI Santo Domingo 2609, no. 47
**Date**: 1781
**Section**: Pensacola
**Abstract**: La rendicion de Panzacola verificada el 9 de Mayo de este ano

**Author**: Robert Farmer, June 20$^{th}$ to 12$^{th}$ of July
**Location**: Journal Siege Pensacola, Library of Congress microfilm
**Date**: 1781
**Section**: Pensacola
**Abstract**: Arrived at Havana where remained until the 30$^{th}$ to take provision and water when we sailed for New York where we arrived upon the 12$^{th}$ of July. The different corps ordered to be quartered in and about New Town Long Island.

**Author**: Chester, Peter
**Title**: Chester to George Germain, 2$^{nd}$ July
**Location**: PRO CO 622
**Date**: 1781
**Section**: New York
**Abstract**: Surrender of the Province to West Florida to the army of Spain after Spanish army appeared on the 9$^{th}$ of March. In a few days they entered the harbor of Pensacola and obligated to capitulate on the 8$^{th}$ of May because the principal advanced work was blown up by Spanish shell. General Campbell and Captain Dean were sent to Havana. Mayor of Brigade Campbell was sent to New Orleans. The remainder of the prisoners went to New York.

**Author**: Huntington, Samuel
**Title**: Samuel Huntington to George Washington, 2$^{nd}$ July
**Location**: Library of Congress, DC
**Date**: 1781
**Section**: Pensacola
**Abstract**: ...The prisoners lately taken at Pensacola were to be sent to New York.

**Author**: O'Neill, Arturo
**Title**: Military Stores at Pensacola, 4th July
**Location**: ANC, fondos Floridas
**Date**: 1781
**Section**: Pensacola
**Abstract**: Relacion de la Artilleria, Montajes, Carruajes, Pertrechos, Municiones y demás Generas que se hallan en la fortalezas y reales almacenes de Panzacola hoy día de la fecha con expression de bueno, mediano e inutil, y lo que se necesita y falta, segun la dotacion hecha por asi d. Manual Izquierdo subteniente del Real Cuerpo de Artilleria y Comandante de ella en este destino por orden del Teniente Coronel de Infanteria y Gobernador del citado destino, 13 pages

**Author**: Galvez, Bernard
**Title**: Bernard Galvez to Joseph Galvez, 19th of July
**Location**: AGI Santo Domingo 87-3-10
**Date**: 1781
**Section**: New Orleans
**Abstract**: The inhabitants of Natchez authorized with patents sent by General Campbell attacked Fort Panmure that surrendered to them on noon. This occurrence, which happened when I was out of the colony, could have had more fatal consequences. The dislodging of the Militia, at the orders of Captain Steven Lamorandiere, resulted in the placement in my power of the chief of those who attacked the fort.

**Author**: Jones, Joseph
**Title**: Joseph Jones to Edmund Pendleton, 24th of July
**Location**: William L. Clements Library, Ann Arbor, Michigan
**Date**: 1781
**Section**: Pensacola
**Abstract**: You must have heard of the Extraordinary Capitulation agreed to by the Spanish Commander on the Reduction of Pensacola, whereby it was left open to the Enemy to transport their Troops to New York, where part of them have already arrived, and will be no doubt be in Arms for the defense of that Post.

**Author**: Partridge, George
**Title**: George Partridge to John Hancock, 2nd of October
**Location**: Smithsonian Institution (Walter Fuller Don Collection), DC
**Date**: 1781
**Section**: Pensacola
**Abstract**: A gentleman has lately arrived here from the Havana who conversed with General Galvez before he came away and says that the General has been informed that the Capitulation at Pensacola was disapproved of by the U. States, which gave him much uneasiness; that the General informed him that it was fully understood at the time of Capitulation, that the troops of that Garrison should not Bear Arms against the U. States; and that he should consider their taking up arms here, as a Breach of that Capitulation, for the fulfillment of which he had a sufficient number of Hostages.

**Author**: Galvez, Bernard
**Title**: Bernard Galvez to Joseph Galvez, 31st of December
**Location**: AGI Indiferente General 146-2-3
**Date**: 1781
**Section:** New Orleans
**Abstract**: ...When the defeat of Cornwallis presented a favorable occasion to invade Florida, if the Americans intended to attack Charlestown or Savanna...

**Author**: Galvez, Bernardo de
**Title**: Federico Varon de Witenfeld ordered to conduct prisoners to New York and treat with the Chief of the British Arms, 14th January
**Location**: AGI Indiferente General 146-2-3
**Date**: 1782
**Section**: Havana Cuba
**Abstract**: Provide information to the Commander of the British Forces in New York of my intentions and give information about what happened in Pensacola between General Campbell and myself with the reasons why I can not agree to the remission of the prisoners made in Mississippi and Mobile and suggest that he name an individual to serve as commander of the English soldiers...

**Title**: Copias de la Correspondencia tenido en Pensacola con el general Campbell, 26 de Octobre ultimo numero ... 31 Diciembre
**Location**: AGI Santo Domingo 2548
**Date**: 1782, January 23rd
**Section**: Pensacola

**Title**: expedientes sobre la evacuacion de la Florida Occidental; comprende varias instancias de vasalllos británicos, habitants de este territorio, por este motivo
**Location**: AGI Santo Domingo 2660
**Date**: 1783-1786
**Section**: West Florida

## Articles

**Author**: Siebert, Wilbur H.
**Title**: The Loyalists in West Florida and the Natchez District.
**Citation**: Mississippi Valley Historical Review 2:465-483
**Publication**: 1916
**Section**: British West Florida
**Abstract**: Review of participation of the loyalists in the affairs of West Florida and fate after conquest by Spaniards. The veterans of the Loyal American regiment, and the Pennsylvania and Maryland Loyalists were evacuated to New York and resettled in Canada (New Brunswick/Nova Scotia).

**Author**: Waldeck, Herr
**Title**: Waldeck Chaplain at Pensacola in West Florida
**Citation**: Letters from America, 1776-1779. Ray W. Pettengill, translator. Boston and New York. Houghton Mifflin Company.
**Publication**: 1924 (1779, March 18th)
**Section**: Pensacola
**Abstract**: Nothing grows, not even a stalk of lettuce. No churches, not even a preacher.

**Author**: Dent, Henry P., editor
**Title**: The Capture of Baton Rouge by Galvez, September 21st, 1779.
**Citation**: Louisiana Historical Quarterly 12 (April) 255-266
**Publication**: 1929
**Abstract**: Spanish captured western part of province before Pensacola knew war had been declared (London Gazette, Saturday April 1, 1780). Letter sent on Capitulation to Spanish of Alexander Dickson, Lieutenant Colonel, of the troop under his command (letter to Major-General Campbell from New Orleans, October 20, 1779). Manchac indefensible against cannon so removed soldiers to redoubt at Baton Rouge. After incessant firing on both sides for more than three hours was obliged to surrender to Galvez (copy of Lieutenant-Colonel Dickson reason's for removing to Baton Rouge, September 22, 1779).

**Author**: Abbey, Kathryn Trimmer
**Title**: Spanish Projects for the Reoccupation of the Floridas during the American Revolution.
**Citation**: Hispanic American Historical Review 9 (August) 265-285
**Publication**: 1929
**Abstract**: Marked distrust rapidly materialized between the English and Spanish during 1777 and 1778. The Spaniards supported the idea of Americans moving against Pensacola. They also feared a British invasion. Galvez launched his own invasion of British territory in 1779 and in one month and a day captured eight ships, taken three forts, made prisoners of twenty-eight officers and five hundred and fifty men, and gained four hundred and thirty leagues of territory. Subsequently, his intention to invade Pensacola having been changed to Mobile, Galvez ordered the embarkation of his forces for Mobile.

**Author**: Nachbin, Jac
**Title**: Spain's Report of the War with the British in Louisiana
**Citation**: Louisiana Historical Quarterly 15 (July) 468–481
**Publication**: 1932
**Section**: Natchez
**Abstract**: This report was first published in the Suplemento a la Gazeta de Madrid, issued on January 14, 1780. It describes the men of the small army that left, on the 27th of August, for English territory. This army surprised and captured Manchak. A rapid march to Baton Rouge, followed by a battery attack on the 21st of September, dismantled the fort and caused it to surrender and also the Fort Panmure of Natchez. An American schooner captured the English cruising sloop called the West Florida on Lake Pontchartrain while another English sloop was overcome by a band of Creoles.

**Author**: Abbey, Kathryn T.
**Title**: Peter Chester's Defense of the Mississippi after the Willing Raid.
**Citation**: Mississippi Valley Historical Review 22 (June, 1935)
**Publication**: 1935
**Section**: Natchez
**Abstract**: The "Willing Raid" went down the Mississippi against Natchez and Manchak. Hutchins broke his parole and met Harrison's party at White Cliffs, totally defeating them. Subsequently Chester assembled men at Natchez and restored the fort at Manchak. It is based upon Colonial Office Papers Photostats at the Library of Congress but also cited are **AGI** (Papeles de Cuba 174), **Archivo General de Simancas** 181, Letters of Delegates to Congress, **Rowland** (1930) and **Pollock Papers (in Library of Congress)**.

**Author**: Padgett, James A., editor
**Title**: The Reply of Peter Chester, Governor of West Florida, to Complaints Made Against His Administration
**Citation**: Louisiana Historical Quarterly 22 (January) 31–46
**Publication**: 1939
**Abstract**: Brief account of the defeat of American invasion in Natchez district of 1778 with convoking and dissolution of an assembly of freeholders within the province of West Florida.

**Author**: Padgett, James A. (editor)
**Title**: Bernardo de Galvez's Siege of Pensacola in 1781 (as related in Robert Farmer's Journal).
**Citation**: Louisiana Historical Quarterly 26, 2, 311–229
**Publication**: 1943
**Section**: Pensacola
**Abstract**: Gives events, from March 9th to May 10th, in 1781 on siege. English evacuated town of Pensacola and took stations at the redoubts. They surrendered after shell thrown in at the door of the magazine killed 40 seamen and 45 men of Pennsylvania loyalist regiment.

**Author**: Padgett, James A. (editor)
**Title**: Governor Peter Chester's Observations on the Boundaries of British West Florida, about 1775
**Citation**: Louisiana Historical Quarterly 26, 1, 5–11
**Publication**: 1943
**Section**: British West Florida
**Abstract**: Boundaries between Louisiana and West Florida, naming the lakes, rivers and islands marking this boundary.

**Author**: Osborn, George C.
**Title**: Major-General John Campbell in British West Florida
**Citation**: Florida Historical Quarterly 27, 317-339
**Publication**: 1949
**Section**: British West Florida
**Abstract**: Campbell found British forces ill equipped to defend West Florida. He achieved some success in re supplying and re equipping his forces but Galvez quickly took over the western part of the province. Pennsylvania and Maryland loyalists, depleted by "death and desertion," combined into one force. Raised two troops of light Dragoons from the inhabitants. Mobile capitulated to Spanish forces and British, retarded by heavy rains, swollen streams and muddy roads, did not arrive in time to defeat them. Spanish forces converged on Pensacola. Shells on an advanced redoubt protecting Fort George precipitated an explosion and forced a capitulation.

**Author**: Worcester, Donald E., translator
**Title**: Miranda's Diary of the Siege of Pensacola, 1781,
**Citation**: Florida Historical Quarterly 29: 163-196
**Publication**: 1951
**Section**: Pensacola
**Abstract**: Information on travel, on board a Spanish ship, to Pensacola and details regarding the subsequent siege. It provides useful data concerning the activities of the besieging troops and surrender of the British.

**Author**: Osborn, George C.
**Title**: Relations with the Indians in West Florida during the Administration of Governor Peter Chester, 1770-1781
**Citation**: Florida Historical Quarterly 31: 239-272
**Publication**: 1953
**Section**: British West Florida
**Abstract**: British attempted to obtain land from Indians and at same time form an alliance with them against the Spaniards and Americans. Spaniards were trying to do the same things with Galvez holding a conference with tribal chiefdoms at Point Coupee. A blow at amiable relations took place by the death of superintendent John Stuart but the immense consumption of English provisions continued and only ended with the surrender of the English to Spanish forces.

**Author**: Haarmann, Albert W.
**Title**: The Spanish Conquest of British West Florida, 1779-1781.
**Citation**: Florida Historical Quarterly 39: 107-134
**Publication**: 1960
**Section**: British West Florida
**Abstract**: Description of the conquest of West Florida, in 1779, 1780 and 1781, by the Spaniards. Sources are Caughey (1934), Alden (1954), Kinnaird (1949), London Morning Chronicle (1780, reprinted Louisiana Historical Quarterly, 12, 1929), Hamilton (1910), von Eelking (1863), Smith (1860), Galvez (1917), Mackenzie (1930) and Miranda (1951). Of these the contemporary accounts are **London Morning Chronicle** (1780), **von Eelking** (1863), **Smith** (1860), **Galvez** (1917), **Mackenzie** (1930) and **Miranda** (1951). This is a competent, complete and detailed discussion of the conquest of the British colony.

**Author**: Murphy, W. S.
**Title**: The Irish Brigade of Spain at the Capture of Pensacola, 1781.
**Citation**: Florida Historical Quarterly 38(3): 216-225.
**Publication**: 1960
**Abstract**: Count Bernardo de Galvez, with a Spanish army of more than 7,000 men, (including 580 officers and men of the "Irish Brigade") besieged British forces at Pensacola for two months and captured them on 2 May 1781. Provides information on the role of a regiment of that Brigade during the capture of Pensacola and subsequent service records in the Archivo General de Simancas. These records are not complete and often run beyond the 1780's.
**Section**: Pensacola

**Author**: Scott, Kenneth, editor
**Title**: Britain Loses Natchez, 1779. Unpublished Letter.
**Citation**: The Journal of Mississippi History 26
**Publication**: 1964
**Section**: Natchez
**Abstract**: List of 59 inhabitants of Natchez.

**Author**: Haarmann, Albert W.
**Title**: The Siege of Pensacola, An Order of Battle
**Citation**: The Florida Historical Quarterly 44
**Publication**: 1966
**Section**: Pensacola
**Abstract**: Details the number of troops, and their organization, of the Spanish, British and French, in the siege of Pensacola (1781). The British troops included the General staff (69), 16$^{th}$ Regiment of Foot (110), Royal Americans (133), Royal Artillery (36), Royal Navy (246), German 3$^{rd}$ Regiment of Waldeck (303), provincial Pennsylvania Loyalists (62), provincial Maryland (135) and provincial Cavalry (19).

**Author**: Rea, Robert R.
**Title**: Graveyard for Britons, West Florida, 1763-1781.
**Citation**: Florida Historical Quarterly 47(4): 345-364.
**Publication**: 1969
**Section**: Mobile, Pensacola
**Abstract**: When British forces occupied West Florida late in 1763 following Spanish withdrawal, bark huts without fireplaces served as troop barracks in Pensacola, and crowded Mobile's Fort Conde (Charlotte) was in a neglected state. Appointed surgeon to the military hospitals, John Lorimer arrived in Pensacola in August 1765. With simultaneous epidemics of yellow fever, dysentery, and either typhus or typhoid, along with malaria, a single regiment in one month lost four officers, five officers' wives, and nearly a hundred men.

Taking command in March 1767 Brigadier General Frederick Haldimand immediately began improvements at Pensacola such as moving the stockade palisades farther away from the crowded barracks, planting vegetable gardens, building a hospital, beginning swamp drainage, and bringing in fresh drinking water. Despite Lorimer's recommendations for removal of Fort Charlotte to the eastern side of Mobile Bay, for clearing and draining the area, and for erecting two-story barracks. Mobile remained a fever-ridden camp in the "graveyard for Britons" at the Spanish takeover in 1781. The penurious policy of the Government toward the American command resulted in shortage of medical supplies and hospital space and a lack of such basic necessities as a balanced diet to blankets for cold weather. Based partly on the Gage Papers in the William L. Clements Library and the Haldimand Papers in the Public Archives of Canada

**Author**: Rea, Robert R.
**Title**: Resources and Research Opportunities for British West Florida, 1763-1783
**Citation**: Ernest F. Dibble and Earle W. Newton, editors, In Search of Gulf Coast Colonial History. Pensacola, Florida. 23-45.
**Publication**: 1970
**Section**: Pensacola
**Abstract:** Information in papers of Public Record Office (London), Haldimand Papers (British Museum, London), General Thomas Gage papers (Clements Library, University of Michigan), Carleton Papers (Colonial Williamsburg), collections of Royal Society of London, Linnean Society and American Philosophical Society, letter book of John Fitzpatrick, letter book of Charles Strachan, etc.

**Author**: Proctor, Samuel
**Title**: Bibliographical Resources in the United States for Gulf Coast Studies
**Citation**: Ernest F. Dibble and Earle W. Newton, editors, In Search of Gulf Coast Colonial History. Pensacola, Florida. 46-78.
**Publication**: 1970
**Section**: British West Florida
**Abstract**: The material noted here is, mostly, collection of data from Mexican, American, and Spanish archives held by repositories in the United States. Of special interest is the John Willard Brister Library (Memphis State University) that has copies of holdings of AGN material pertaining to West Florida, Howard Memorial Library (New Orleans) with transcripts and translations of pertinent Spanish letters (including those of Don Bernardo de Galvez to his uncle Don Jose de Galvez), Library of Congress West Florida Papers including Robert Farmer's Journal on the Siege of Pensacola (March 9–May 10 1781) and Reply of Peter Chester to Complaints Against his Administration. The P. K. Yonge Library of Florida History (University of Florida, Gainesville) is the largest collection but the majority of the holdings are from the Archivo General de Indias.

**Author**: Griffith, Lucille
**Title**: Peter Chester and the End of the British Empire in West Florida
**Citation**: Alabama Review 30:1:14-33
**Publication**: 1977
**Section**: British West Florida
**Abstract**: When the government of British West Florida was given to Peter Chester the result was the rule of a man who headed that administration for more than a decade. It was his policy to do as little as possible while allowing the settlers to administer their own affairs. No supporter of legislative powers, he for the most part, ruled without one. He had never refused to raise troops for defense but was handicapped by insufficient funds, unreliable leadership and lack of a militia law. Finally it should be noted that Chester did not stand alone before his critics, for he also had loyal and vocal supporters. In the end, even with the loyal support and cooperation of the military forces it is problematical that Chester could have saved the colony from the Spanish. The final division of territory was made at the conference table as it had been after each of the previous colonial wars.

**Author**: Rea, Robert R.
**Title**: Life, Death, and Little Glory: The British Soldier on the Gulf Coast, 1763-1781
**Citation**: William S. Coker, editor, The Military Presence on the Gulf Coast. Pensacola, Florida. 21-35.
**Publication**: 1978
**Section**: Pensacola
**Abstract**: The British soldier suffered much but gained little glory by his garrison of the posts in British West Florida. Women, wives and otherwise, were associated with the military but neither men nor women received special care. Three companies were forces to bivouac in tents because the huts were uninhabitable. Bedding and firewood proved to be a major economic problem because the Quartermaster General did not expect to provide either. Normal military assemblies and drill filled but a part of the time of the soldier for much of his life consisted of the dullest routine. As every British military authority has agreed since 1763, the fate of West Florida rested in the hands of the Royal Navy and those hands were too weak and too busy elsewhere in 1781. Campbell's redcoats were a sacrifice on the altar of war.

**Author**: Fabel, Robin F. A.
**Title**: Anglo-Spanish Commerce in New Orleans During the American Revolutionary Era
**Citation**: William S. Coker, Robert R. Rea, editors, Anglo-Spanish Confrontation on the Gulf Coast during the American Revolution. Pensacola, Florida. 25-53.
**Publication**: 1982
**Section**: New Orleans
**Abstract**: Trade in British goods by British, or American, merchants, continued throughout the period with only temporary interruptions. The balance was in British goods to the Spanish colony rather than Spanish goods to England. The difference was made up by coined Spanish currency.

**Author**: Cummins, Light T.
**Title**: Spanish Historians and the Gulf Coast Campaigns
**Citation**: William S. Coker, Robert R. Rea, editors, Anglo-Spanish Confrontation on the Gulf Coast during the American Revolution. Pensacola, Florida. 194-205.
**Publication**: 1982
**Section**: Pensacola
**Abstract**: There are two major viewpoints represented in the discussion of Spanish historians, these are the Latin American and peninsula orientations. The Latin American interpretation, which includes Spanish historians: (1) emphasizes the role of events in the Americas, (2) use a broad base of primary and secondary sources, (3) the prevailing orientation falls within the non peninsular framework.

**Author**: Green, Michael D.
**Title**: The Creek Confederacy in the American Revolution: Cautious Participants
**Citation**: William S. Coker, Robert R. Rea, editors, Anglo-Spanish Confrontation on the Gulf Coast during the American Revolution. Pensacola, Florida. 54-75.
**Publication**: 1982
**Section**: Pensacola
**Abstract**: Creek support of the British at Pensacola was weak because the Creek did not need Pensacola for trade purposes and the British commanding general felt that he could survive without their help.

**Author**: O'Donnell III, James H.
**Title**: Hamstrung by Penury: Alexander Cameron's Failure at Pensacola
**Citation**: William S. Coker, Robert R. Rea, editors, Anglo-Spanish Confrontation on the Gulf Coast during the American Revolution. Pensacola, Florida. 76-89.
**Publication**: 1982
**Section**: Pensacola
**Abstract**: Cameron, as the new superintendent of the Mississippi District, was required not to exceed 1,955 pounds. Furthermore he was expected to spend most of the year traveling in the Indian country, visiting the tribes for whom he was responsible, and cultivating their loyalty to the crown. He was required to spend money freely and was no longer allowed to do so. Nor was roving ambassador to the Indians an idea of a role befitting his situation. Neither Cameron, nor his antagonist General Campbell, could persuade Governor Peter Chester to disburse the 1,000 pounds in his budget for the entertainment of Indians.

**Author**: Holland, Kathryn
**Title**: Anglo-Spanish Contest for the Gulf Coast as Viewed from the Town square.
**Citation**: William S. Coker, Robert R. Rea, editors, Anglo-Spanish Confrontation on the Gulf Coast during the American Revolution. Pensacola, Florida. 90-105.
**Publication**: 1982
**Section**: Pensacola
**Abstract**: Choctaw attracted by Spanish trade goods, received Spanish trinkets. British traders, attempting to end the Spanish connection, forced many chiefs to reconsider their position. Six Village chiefs proved more difficult and some still maintained a Spanish relationship. Creeks continued to support the British after the fall of Pensacola.

**Author:** Borja Medina Rojas, Francisco de
**Title:** Jose de Ezpeleta and the Siege of Pensacola
**Citation:** William S. Coker, Robert R. Rea, editors, Anglo-Spanish Confrontation on the Gulf Coast during the American Revolution. Pensacola, Florida. 106-124.
**Publication:** 1982
**Section:** Pensacola
**Abstract:** Major General of the besieging army and colonel of the Spanish Regiment of Navarre, from the occupation of Mobile, Jose de Ezpeleta took part in all aspect of planning and execution of the conquest of Pensacola. The West Florida campaign began for Ezpeleta when at the end of January 1780 he was appointed to command the veteran troops from the garrison of Havana operating against Mobile under Bernardo de Galvez. He was appointed governor For Carlotta (old British Fort Charlotte) and commander of the Mobile District. For the next several months he formulated plans to capture Pensacola. Ultimately he would sail to Pensacola, land troops at Bon Secour Bay and then to Rose island and cross to the mainland. He participated in subsequent the campaign against the English and with the capture of the Queen's Redoubt, he obtained the final capitulation of Pensacola.

**Author**: Beerman, Eric
**Title**: Jose Solano and the Spanish Navy at the Siege of Pensacola
**Citation**: William S. Coker, Robert R. Rea, editors, Anglo-Spanish Confrontation on the Gulf Coast during the American Revolution. Pensacola, Florida. 125-144.
**Publication**: 1982
**Section**: Pensacola
**Abstract**: Vice Admiral Jose Solano sailed out of Cadiz Bay on April 28th (1780), commanding a fleet of seventeen warships that escorted 140 transport vessels carrying nearly twelve thousand crack infantrymen. His expedition aimed at clearing the British from the Gulf of Mexico and the Caribbean. His first objective was Fort George at Pensacola.

Scattered by a hurricane in October, another invasion attempt against Pensacola was approved in January. With no opposition, the Spaniards captured Rose island and Galvez forced the bay on his brig Galveztown, accompanied by the Valenzuela and two armed launches. Galvez and Campbell negotiated the neutrality of Pensacola and the English troops moved to Fort George and the two outlying redoubts.

On April 22, Solano's fifteen ships of the line and seven frigates, arrayed off the southern shore of Rose island, presented an intimidating sight for the English defenders of Pensacola. Forty launches forced the bay with 1,600 of Cagigal's troops, 1,500 of Solano's men and 700 of Monteill's Frenchmen joining the siege of Fort George. Finally, on May 8th, a Spanish howitzer round struck the Queen's Redoubt, setting fire to inflammable walls, causing the powder magazine to explode, and killing 105 defenders. This caused Campbell to run up the white flag and the siege ended.

**Author**: Holmes, Jack D.
**Title**: French and Spanish Military Units in the 1781 Pensacola Campaign
**Citation**: William S. Coker, Robert R. Rea, editors, Anglo-Spanish Confrontation on the Gulf Coast during the American Revolution. Pensacola, Florida. 145-157.
**Publication**: 1982
**Section**: Pensacola
**Abstract**: Lists Spanish and French units that served in this campaign and describes the contribution of the Spanish units.

**Author**: Fabel, Robin F. A.
**Title**: Ordeal by Siege: James Bruce in Pensacola, 1780-1781.
**Citation**: Florida Historical Quarterly 66(3): 280-297.
**Publication**: 1988
**Section**: Pensacola
**Abstract**: The Spanish siege of British-held Pensacola in 1781 has garnered much attention. Most historians focus on military records and witnesses. The author prints six letters written by James Bruce, a large landowner and customs collector that present a different perspective on the attack.

**Author**: Parks, Virginia
**Title**: The British Fort at Pensacola
**Citation**: Pensacola History Illustrated 3 (4):11-18
**Publication**: 1990
**Abstract**: Outlines the history of the British fort at Pensacola during the late 18th century, including its various military contingents and commanders. Provides firsthand accounts of the fort's layout and appearance, and different periods of renovation and reconstruction.
**Section**: Pensacola
**Period**: 1763-81.

**Author:** Vickers, Elizabeth D.
**Title:** Disease: The Unconquerable Foe in British West Florida
**Citation:** Pensacola History Illustrated 3 (1990) 4: 29-32
**Publication:** 1990
**Section:** Pensacola
**Abstract:** British military forces found disease to be their most formidable foe. Upon arriving in Mobile they were already sickly from a campaign in Havana. Those in Pensacola suffered from a "most inveterate scurvy." An epidemic soon carried off four officers, five officers wives and about 100 men. Dressed for northern Europe, dehydration must have been a significant problem. During the eighteen year occupation of Pensacola the incidence of typhoid, dengue, typhus and yellow fever was high. Malaria was endemic and Pneumonia, Smallpox and venereal diseases were additional problems. The sickness rate was so high that in 1781 only 700 of 1200 troops were fit for duty during the siege of Pensacola.

**Author:** Rea, Robert R.
**Title:** British Pensacola
**Citation:** Pensacola History Illustrated 3 (1990) 4: 3-10
**Publication:** 1990
**Section:** Pensacola
**Abstract:** Traces the history of Pensacola from 1763 to 1779 giving early history as frontier, relations with nearby Indians, commercial activity, growth and development, and fall to Spanish forces during the American Revolution.

**Author**: Mills, Bill
**Title**: Merchant and Naval Shipping of British Pensacola, 1763-1781
**Citation**: Pensacola History Illustrated 4 (Winter 1991) 1, 7-19
**Publication**: 1991
**Section**: Pensacola
**Abstract**: Pilots were vital in getting any large ship across the bar and past the shoals on either side but was not a guarantee of safety as when a pilot was responsible for one vessel running aground on Pelican Island. Laws were enacted to deny access to the gulf of any vessel not holding a proper Fort Pass or even clearance from customs.

Guard ships, gunboats or something similar were required to protect the provincial capital from invasion by sea. The number of vessels lost by capture to unfriendly forces were small compared to those rendered not seaworthy by the forces of nature requiring the need for annual inspections of every vessel in warmer waters. Pensacola, without areas of bedrock to construct a basing and since dry docks were too expensive, careening was conducted at a wharf.

Due to natural disasters, war and decay, the British were constantly acquiring vessels for duty at stations in the gulf region. His Majesty's ships Mentor and Stork, two sloops named Florida and West Florida were acquired by purchase of privately owned or condemned vessels. All of these vessels except the West Florida are known to have been lost in Pensacola Bay.

**Author**: Alsedo y Bustamante, Francisco de.
**Title**: [Letter Concerning an Expedition to Western Florida]
**Citation**: Revista de Historia Naval [Spain] 11 (41): 123-128
**Abstract**: Letter to mother of author (19 November 1780) on preparations of Spanish governor of Louisiana regarding 1781 expedition against British Pensacola and difficulties encountered during these preparations.
**Section**: Pensacola
**Publication**: 1993

## Books

**Author**: Romans, Bernard
**Title**: A Concise Natural History of East and West Florida
**Publication**: 1775 (1962)
**Section**: British West Florida
**Abstract**: This is a detailed description of the land and flora of the peninsula of Florida. It is not, except incidentally, a historical account. Rather it tells how one travels in different routes throughout the peninsula. Thus it notes that "Pensacola has about an hundred and eighty houses in it, built in general in good taste, but of timber: the town is laid out in an oblong square, near the foot of an hill, called Gage-hill....". However no information is provided on how the town was founded or its subsequent history. It goes on to detail the route taken into the backcountry and a return to Mobile. Information is provided on the different plants and foods grown in the land. The date of the volume is 1775 for at that time the author abandoned his career as a surveyor and went over to the rebels as a soldier. It ends four years before the campaigns of Galvez.

**Author**: Bartram, William
**Title**: The Travels of William Bartram
**Citation**: Library of Congress Catalogue
**Publication**: 1778 (1958, 1998)
**Section**: Pensacola, Mobile
**Abstract**: Brief description of Mobile and Pensacola in 1778. Mobile was largely in ruins, but a few "buildings were inhabited by French gentlemen, English, Scotch and Irish, and emigrants from the Northern British colonies." In Pensacola the secretary introduced him to Governor Chester who observing that a complete investigation "would require the revolution of the seasons to discover." offered to "bear my expenses and [have] a residence in his own family as long as I chose to continue in the colony."

"There are several hundred habitations in Pensacola: the governor's palace is a large stone building ornamented with a tower, built by the Spaniards. The town is defended by a large stockado fortress, the plan a tetragon with salient angles at each corner, where is a block-house or round tower, one story higher than the curtains, where are light cannon mounted, it is constructed of wood. Within this fortress is the council chamber, here the records are kept, houses for the officers and barracks for the accommodation of the garrison, arsenal, magazine, etc. The secretary resides in a spacious, neat building: there are several merchants and gentlemen of other professions, who have respectable and convenient buildings in the town."

**Author**: Anonymous
**Title**: [The German Allies in the North American Wars for Liberation]
**Publication**: 1779–1781 (1863)
**Section**: Pensacola
**Abstract**: Forts built of logs and held together with saplings, intertwined, and sand heaped about. Waldecker Grenadiers left for Baton Rouge and the Mississippi. Spanish seized several British ships on the Mississippi. Dixon could not hold Mohawk in face of overwhelming numbers but determined to withstand them as long as possible. After two attacks Dixon decided to accept the terms of Galvez. On $5^{th}$ of March 1780, the $60^{th}$ Regiment and on the $6^{th}$ the rest of the Waldecker Regiment left for Mobile. The aid was too late and Captain Durnford was compelled to surrender. March $28^{th}/29^{th}$ Spanish flotilla anchored in Pensacola bay and then vanishes. British counterattack on Mobile outposts (January $3^{rd}$ 1781) fails and Colonel von Hanxleden is killed. March $9^{th}$ to May $8^{th}$, the Spanish return to Pensacola and capture it.

**Author**: Saavedra de Sangronis, Francisco
**Title**: Journal from 25 June 1780 until 20$^{th}$ of the same month of 1783
**Publication**: 1780-1783 (1989)
**Section**: Pensacola
**Abstract**: English attack on Mobile repulsed by Spaniards with death of Colonel Hanxleden. Launching of the Pensacola expedition on 18$^{th}$ of February which set sail on the 28$^{th}$ of February for Pensacola. Received word on the 5$^{th}$ of April regarding the entrance of the brigantine Galveztown, and other ships, into the bay of Pensacola. The warship San Roman, considered her mission accomplished and retired to Havana. On the 10$^{th}$ of April, a reinforcement of 1,627 men detached from various regiments and divided into two brigades, left Havana for Pensacola in a fleet of fifteen ships-of-the-line, three frigates, one brigantine and two cutters commanded by Don Jose Solano. This fleet arrived at Pensacola on the 20$^{th}$ of April and the commanders met with Galvez on the 21$^{st}$. The Spaniards began the siege of Pensacola and, with the explosion on May 8$^{th}$ of a shell in Fort Half Moon (the northern most and highest of their fortifications), the English evacuated it and surrendered all their troops the 10$^{th}$.

**Author**: Galvez, Bernardo de
**Title**: Diario de las Operaciones de la Expedicion contra la Plaza de Panzacola concluida por las Armas de S.M. Catolica, bajo las Ordenes del Mariscal de Campo
**Publication**: 1781 (republished 1966)
**Section**: Pensacola
**Abstract**: Description of the conquest of Pensacola by the Galvez led expedition. Includes events from landing in Pensacola to the British surrender plus Articles of Capitulation, Relation of deaths and wound, summary of arms and munitions; 48 pages long.
**Period**: 1781

**Author**: Hutchins, Thomas
**Title**: A Historical Narrative and Topographical Description of Louisiana and West Florida.
**Publication**: 1784 (republished 1968)
**Section**: Natchez, Pensacola, Mobile
**Abstract**: Mobile had a fort, built with brick, and barracks for the officers and soldiers. Pensacola is of an oblong form and lies almost parallel to the beach. It is about a mile in length and a quarter of a mile in breadth, but contracts at both ends. The fort takes up a large space of ground just in the middle of the town dividing it into two parts. Natchez district is timbered with different types of trees while the inhabitants cultivate indigo, rice, tobacco, maize and some wheat. They raise cattle, horses, mules, hogs, sheep and poultry. The district was settling very fast by daily emigrations from the northern states but the capture of the British troops, in 1779, put a stop to it. Further details on the people, flora and geography of the area are given in the book.

**Author**: His Majesties Loyal Subjects
**Title**: Case and Petition of His Majesties Loyal Subjects Late of West Florida
**Citation**: Library of Congress catalogue citation but this very thin book was in the library of the State of Virginia. I used a scanned copy of the volume.
**Publication**: 1787
**Section**: Pensacola
**Abstract**: Former British planters, merchants, officers and others of West Florida request compensation for the loss due to the Spanish conquest of the territory. Claim that they refused to revolt against the English and spent efforts in defeating American attempt at invasion.
**Period**: 1779-1781

**Author**: Vignoles, Charles
**Title**: Observations upon the Floridas
**Publication**: 1823 (1977)
**Section**: Pensacola
**Abstract**: Does not have any information on the British period of Florida history. Has some information on topography, soil, culture, temperature and climate.

**Author**: Allen, Joseph
**Title**: Memoir of the Life and Services of Admiral Sir William Hargood
**Publication**: 1841
**Section**: Pensacola
**Abstract**: Brief description (pages 25-30) of the conquest of Pensacola by the Spanish. Does not provide any information not found elsewhere.

**Author**: Pickett, Albert J.
**Title**: History of Alabama
**Publication**: 1851 (1962)
**Section**: Pensacola, Mobile, Natchez, Manchac
**Abstract**: This book, whose emphasis is on the Post British period, covers the Spanish conquest of the British territories in two pages. It does not provide any new data.

**Author**: Durnford, Mary
**Title**: Family recollections of Lieut. General Elias Walker Durnford, a colonial commandant of the Corps of Royal Engineers
**Publication**: 1863
**Section**: Mobile
**Abstract**: Durnford, captain of engineers and Lieut.-Governor of West Florida, commanded garrison of Mobile. This consisted of ninety-seven regulars of the 60$^{th}$ regiment, sixteen royal Marylanders, three artillerymen, sixty seamen, fifty-four inhabitants, and fifty-one armed Negroes, with two surgeons and a laborer, - amounting to 284 of all sorts. The Spaniards attacked on the 12 of March, with eight eighteen and one twenty-four pounder. The fire had considerable effect on the embrasures and parapets of the two faces of the fort and, two garrison guns being dismounted, they hung out a white flag that sunset. The capitulation was not signed until the 14th, when the fort was given up and the garrison surrendered as prisoners of war.

**Author**: Campbell, Richard L.
**Title**: Historical Sketches of Colonial Florida
**Publication**: 1892 (1975)
**Section**: British West Florida
**Abstract**: This work provides twenty eight pages on the Spanish conquest of British West Florida. The only primary source cited is Von Elking who gives a detailed report of the experiences of the Waldeck troops. A secondary (nineteenth century) source also cited is Sparks (Diplomatic Correspondence of the American Revolution, 1829-30). Other material was known from the details on the conquest. The information is useful but the emphasis is on interaction between Europeans rather than the role of the United States (which was minimal).
**Period**: 1779-1781

**Author**: Hamilton, Peter Joseph
**Title**: Colonial Mobile
**Publication**: 1910
**Section**: Mobile
**Abstract**: Mobile was French before it became British but these notes are concerned with the British phase of its history (1763-1780). By the treaty of Paris, February 10, 1763, Mobile became a province of West Florida. The military command, in 1763, was General Thomas Gage. Mobile, thanks to its location surrounded by swamps, was not considered healthy. Except for the fort at Mobile itself, most the territory was subsequently evacuated by British troops. At the same time parts of the interior was occupied by British settlers coming from Europe and the older colonies. The center of British settlement was not Mobile but rather the Tombigbee river. The military history of this colony, especially the defeat of the British, is not very accurate and one should use other more primary sources.

**Author**: Dunbar Shields, Joseph
**Title**: Natchez, Its Early History
**Publication**: 1930
**Section**: Natchez
**Abstract**: This book has a brief, and secondary, paragraph on the Spanish campaigns against Natchez, Baton Rouge, Mobile and Pensacola (p. 19). The next page (p. 20) comments on the temporary capture of Fort Panmure by the British.
**Period**: 1779-1781

**Author**: Dunbar, William (Dunbar Rowland, editor)
**Title**: Life, Letters and Papers
**Publication**: 1930
**Section**: Baton Rouge, Natchez
**Abstract**: Mostly concerns a time beyond the purview of this bibliography but does mention the Willing raid of 1778. He removed his Blacks before the arrival of Willing but had his house plundered by Willings followers.

**Author**: Shaw, Helen Louise
**Title**: British Administration of the Southern Indians, 1756-1783
**Publication**: 1931 (1981)
**Section**: British West Florida
**Abstract**: Plans include capture of New Orleans but Spain captures Fort Charlotte in 1780 and Cameron blames Campbell for its loss; the criticism and controversy over treatment of Indians leads to fall of Pensacola.

**Author**: Holmes, Jack D. L.
**Title**: Honor and Fidelity, The Louisiana Infantry Regiment and the Louisiana Militia Companies, 1766-1821
**Publication**: 1965
**Section**: British West Florida
**Abstract**: Eight pages on the Galvez campaigns. This is a secondary source derived mostly from Papeles de Cuba, Museo Naval and Archivo Historico Nacional papers. A succinct description of the campaigns against Manchak, Baton Rouge, Mobile and Pensacola is included in this volume.

**Author**: Rush, N. Orwin
**Title**: Spain's Final Triumph over Great Britain in the Gulf of Mexico: The Battle of Pensacola, March 9 to May 8, 1781
**Citation**: Kislak Collection, rare books and manuscripts division of LC
**Publication**: 1966
**Section**: British West Florida (Pensacola)
**Abstract**: Preliminary information on the capture and/or conquest of Manchac, Baton Rouge, and Mobile plus the surrender of Fort Panmure at Natchez. Most of the book concerns the conquest of Pensacola based upon the Royal Proclamation of Charles III citing Galvez's many deeds (1783) and as detail in information on the battle from: (1) Diario de las Operaciones ... contra ... Pensacola translated into English from an eighteenth century printing. The original, which was not seen for this work, may be in the Biblioteca Central Militar (Madrid), (2) Diario de lo Ocurrido ... of Jose Solano, (3) Diario of [Francisco de Miranda] as in Florida Historical Quarterly 29:164-195, (4) A Journal of the Siege of Pensacola, West Florida, 1781 of Robert Farmer (Buckingham Smith, editor), (5) New York and Weekly Gazette, July 29, 1781. There are also Campbell reports (Campbell to Clinton, PRO Carleton Paper 30/55) of April 9th, May 7th and May 12th, all for 1781. The maps come from Museo Naval Madrid (7), Clinton Papers – British Headquarters of University of Michigan Library (6), drawings from Crown collection at University of Michigan (2), maps of the Biblioteca Central Militar Madrid (4), Archivo General de Indias Seville (2), Biblioteca Nacional Madrid (3), the harbor of Pensacola in the library of the University of Michigan (1) and in the British Museum (1).

**Author**: James, James Alton
**Title**: Oliver Pollock, The Life and Times of an Unknown Patriot
**Publication**: 1970
**Section**: New Orleans and Natchez
**Abstract**: Arriving in New Orleans in 1767, he traded in goods from Philadelphia and blacks from Africa in return for the produce of Louisiana. In 1776 he obtained a supply of gunpowder for the Americans. The new governor of Luisiana, Bernardo Galvez, assured Pollock that the port of New Orleans would be open and free to American commerce and to the admission and sale of prizes made by Americans. Further supplies of gunpowder, arms, quinine etc. were sent in the year 1777 and 1778. Pollock appointed, in March 1778, as commercial agent for the United States. Willing's raid on Natchez supported by Pollock, who guided him to New Orleans. Pollock granted permission by Galvez to fit out a captured British sloop, sailing under American colors. Clark received support from Pollock, who honored his expenses and paid their face value in silver. Pollock supported the Spanish advance on Natchez and participated in it. Subsequently, Pollock returned to the United States and by 1811 most of his claims against the Federal government and Virginia had been met. He died, in the State of Mississippi in 1814.
**Period**: 1767-1811

**Author:** Anonymous
**Title:** The 14th Colony
**Publication:** 1975 [?]
**Section:** British West Florida
**Abstract:** This consists of 44 pages on the history of British West Florida. Johnstone was its first governor. Relieved in 1767, he was replaced by Eliot but Browne, the Lt. Governor, assumed control until the arrival of Eliot. Gage recalled most of the British garrison in 1768, leaving only one regiment in Pensacola. Eliot arrived at the end of 1768 but shortly afterwards committed suicide leaving Browne in charge. Durnford was named Lt. Governor in 1769 and remained acting governor until the arrival of Chester in 1770. White settlers arrived in the British colony beginning around 1770 and occupied grants of land along the Mississippi river. The tensing of relation with Spain, especially with the arrival of Bernardo Galvez as governor in New Orleans, led to war in 1779. Galvez defeated the British at Baton Rouge (1779), Mobile (1780) and Pensacola (1781) resulting in the annexation of the colony of British West Florida.
**Period:** 1763-1781

**Author**: Haynes, Robert V.
**Title**: The Natchez District and the American Revolution.
**Publication**: 1976
**Section**: Natchez
**Abstract**: Information is provided on the area, British forces in the region, American raid of James Willing and Spanish conquest of the region. Although mention is made of the Spanish conquest of Mobile and Pensacola, the focus is on the conquest of the Natchez district. The author provides citations for the primary sources used for this modern description and history.

The English sources are the transcripts of documents from the Public Records Office in the Mississippi Department of Archives and History, as well as the legislative proceedings of British West Florida in the Records of the States of the United States, **Oliver Pollock** Papers (Library of Congress), **General Edward Hand and Abraham Skinner Papers** (Gratz Autograph Collection in the Historical Society of Pennsylvania). Information about the social and economic life of the Old Natchez District may be found in the Letter books of **John Fitzpatrick** (New York Public Library), the **Thomas Gage and Earl of Shelburne Papers** (William L. Clements Library) and **William Dunbar** Papers of Mississippi Department of Archives and History.

Contemporary descriptions include **Bernard Romans** (*A Concise Natural History of East and West Florida*), **Thomas Hutchins** (*An Historical Narrative and Topographical Description of Louisiana and West Florida*), and **William Bartram** (*Travels of William Bartram*). Other contemporary accounts include the *Life, Letters and Papers of* **William Dunbar** (Eron O. Rowland, editor, 1930).

**Author**: Meyers, Rose
**Title**: A History of Baton Rouge, 1699-1812
**Publication**: 1976
**Section**: Baton Rouge
**Abstract**: Spain declared war on Great Britain in June 1779. Galvez invaded Spanish West Florida on August 27th. The fort of Bute was taken by surprise on September 7th. Lieutenant Colonel Alexander Dickson, who was in command of British forces in the Baton Rouge District, had previously abandoned it for the Watts and Flowers' plantation in Baton Rouge; only a token garrison remained in the fort.

Troops, artillery and stores were moved to the new redoubt, called Fort New Richmond or Baton Rouge Redoubt. Surrounded by a ditch, eighteen feet wide and nine feet deep, inside was an earthen wall and outside a wall of palisades. It had thirteen cannon, four hundred regular troops and about one hundred armed civilians. Galvez made a commotion on one side and, when the British were distracted, attacked on the opposite side. The damage was so severe that the English surrendered, not only this fort but also Fort Panmure at Natchez. A subsequent rebellion, in 1781, by the English colonists led by Captain John Blomart had initial success but when the news of the surrender of Pensacola to Galvez reached Natchez, the rebellion collapsed and many fled into the wilderness.
**Period**: 1779-1781

**Author**: Mathews, Hazel C.
**Title**: British West Florida and the Illinois Country
**Publication**: 1977
**Section**: Pensacola, Mobile, Natchez, Manchac
**Abstract**: This is a history of the people of British West Florida based upon, in great part, the papers of the Colonial Office in the Public Record Office as copied for the P.K. Yonge Library of Florida History in the University of Florida at Gainesville. The emphasis is the eighteenth century colonization of this area by the British and the Spanish conquest is given as a postscript.

**Author**: Dalrymple, Margaret Fisher (editor and author)
**Title**: The Merchant of Manchac, The Letter books of John Fitzpatrick, 1768-1790.
**Publication**: 1978 (1768-1790)
**Section**: Manchac
**Abstract**: Provides details on the buying and selling of goods in a small town (Manchac) and these type of transactions between one resident of this town and people in Pensacola, New Orleans, Mobile, Natchez and elsewhere. However little information is given on the political matrix in which this takes place.

**Author**: Galvez, Bernardo de
**Title**: Yo Solo, the Battle Journal of Bernardo de Galvez during the American Revolution
**Publication**; 1978 (1781)
**Translator**: E. M. Montemayor
**Section**: Pensacola
**Abstract**: The book is divided into different sections but, excluding preliminary and subsequent material, it is in four parts: Operations [12th of May 1781], Articles of Capitulation [May 1781], Report of Dead and Wounded [12th of May 1781], and List of Weapons [26th of May]. The 30 pages of Operations is a compilation of several eighteenth century reports while three subsequent reports are literal translations from the Spanish. The book has a "Plan in Sections" of the British "Fort at Pensacola."

**Author**: Rea, Robert R. with Milo B. Howard, Jr., compilation and introduction
**Title**: The Minutes, Journals, and Acts of the General Assembly of British West Florida
**Publication**: 1979 (1766–1778)
**Section**: British West Florida
**Abstract**: Laws passed and proposed by the First through the Seventh General Assembly. The Assembly had an ongoing conflict with the Royal governors and, while they neither revolted nor rioted against the Crown, passage of laws was not possible without their consent. The governor through much of this period (1770–1781), Peter Chester, preferred to govern without their presence and for most of this time the General Assembly was not called into existence. The session of 1778 was accomplished little, only a bill for establishing the number of representatives for different towns was passed, and subsequently the conquest by the Spaniards ended this institution.

**Author**: Woodward, Ralph Lee, Jr., editor
**Title**: Tribute to Don Bernardo de Galvez
**Publication**: 1979
**Section**: British West Florida
**Abstract**: An introduction to the role of Bernardo de Galvez in the American Revolution, it provides the Reales Cedulas which granted him the title of Count and a "heroic romance" [poem] that was published upon the occasion of his death. Neither of these two accounts provide new data on the exploits of Bernardo de Galvez but the essay of Woodward and the many eighteenth century references will be useful for those interested in this topic.

**Author**: Borja Medina Rojas, F. de
**Title**: Jose de Ezpeleta, Gobernador de la Mobila, 1780-1781
**Publication**: 1980
**Section**: Mobile
**Abstract**: This book deals with Mobile under Spanish occupation and it does provide the earliest Spanish census documents for the English inhabitants of Tombechec, Tensa, Mobile (1780). The reference for these texts is AGI Cuba 2359.

**Author**: Coker, William S.
**Title**: The siege of Pensacola, 1781, in Maps
**Publication**: 1981
**Section**: Pensacola
**Abstract**: Details on the attack and conquest of Pensacola in 1781 dividing into the following sections: expeditions to reinforce Mobile and for the Pensacola campaign, 10 February - 30 December 1780; British attack upon the village, 5 - 7 January 1781; the fourth expedition to Pensacola and the arrival of the reinforcements, 28 February - 27 March 1781; movement to Suttons lagoon and the final Spanish camp, 23 March - 12 April 1781; reinforcements from Havana and the enlargement of Spanish camp, 7 -23 April 1781; Spaniards selected site for batteries, marked and dug entrenchments and built redoubts, 24 April - 2 May; the Finale, 2 - 11 May 1781.

**Author**: Servies, James A.
**Title**: The Siege of Pensacola, 1781: A Bibliography
**Publication**: 1981
**Section**: Pensacola
**Abstract**: This work provides a list of the manuscripts, articles and books pertaining to the conquest of Pensacola. It also includes essays on British West Florida, The Spanish Campaign, general works on the Siege of Pensacola, British Participation in the Siege, Spanish Participation in the Siege, French Participation in the Siege, and Bernardo de Galvez. The listing provided here is based, in part, upon this previously published compilation.

**Author**: Coker, William S.
**Title**: The Siege of Mobile, 1780, in Maps
**Publication**: 1982
**Section**: Mobile
**Abstract**: Details on the attack and conquest of Mobile in 1780 dividing into the following sections: preparation for the Mobile campaign (17 August 1779 to 11 January 1780); sailing of the expedition from New Orleans to Mobile (12 January to 9 February 1780); expedition stopped at Mobile pass (9 to 17 February 1780); reinforcements from Havana and the movement to the first Spanish encampment (18 to 25 February 1780); preliminary negotiations with the British and the movement to the second Spanish encampment (26 February to 5 March 1780), reinforcements from Pensacola and the construction of the Spanish battery (5 to 11 March 1780); bombardment and surrender of Fort Charlotte; the arrival and departure of the Spanish fleet (12 March to 20 May 1780). References include AGS (Guerra Moderna 6912), American Historical Review (1896: 1:696–699), Florida Historical Quarterly (1949: 27; 1960: 39), Alabama Historical Quarterly (1976: 38), London Gazette (1781: 12232) et. al.

**Author**: Rea, Robert R. (introduction) and James A. Servies (editor)
**Title**: The Log of H.M.S. Mentor, 1780-1781
**Publication**: 1982
**Section**: Pensacola and Mobile
**Abstract**: This work provides a detailed (primary) description of events on H.M.S. Mentor from the date of commissioning of the ship in March 1780 to the end of the log and dispersal of the crew in May 1781. The entries provide the "Courses," "Winds," and Remarks regarding that particular day; these mostly pertain to location and weather but also information on other ships (i.e. location, etc.). Provides data on opening cask of pork, exercised small arms, etc. Please note "its entries are succinct; its focus is the ship, not the affairs of men; its character is bureaucratic rather than individualistic; and its structure is so rigid that routine matters are given the same space as exciting events." The manuscript, of which this is an edited version, is the log book of Robert Deans, University of West Florida, John C. Pace Library, Special Collections Group 75-15

**Author**: Eugene Lyon and Teresa de Balmaseda Milam
**Title**: Spain in Florida and the American West
**Publication**: 1994
**Section**: Natchez, Baton Rouge, Mobile and Pensacola
**Abstract**: Brief description of the Galvez conquest of these areas. This is a secondary treatment of the British period. The focus of the book is on other periods of Florida history.

## References Cited

Adams, Katherine J. and Lewis L. Gould, editors
   1999. Inside the Natchez Trace Collection. Louisiana State University Press, Baton Rouge.

Abbey, Kathryn Trimmer

   1929. Spanish Projects for the Reoccupation of the Floridas during the American Revolution. Hispanic American Historical Review 9 (August) 265-285

   1935. Peter Chester's Defense of the Mississippi after the Willing Raid. Mississippi Valley Historical Review 22 (June)

Allen, Hargood
   1841. Memoir of the Life and Services of Admiral Sir William Hargood. Printed for private circulation only, Greenwich

Alsedo y Bustamente, Francisco de
   1993. [Letter Concerning an Expedition to Western Florida]. Revista de Historia Naval [Spain] 11 (41): 123-128

Anonymous
   1863. The German Allies in the North American Wars for Liberation. SEE Eelking 1863

Bartram, William
   1778. The Travels of William Bartram. (Edited with commentary and an annotated index by Francis Harper, University of Georgia Press, Athens, Georgia 1998)

Beerman, Eric
   1982. Jose Solano and the Spanish Navy at the Siege of Pensacola *in* William S. Coker, Robert R. Rea, editors, Anglo-Spanish Confrontation on the Gulf Coast during the American Revolution. Pensacola, Florida. 125-144.

Borja Medina Rojas, Francisco de

   1980. Jose de Ezpeleta, Gobernador de la Mobila, 1780-1781. Escuela de Estudios Hispano-Americanos de Sevilla. Seville, Spain

1982. Jose de Ezpeleta and the Siege of Pensacola, 106-124, *in* Coker, William S. Coker and   Robert R. Rea, editors, Anglo-Spanish Confrontation on The Gulf Coast during the American Revolution, Gulf Coast History and Humanities Conference, Pensacola, Florida.

Campbell, Richard L.
    1892. Historical Sketches of Colonial Florida. (University Presses of Florida, Gainesville, Florida. 1975)

Carter, Clarence Edwin, editor
    1969. The Correspondence of General Thomas Gage. Archon Books (Yale University Press, 1933)

Caughey, John Walton
    1934. Bernardo de Galvez in Louisiana, 1776-1783.
    (Pelican Publishing Company, Gretna, Louisiana, 1972)

Coker, William S., editor,
    1977. The Military Presence on the Gulf Coast. Pensacola, Florida

Coker, William S. and Hazel P. Coker

    1981. The Siege of Pensacola, in Maps. Pensacola, Perdido Bay Press

    1982. The Siege of Mobile, in Maps. Pensacola, Perdido Bay Press

Coker, William S. and Robert R. Rea, editors

    1979. Anglo-Spanish Confrontation on the Gulf Coast during the American Revolution. Pensacola, Florida.

    1981. Anglo-Spanish Confrontation on the Gulf Coast during the American Revolution, Pensacola, Florida,

Cummins, Light T.
    1981. Spanish Historians and the Gulf Coast Campaigns *in* William S. Coker, Robert R. Rea, editors, Anglo-Spanish Confrontation on The Gulf Coast during the American Revolution. 194-205. Pensacola, Florida.

Dalrymple, Margaret Fisher, editor
    1978. The Merchant of Manchac, The Letterbooks of John Fitzpatrick, Louisiana State University Press, Baton Rouge and London.

De Villa, Winston
    1986. English Land Grants in West Florida, A Register for the States of Alabama, Mississippi, and Parts of Florida and Louisiana, 1766-1776. Ville Platte, Louisiana.

Dent, Henry P., editor
    1929. The Capture of Baton Rouge by Galvez, September 21st, 1779.
    Louisiana Historical Quarterly 12 (April) 255-266

Dibble, Ernest F. and Earle W. Newton, editors
    1970. Search of Gulf Coast Colonial History. Pensacola, Florida

Dunbar, William (Dunbar Rowland, editor)
    1930. Life, letters, and papers of William Dunbar: of Elgin, Morayshire,
    Scotland, and Natchez, Mississippi. Compiled and prepared from
    original documents by Mrs. Dunbar Rowland (Eron Rowland).
    Press of the Mississippi Historical Society, Jackson, Mississippi

Dunbar Shields, Joseph
    1930. Natchez, Its Early History. John P. Morton & Company,
    Louisville Kentucky.

Durnford, Mary
    1863. Family Recollections of Lieut. General Elias Walker Durnford.
    Printed by John Lovell, Montreal, Canada.

Eelking, Max von
    1863. "The German allies, 1776-1783, in the North American wars for
    liberation." Translated in 1938 by Louis Krupp as "German Mercenaries
    in Pensacola During the American Revolution, 1779-1781" and published
    by the Pensacola Historical Society Quarterly (November 1977).

Fabel, Robin F. A.

    1981. Anglo-Spanish Commerce in New Orleans During the American
    Revolutionary Era *In* William S. Coker and Robert R. Rea, editors,
    Anglo-Spanish Confrontation on the Gulf Coast during the
    American Revolution, Pensacola, Florida, 25-53

    1986. The Economy of British West Florida, 1763-1783.
    University of Alabama Press, Tuscaloosa and London

    1988. Ordeal by Siege: James Bruce in Pensacola,
    1780-1781 *in* Florida Historical Quarterly 66: 280-297.

Forbes, James Grant
    1821. Sketches, historical and topographical, of the Floridas, more
    particularly of east Florida. Copy republished in 1964,
    Gainesville, University of Florida Press

Galvez, Bernardo

    1781. Diario de las operaciones de la expedicion contra la plaza de Panzacola concluida por las armas de S. M. católica. A facsimile reproduction of the 1st ed., with a foreword by N. Orwin Rush. Tallahassee, Fla., 1966

    1978. Yo solo: the battle journal of Bernardo de Gálvez during the American Revolution. Translated and with an epilogue by E.A. Montemayor ; introduction by Eric Beerman ; a message by His Majesty Juan Carlos I ; and a proclamation by Gerald R. Ford ; Winston De Ville, general editor. 1st English ed. New Orleans, Polyanthos, 1978

Gardner Griffin, Grace

    1946. A Guide to Manuscripts relating to American History in British Depositories reproduced for the Division of Manuscripts of the Library of Congress. Library of Congress, DC.

Green, Michael D.

    1978. The Creek Confederacy in the American Revolution: Cautious Participants *in* William S. Coker and Robert R. Rea, editors, Anglo-Spanish Confrontation on the Gulf Coast during the American Revolution. Pensacola, Florida. 54-75

Griffith, Lucille

    1977. Peter Chester and the End of the British Empire in West Florida Alabama Review 30:1:14-33

Haarman, Albert W.

    1960. The Spanish Conquest of British West Florida, 1779-1781. Florida Historical Quarterly 39: 107-134

    1966. The Siege of Pensacola, An Order of Battle. The Florida Historical Quarterly 44

Hargood, Admiral Sir William

    1841. Memoir of the Life and Services of. Printed for Private Circulation by Henry S. Richardson, Greenwich

Hamilton, Peter Joseph

    1910. Colonial Mobile. Copy reprinted by University of Alabama Press, University, Alabama, 1976

Haynes, Robert V.

    1976. The Natchez District and the American Revolution. University Press of Mississippi, Jackson

His Majesties Loyal Subjects
   1787. Case and Petition of His Majesties Loyal Subjects Late of West Florida

Holland, Kathyrn
   1982. Anglo-Spanish Contest for the Gulf Coast as Viewed from the Town square *in* William S. Coker, Robert R. Rea, editors, Anglo-Spanish Confrontation on the Gulf Coast during the American Revolution. Pensacola, Florida. 90-105

Holmes, Jack D. L.
   1965. Honor and Fidelity: The Louisiana Infantry Regiment and the Louisiana Militia Companies, 1766-1821. Birmingham, Alabama.

   1982. French and Spanish Military Units in the 1781 Pensacola Campaign *in* William S. Coker and Robert R. Rea, Editors. Anglo-Spanish Confrontation on the Gulf Coast during the American Revolution, 145-157, Pensacola, Florida

Hutchins, Thomas
   1784. An Historical Narrative and Topographical Description of Louisiana and West-Florida. Copy reprinted in 1968 for University of Florida Press, Gainesville

James, James Alton
   1970. Oliver Pollock, The Life and Times of an Unknown Patriot. Reprint of 1937 edition, Books for Libraries Press, Freeport, New York

John Appleyard Agency
   1975. The 14th colony, British West Florida, 1763-1781. Pensacola Home and Savings Association. Pensacola, Florida

Johnson, Cecil
   1971. British West Florida, 1763-1783. Archon Books. (Yale University Press, 1943)

Lyon, Eugene (Teresa de Balmaseda Milam, editor)
   1994. Spain in Florida and the American West. Jax Xpress Print Inc., Jacksonville Florida.

Mathews, Hazel
   1977. British West Florida and the Illinois Country. Printed by Earl Whynot & Associates Graphics Limited, Halifax, Nova Scotia

Meyers, Rose
    1976. A History of Baton Rouge, 1699–1812. Louisiana State
        University Press, Baton Rouge

Mills, Bill
    1991. Merchant and Naval Shipping of British Pensacola, 1763–1781.
        Pensacola History Illustrated 4 (Winter) 1, 7–19

Murphy, W. S.
    1960. The Irish Brigade of Spain at the Capture of Pensacola, 1781.
        Florida Historical Quarterly 38(3): 216–225

Nachbin, Jac
    1932. Spain's Report of the War with the British in Louisiana.
        Louisiana Historical Quarterly 15 (July) 468–481

O'Donnell III, James H.
    1982. Hamstrung by Penury: Alexander Cameron's Failure at
        Pensacola *in* William S. Coker and Robert R. Rea, editors,
        Anglo-Spanish Confrontation on the Gulf Coast during the
        American Revolution. Pensacola, Florida. 76–89

Osborn, George C.

    1949. Major-General John Campbell in British West Florida.
        Florida Historical Quarterly 27, 317–339

    1953. Relations with the Indians in West Florida during the
        administration of Governor Peter Chester, 1770–1781.
        Florida Historical Quarterly 31: 239–272

Padgett, James A., editor

    1939. The Reply of Peter Chester, Governor of West Florida, to
        Complaints made against his administration.
        Louisiana Historical Quarterly 22 (January)

    1943a. Bernardo de Galvez's Siege of Pensacola in 1781 (as related in
        Robert Farmer's Journal). Louisiana Historical Quarterly 26,
        2, 311–229

    1943b. Governor Peter Chester's Observations on the Boundaries of
        British West Florida, about 1775. Louisiana Historical Quarterly 26,
        1, 5–11

Parks, Virginia
    1990. The British Fort at Pensacola. Pensacola History Illustrated 3
        (4): 11–18

Pettengill, Ray W., translator
  1924. Waldeck Chaplain at Pensacola in West Florida *in* Letters from America. Houghton Mifflin Company, Boston and New York.

Pickett, Albert James
  1851. History of Alabama and incidentally of Georgia and Mississippi. Reprinted in 2003 by River City Publishing, Montgomery, Alabama

Proctor, Samuel
  1970. Bibliographical Resources in the United States for Gulf Coast Studies. Ernest F. Dibble and Earle W. Newton, editors, *in* Search of Gulf Coast Colonial History, 46-78, Pensacola, Florida

Rea, Robert R.

  1969. Graveyard for Britons, West Florida, 1763-1781. Florida Historical Quarterly 47(4): 345-364

  1970. Resources and Research Opportunities for British West Florida, 1763-1783. Ernest F. Dibble and Earle W. Newton, editors. *In* Search of Gulf Coast Colonial History, 23-45 Pensacola, Florida

  1975. Life, Death, and Little Glory: The British Soldier on the Gulf Coast, 1763-1781. *In* Gulf Coast History and Humanities Conference, VII, 21-35

  1977. Life, Death, and Little Glory: The British Soldier on the Gulf Coast, 1763-1781. *In* William S. Coker, editor, The Military Presence on the Gulf Coast, 21-35, Pensacola, Florida,

  1990. British Pensacola. Pensacola History Illustrated 3: 4: 3-10

Rea, Robert R. and Milo B. Howard, Jr., compilers and introductions
  1978. The Minutes, Journals, and Acts of the General Assembly of British West Florida. University of Alabama Press, University, Alabama

Rea, Robert and James A. Servies
  1982. The Log of H.M.S. Mentor, 1780-1781. Pensacola, University Presses of Florida

Romans, Bernard
  1775. A Concise Natural History of East and West Florida. Copy reprinted in 1962 by University of Florida Press, Gainesville Florida

Rowland, Mrs. Dunbar [Eron Rowland]

    1925. Peter Chester, Third Governor of the Province of West Florida under British Dominion, 1779-1781, 1-183 *in* Publications of Mississippi Historical Society, Volume 5, Jackson, Mississippi

    1930. Life, Letters and Papers of William Dunbar. Mississippi Historical Society Press, Jackson, Mississippi

Rush, N. Orwin
    1966. Spain's Final Triumph over Great Britain in the Gulf of Mexico: The Battle of Pensacola, March 9 to May 8, 1781.

Saavedra de Sangronis, Don Francisco
    1979. Journal during the commission ... from 25 June 1780 until the 20th of the same month of 1783. University of Florida Press, Gainesville, Florida

Scott, Kenneth, editor
    1964. Britain Loses Natchez, 1779: An Unpublished Letter. Journal of Mississippi History 26: 1: 45-46

Servies, James A.
    1978. The Siege of Pensacola, 1781: A Bibliography. John C. Pace Library, Pensacola, Florida

Shaw, Helen Louise
    1978. British Administration of the Southern Indians, 1756-1783. Reprinted from 1931 edition. Lancaster Press, Lancaster, Pa.

Siebert, Wilbur H.
    1916. The Loyalists in West Florida and the Natchez District. Mississippi Valley Historical Review 2:465-483

Smith, Paul H. et al. editor
    1976-2000. Letters of delegates to Congress, 1774-1789,
        Vol. 14 October 1, 1779-March 31, 1780,
        Vol. 15: April 1, 1780- August 31, 1780.
        Vol. 16: September 1, 1780- February 28, 1781,
        Vol. 17: March 1, 1781-August 31, 1781,
        Vol. 18: September 1, 1781- July 31, 1782.
        Vol. 25, March 1, 1788- July 25, 1789,
        Vol. 26: Cumulative index with a list of delegates to Congress 1774-1789. Library of Congress: Washington D.C.

Starr, Joseph Barton
    1975. Tories, Dons, and Rebels: The American Revolution in British West Florida. University of Florida Press, Gainesville, Florida.

Stewart, Charles H., compiler
   1962.The Service of British Regiments in Canada and North America.
   Department of National Defense Library, Ottawa Canada

Vickers, Elizabeth
   1990. Disease: The Unconquerable Foe in British West Florida.
   Pensacola History Illustrated 3, 4: 29-32

Vignoles, Charles
   1975. Observations upon the Floridas. Reprinted from the 1826
   edition by University Presses of Florida, Gainesville, Florida

Woodward, Ralph Lee, Jr., editor and translator
   1978. Tribute to Don Bernardo de Galvez: royal patents and an epic ballad
   honoring the Spanish Governor of Louisiana. Baton Rouge: Historic
   New Orleans Collection

Worcester, Donald, E., translator
   1951. Miranda's Diary of the Siege of Pensacola, 1781.
   Florida Historical Quarterly 29: 163-196

Wright, J. Leitch, Jr.
   1975. Florida in the American Revolution. University of Florida Press,
   Gainesville, Florida

Zendegui, Dr. Guillermo de
   1944. Catalogo de los fondos de Las Floridas. Archivo Nacional de
   Cuba, Havana, Cuba

www.ingramcontent.com/pod-product-compliance
Lightning Source LLC
Chambersburg PA
CBHW061436300426
44114CB00014B/1711